I Dwell in Possibility

WOMEN BUILD A NATION
1600-1920

For Moira, the bravest woman I know

A determined "Miss Liberty" (OPPOSITE) wields a sword in a 19th-century work of folk art. She leads an array of women on the following pages who helped create the American spirit.

PAGES 4-5 (LEFT TO RIGHT): a Georgia cotton worker; art collector Isabella Stewart Gardner; an impassioned suffragist; artist and museum founder Gertrude Vanderbilt Whitney; western rancher and photographer Evelyn Cameron; Civil War soldier Frances Clalin; Pocahontas; (lower far right): Martha Washington.

PAGES 6-7: World War I-era patriot.

PAGES 8-9: mother and child in a Wyoming wheat field.

PAGES 10-11 (LEFT TO RIGHT): Georgia cotton worker; feminist author and lecturer, Charlotte Perkins Gilman.

PAGES 12-13: a Hudson River dowager and her daughter.

PAGES 14-15 (LEFT TO RIGHT): smiling Eastern European immigrants; a pensive young woman at the turn of the 20th century.

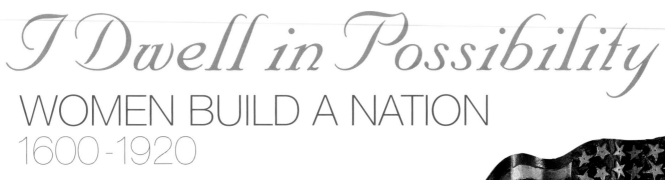

I Dwell in Possibility
WOMEN BUILD A NATION
1600-1920

Donna M. Lucey

NATIONAL GEOGRAPHIC
WASHINGTON, D.C.

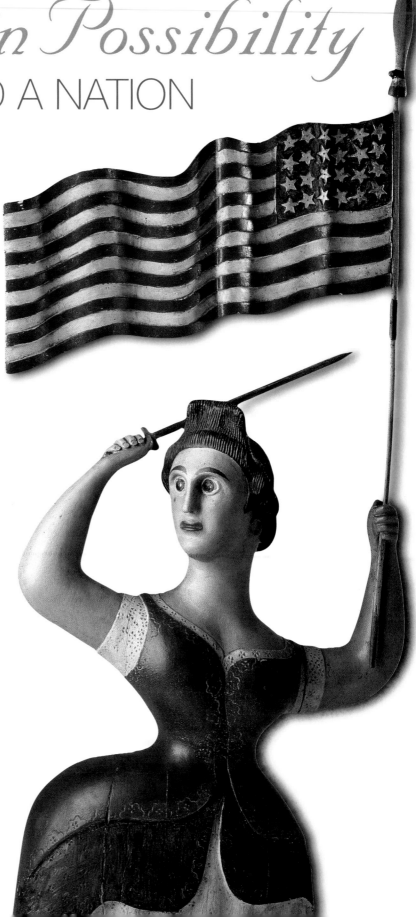

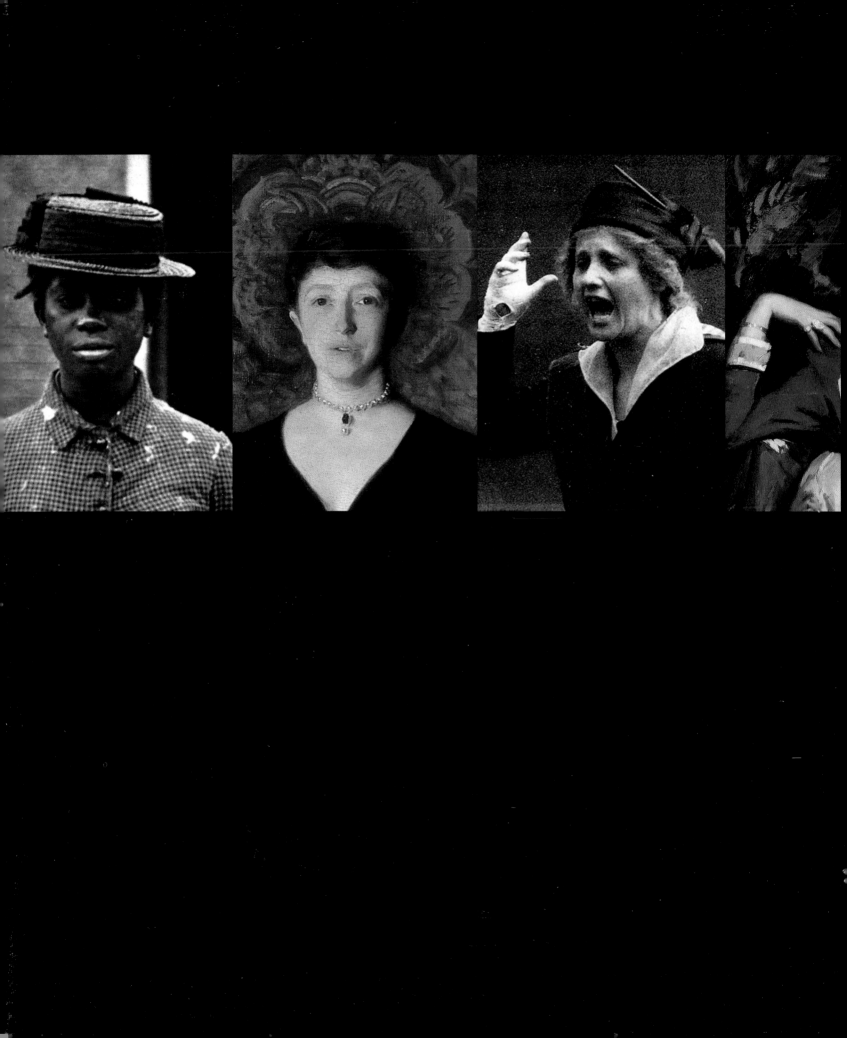

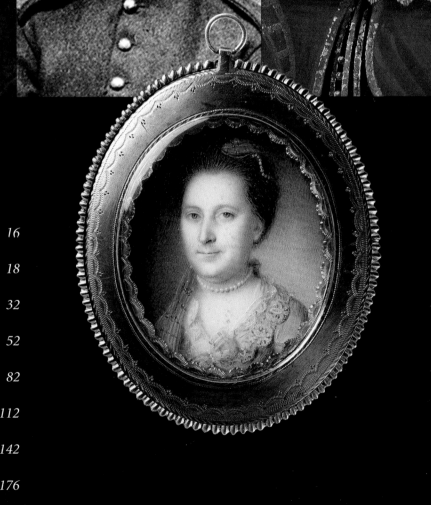

CONTENTS

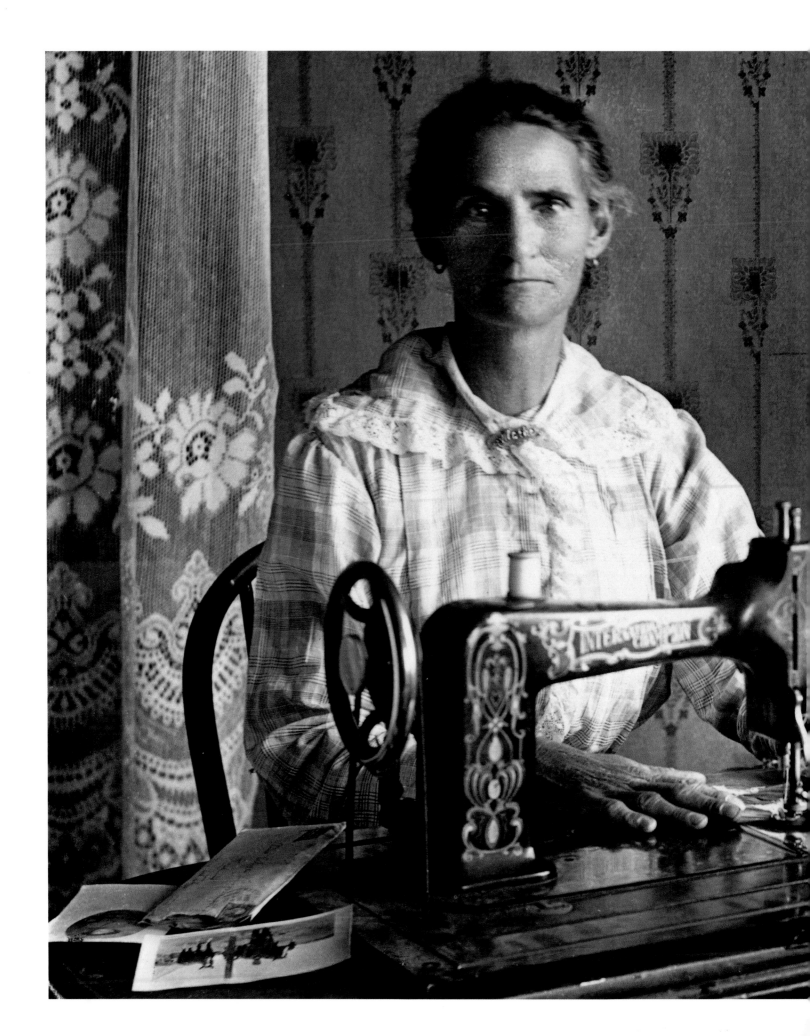

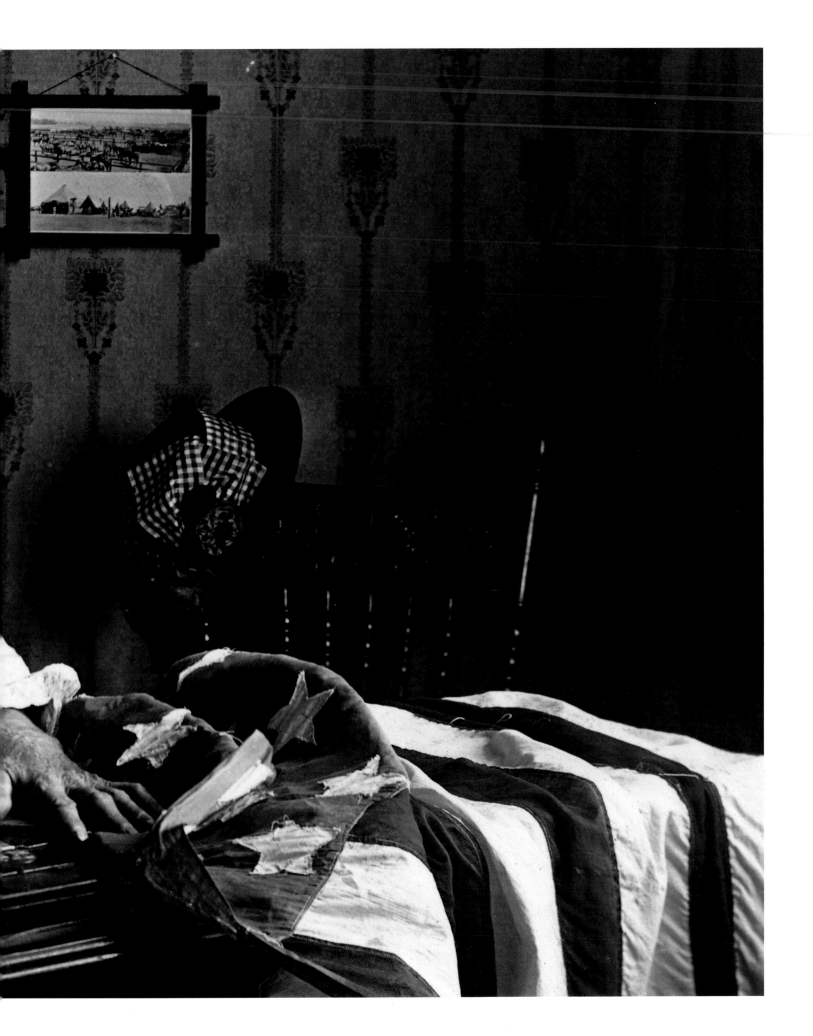

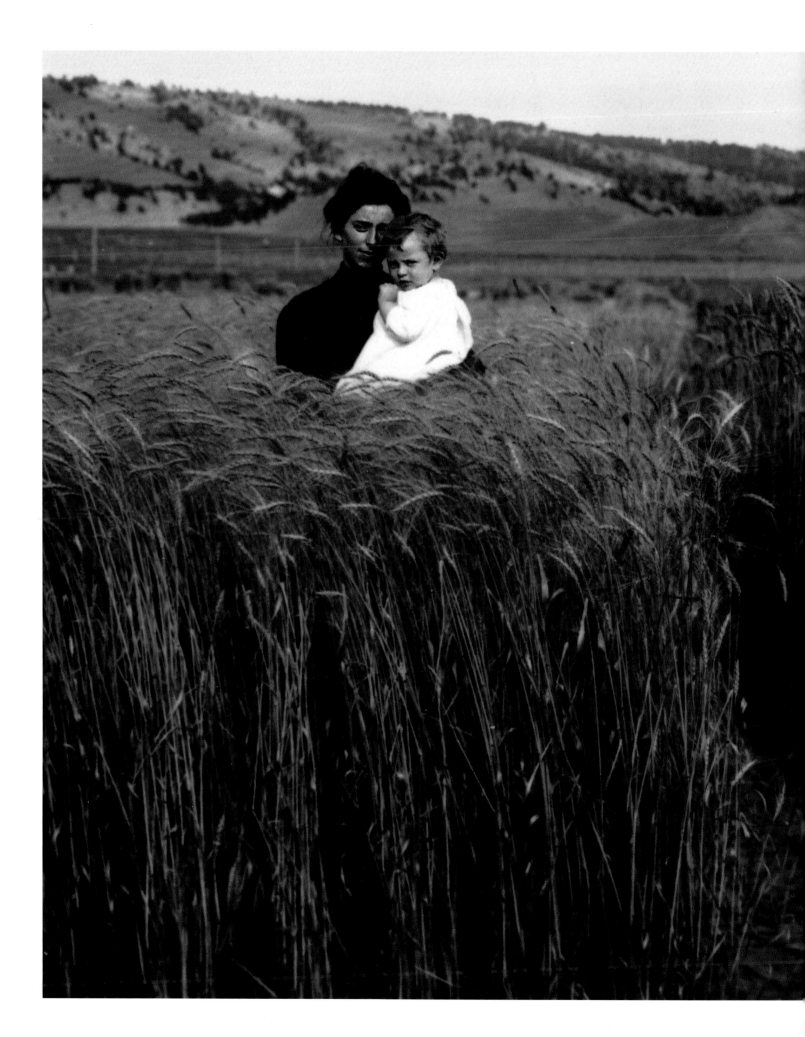

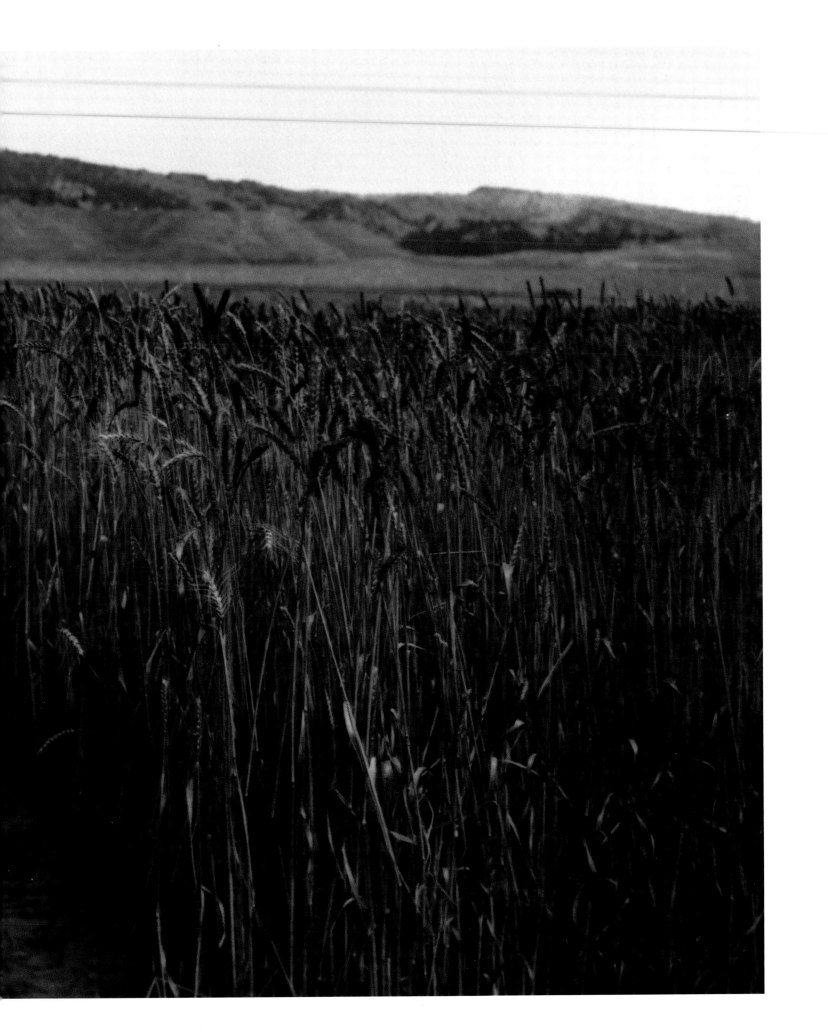

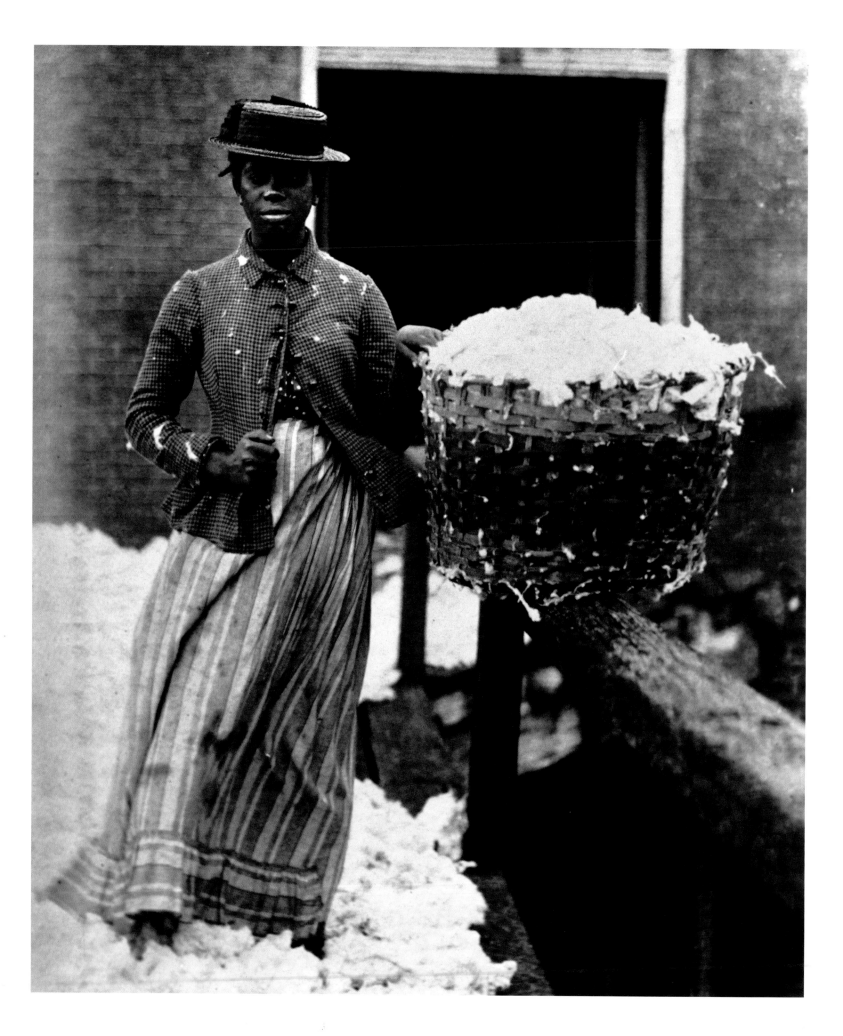

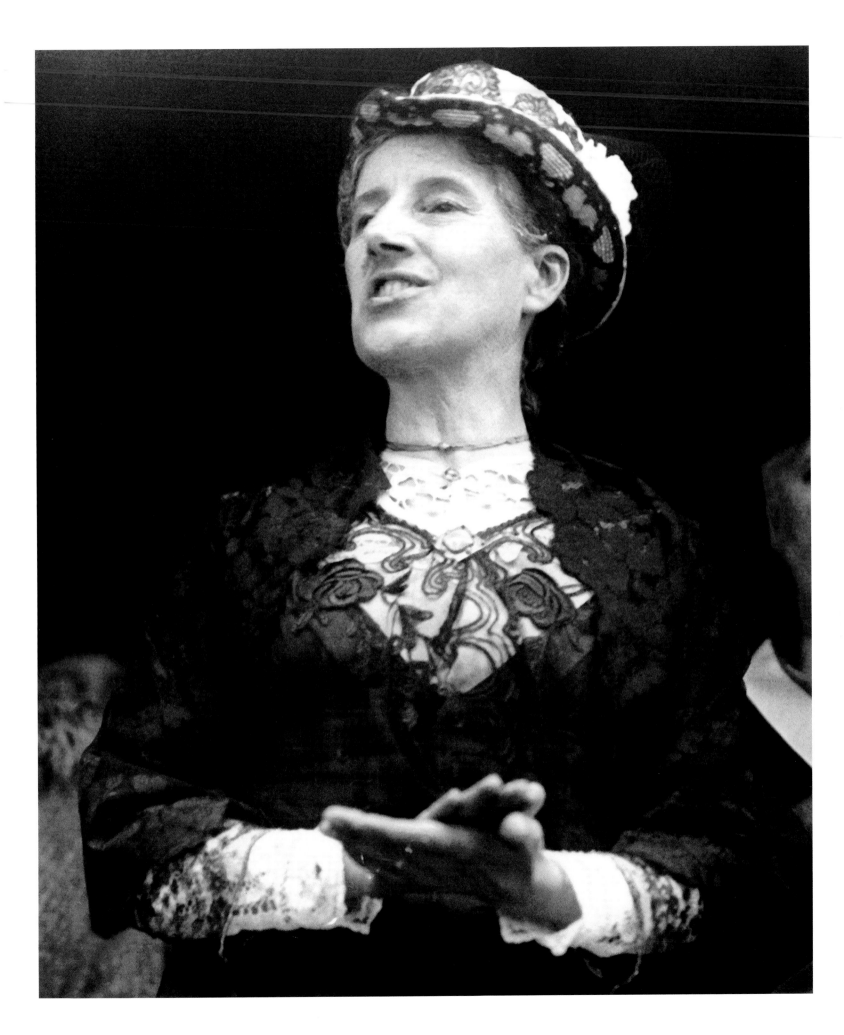

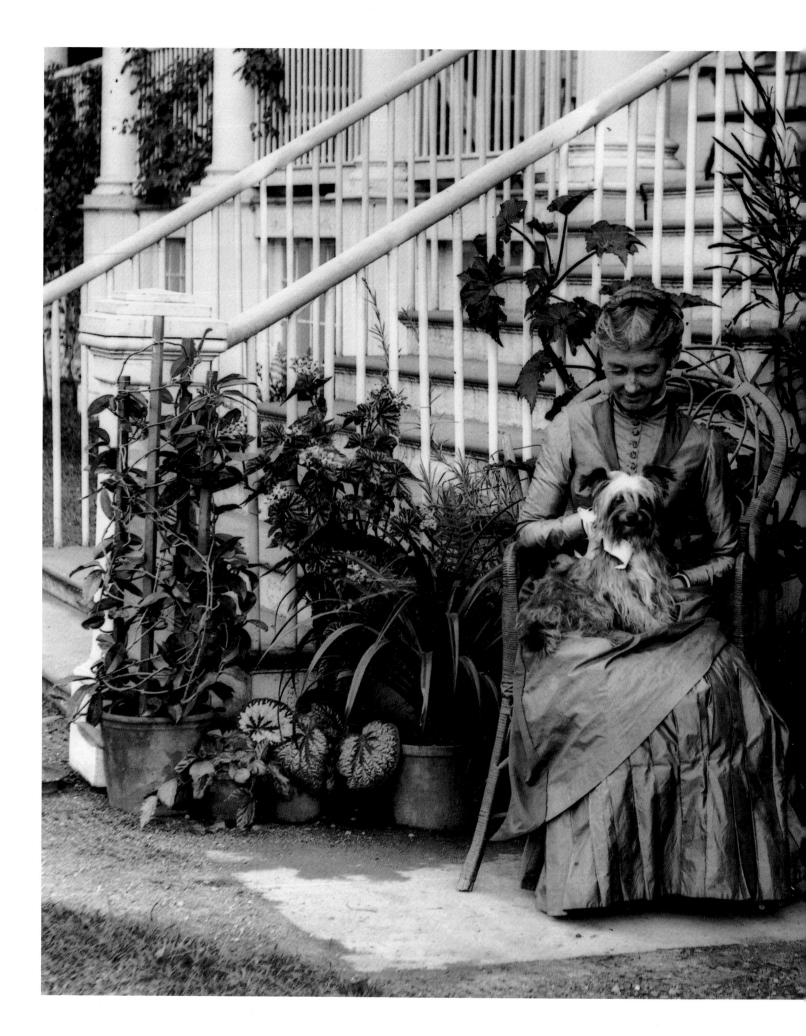

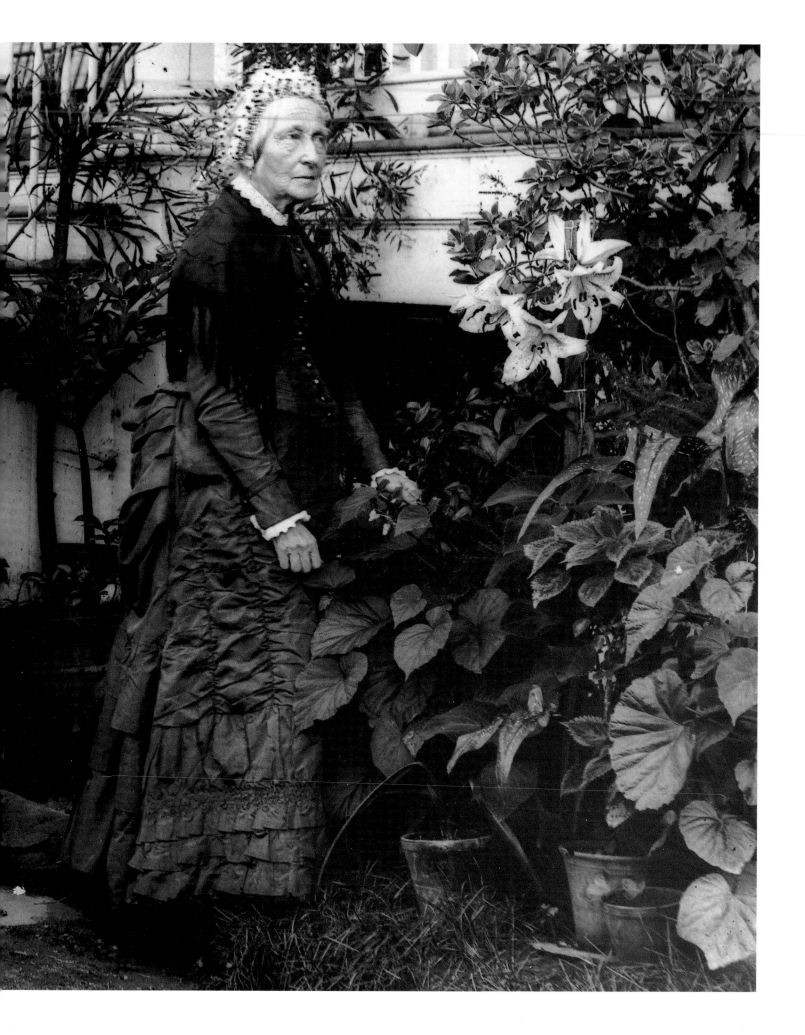

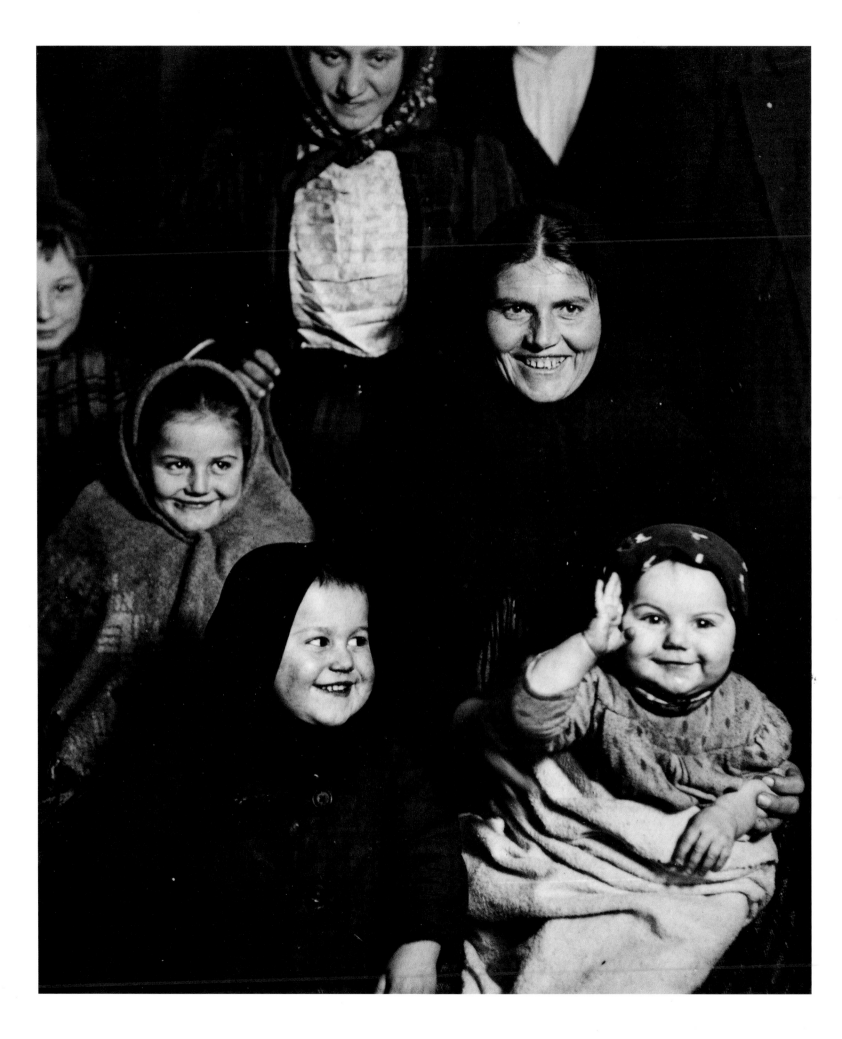

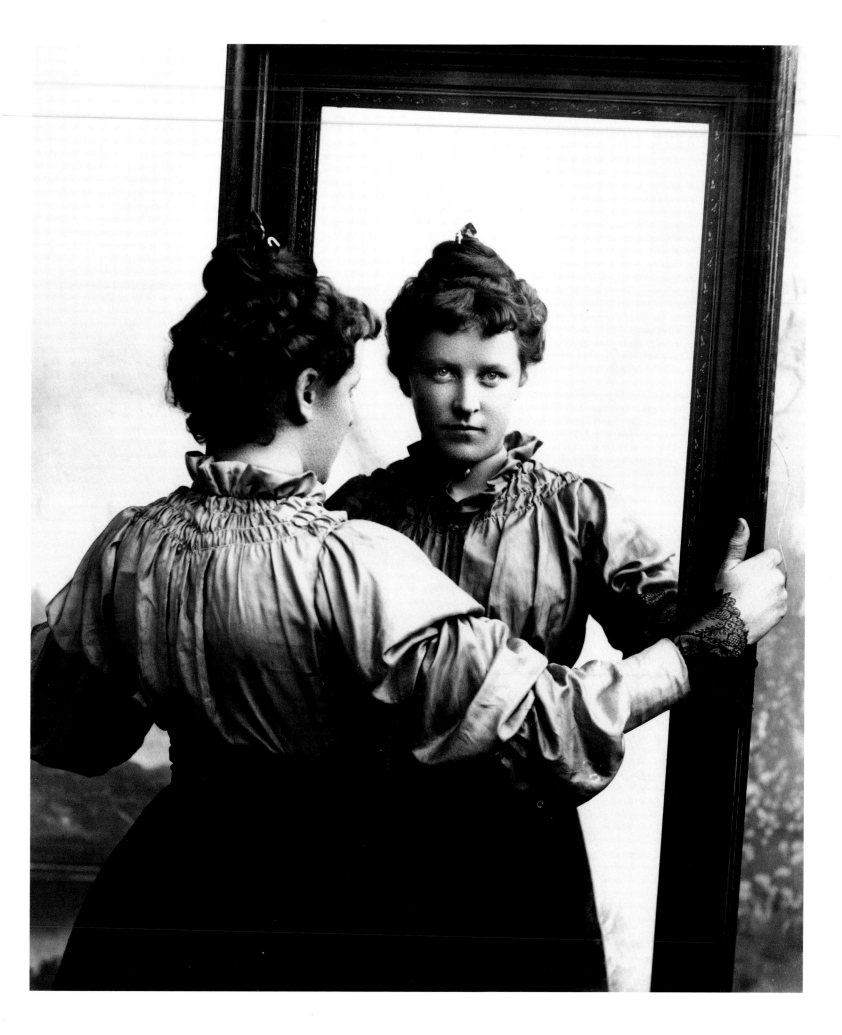

In the old times, women did not get their lives written, though I don't doubt many of them were much better worth writing than the men's.

HARRIET BEECHER STOWE, *THE PEARL OF ORR'S ISLAND*

Let them be sea-captains—if they will!

MARGARET FULLER, *WOMAN IN THE NINETEENTH CENTURY*

UNTIL RECENT TIMES, most histories of the United States ignored women's lives. Generals, male political leaders, battles—this was the fodder for classic histories. Women were not deemed part of that world; they were silent helpmates not critical to great events. It was unspoken—but more or less implied by their absence in these histories—that women did not take a meaningful part in the fabric of American life; they only became powerful after they voted in 1920. Nothing could be further from the truth. Women were never silent, nor powerless in shaping the country. They were just never given any credit.

With imagination, energy, ingenuity, persistence, courage, and sheer willpower, anything is possible. So American women have proven. As co-equals with their male partners, Native American women sowed seeds, controlled crops, took part in religious ceremonies, and made their voices resonate within tribal councils. And when the incursion of Anglos disrupted their world, the native women rushed to the fore to try and save it.

Other women arrived by ship—some forcibly, others voluntarily—to this country.

Restrictions of every kind were placed upon them—religious, political, economic, social. In the case of African-American women, the restrictions were of a more heinous and physical nature—they were literally shackled and subjected to the whims of white slaveholders.

Yet women not only survived; they flourished. They created lives out of nothing. They faced the most basic questions on their arrival in the wilderness: How to survive a winter? How to scrape a living out of this new land? How to protect their children? Such challenges would seem more than enough to face, but many women asked even more profound questions: How to make a just society? How to reform inequities? How to create beauty and meaning in life?

One woman who tried to answer the last question was Emily Dickinson, acknowledged now as one of the greatest poets America has ever produced. She referred to herself once, in jest, as the "belle of Amherst," but she lived a highly restricted—in fact reclusive—life in New England. Her world was very small indeed, but her imagination was boundless. At 31, completely unknown, she sent a few of her poems to a literary critic and asked his opinion: She wondered whether her verses "breathed." He was dumbfounded. Her poetry was of such beauty and startling originality that he did not know what to make of it. The verses were so revolutionary that he was not even sure that they were poems. In part because of its powerful creativity, her work was doomed to obscurity during her lifetime. Yet it gave her the key to her own freedom.

> *"I dwell in Possibility,"* she wrote in one poem, ending her verse with:
> *For Occupation—This—*
> *The spreading wide my narrow Hands*
> *To gather Paradise—*

Her poetry speaks directly to the heart of American women's triumph in this country. Like Dickinson, women worked tirelessly over the centuries without recognition, but they constantly spread their hands—widened their horizons and that of the nation—to help create a better society. They influenced every facet of American life, regardless of the restrictions placed upon them. They dwelt in possibility—and made it a reality. Women truly built a nation. ■

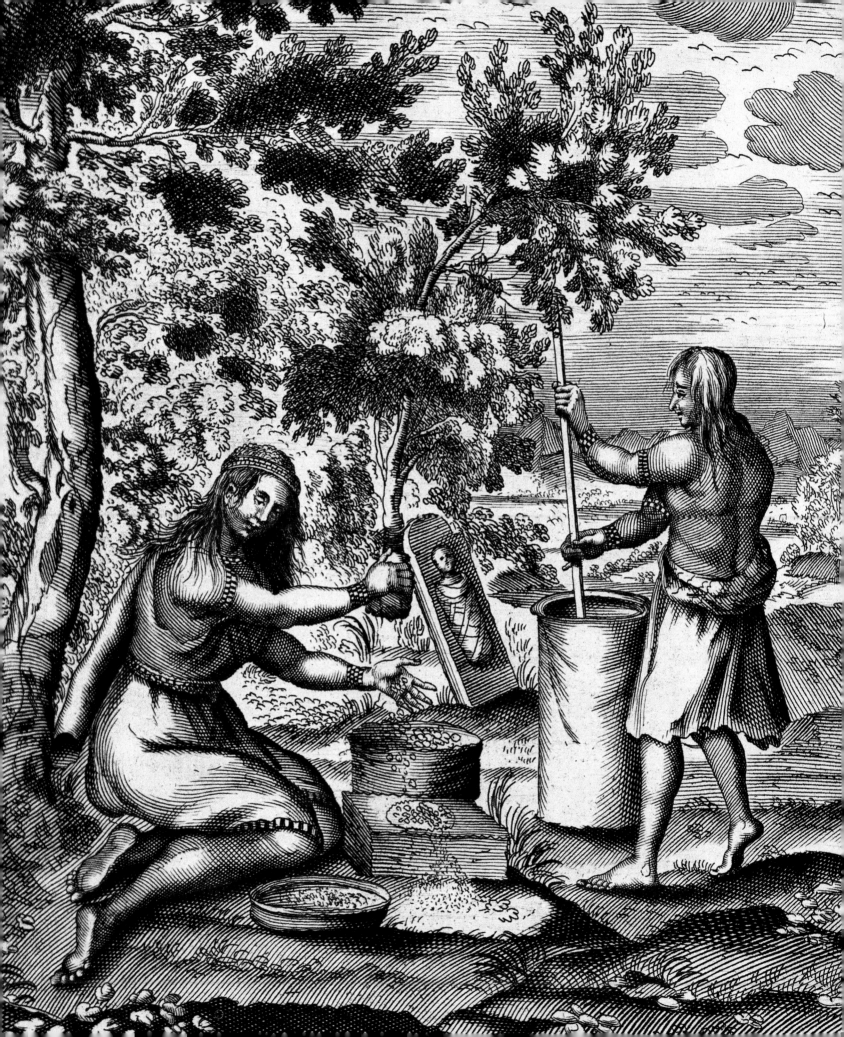

NATIVE AMERICAN WOMEN

OCAHONTAS—the name itself connotes the romantic mingling of Anglo and native cultures. Reportedly a spirited girl who cartwheeled naked with the young boys of colonial Jamestown—her name meant "little wanton" or "plaything"—the alluring image of Pocahontas seems to have little in common with the native women here, who dutifully grind corn or dried berries while caring for the baby on the cradleboard. Pocahontas, the most famous— and most mythologized native woman from early America, was an Indian princess who embraced white ways and dramatically interceded to save the life of Virginia colonist Capt. John Smith just as he was about to be executed. At least that's how Smith wrote it up years after his rescue, in a book entitled *Generall Historie.* (The book related two other incidents where beautiful women saved him from certain death at the last moment, casting shadow on the veracity of his prose.) Historians have argued about the story for over a century.

Details about Pocahontas herself are scarce. Daughter of Powhatan, powerful chief of the Virginia tidewater confederacy of tribes, she was kidnapped in 1613 and became a political pawn between the colonists and her father. While in captivity for a year, she learned English ways, was baptized into the Church of England as "Rebecca," and fell in love with widower John Rolfe. They married, had a son, and then left for England on a publicity junket to attract new investors to Jamestown. Feted by the king and queen, Lady Rebecca was the sensation of London, where pubs changed their names to "La Belle Sauvage" in her honor. How she felt about all this—being paraded about as the "right-thinking savage"—no one knows. Preparing to return to her homeland she became ill—probably with smallpox—and died at around the age of 22. She was buried in England. Her story is a tragic one that really says more about the white culture than native society, but one that remains embedded in the romantic mythology of this country.

The anonymous native women who established an agricultural economy and helped create a society marked by cooperation, harmony, and a deep-seated spirituality left behind a far greater legacy than that of Pocahontas. In the face of the European incursion, native women stoutly defended traditional ways of life, often more passionately than their men did. Their proud, stubborn devotion to old ways earned them the scorn of Europeans. Jesuit missionaries found native women—whom they called "firebrands of hell"—much more difficult to convert than the men. And the work that women did both stunned and horrified the newcomers. Generally, women raised the crops, chopped the firewood, and even built the homes. The white interlopers heartily disapproved. After all, that was men's work. Europeans pitied Native American women, believing they were merely slaves. An English fur trader in the 1690s wrote that native women were treated like sled dogs. Samuel de Champlain referred to Huron women as "mules"; yet his description of how hard these "powerful women of extraordinary stature" worked inspires awe:

It is they who have almost the whole care of the house and the work; for they till the soil, sow the Indian corn, fetch wood for the winter, strip the hemp, and spin it, and with any thread make fishing nets for catching fish...likewise they have the labour of harvesting the corn, storing it, preparing food, and...besides are required to follow and accompany their husbands from place to place...where they serve as mules to carry the baggage, with a thousand other kinds of duties and services.

Viewing native life through the prism of their own culture, the European newcomers completely misunderstood it. Far from being slaves, native women were integral partners in a complex society. Throughout North America they were recognized—and honored—for their central role in giving life and sustaining it. The Cherokee word *selu* means both "woman" and "corn"; for it was women who grew the corn and provided sustenance for the entire tribe. Women were at the center of many native creation myths, including that of the Iroquois Sky Woman who fell from the heavens toward an endless lake. Geese helped break her fall and a turtle rose out of the waters; on his back a muskrat spread earth from the bottom of the lake—and thus was formed the continent of North America. Settling onto the ground, Sky Woman spread seeds from which came the first trees, fruits, and flowers. Sky Woman gave birth to a daughter, the first child of this new world; eventually, the daughter's grave would sprout corn, beans, and squash, the so-called Three Sisters on which life depended.

Native women, particularly those in eastern tribes, controlled agricultural production. Men and women worked together to clear the fields of trees and stones, but only women planted, weeded, harvested, and stored the corn. The fields were the domain of women, and they worked them communally. A white captive adopted by the Seneca tribe of the Iroquois Confederacy described how native women, their children at their sides, worked together "in order to expedite their business, and at the same time enjoy each other's company." Women's clans organized the farming, distributing the land equitably according to the size of each household. In some places, the women cultivated as many as 2,000 acres and they traded surplus land to colonists. (Native women were not terribly impressed with the Europeans as farmers; many colonists failed to keep their fields well weeded, which became a source of joking among the women.)

In many tribes, including those of the Iroquois Confederacy and the Cherokee,

"You ought to hear and listen to what we, women, shall speak...for we are the owners of this land, and it is ours."

DELEGATION OF SENECA WOMEN

property passed from mother to daughter to granddaughter. Family names also came down through the mother, so that children became members of their mother's clan and traced their bloodlines only through their maternal side. Women were at the center of

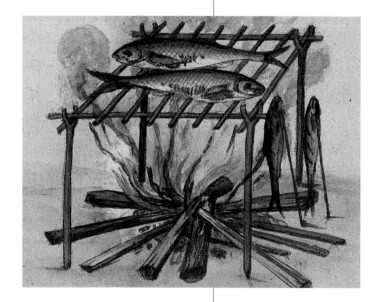

family life and held ultimate power. A husband moved into his wife's household, and if he dared displease his mother-in-law, he could be banished from the home. In effect, women owned the houses, the fields, and the crops.

Women wielded political power as well. When an emissary from President George Washington went to the Seneca to negotiate a peace agreement, he naturally sought out the male leaders. But in short order a delegation of Seneca women presented themselves and announced: "You ought to hear and listen to what we, women, shall speak, as well as to the sachems; for we are the owners of this land, and it is ours. It is we that plant it for our and their use. Hear us, therefore, for we speak of things that concern us." (During the Revolution, Seneca women had suffered terribly during an American punitive campaign in which 40 towns and villages were wiped out, an atrocity that one army officer called "almost incredible to a civilized people.")

The Iroquois system of government was led by males, but it was the matrons who selected chiefs, and could depose them. "They did not hesitate," according to one missionary, "to 'knock off the horns'...from the head of a chief and send him back to the ranks of the warriors." Women's councils met regularly, and grew ever more powerful; in the 18th century there were even reports of Iroquois "she-sachems," or chiefs.

Women helped decide matters of war: To avenge the death of a husband or son, a matron could insist that her male kin wage war to bring back captives. She could then decide the fate of those captured; she could either "send them to the flames," in the words of horrified Europeans, or adopt them into her own family. Father Jogues, a captured Jesuit, had his finger cut off at the behest of one Iroquois woman, but was eventually given to another woman as a replacement for her dead brother. The mourning sister could have decreed that he die "in all the torments...suggested by revenge"; instead she took him in as her own. "As soon as I had entered her cabin, she began to sing a song of

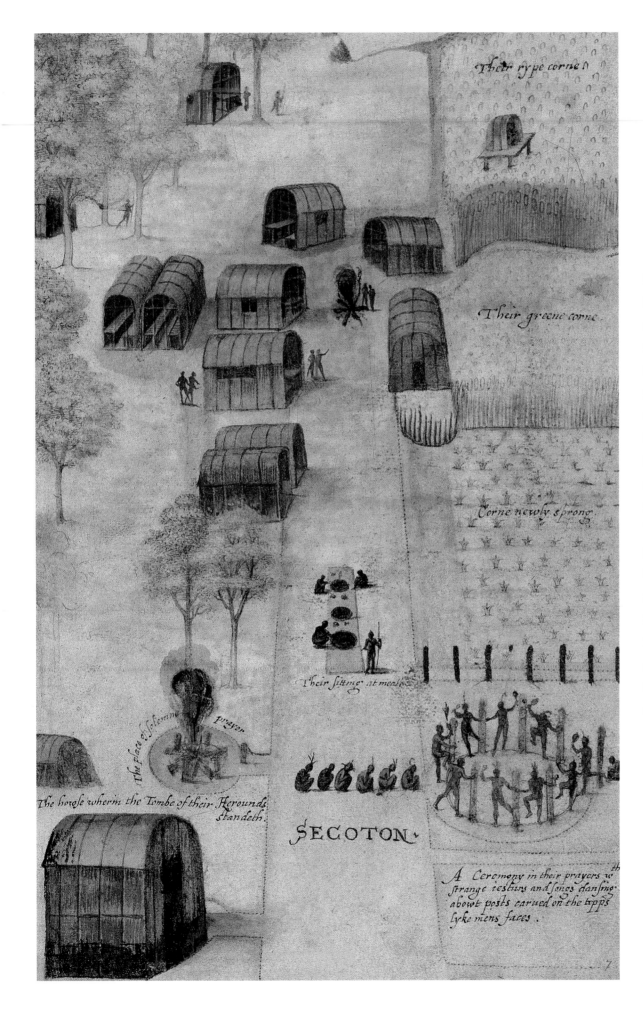

Their rype corne

Their greene corne

Corne newly sprong

Their sitting at meate

The place of solemne prayer

The howse wherin the Tombe of their Herounds standeth.

SECOTON

A Ceremony in their prayers wth strange testurs and sones dansing abowt posts carued on the topps lyke mens faces.

In a 1585 watercolor, artist John White created a bird's-eye view of the Secotan Indians' main village along coastal North Carolina, and in the process, presented a rendering of the native women's domain. Women controlled the houses, the fields, which they tended communally, and the crops. Here the corn is shown in three stages: "newly sprong," "greene," and "rype." Women prepared the meals, like fresh fish (opposite), and drew the admiration of at least one Englishman, who wrote that the Indians cooked with great care and ate moderately. "I would to God that we followed their example," he noted.

An engraving from 1591 shows Florida Indian women planting seeds while men break up the soil. The French artist Jacques Le Moyne drew the scene from firsthand observation, but this later reproduction took some liberties. Though Le Moyne reported that the men used hoes made from fish bones, here the hoes are of a decidedly European cast.

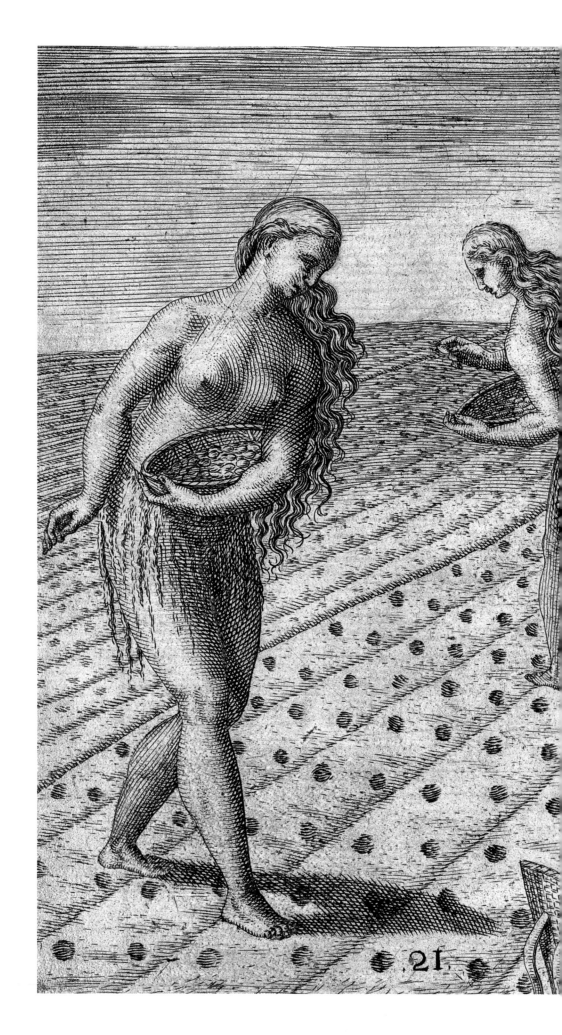

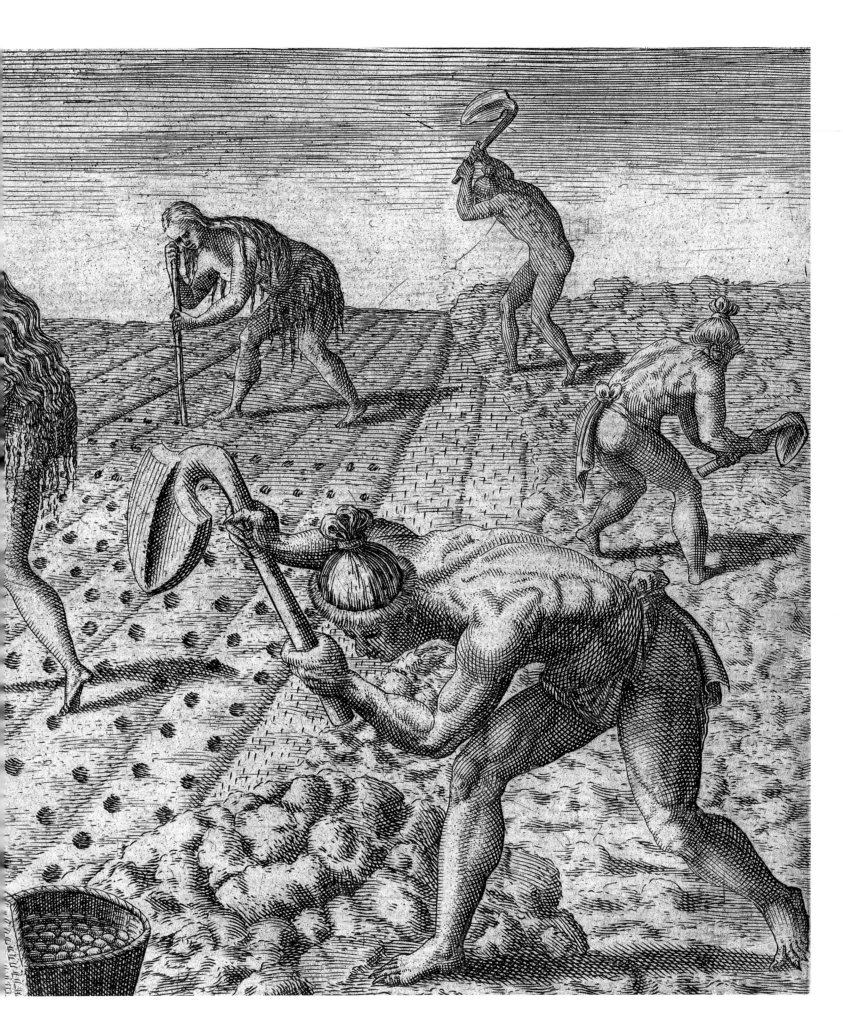

"Nothing is more real than the women's superiority.... The men, on the contrary, are entirely isolated and limited to themselves. Their children are strangers to them. Everything perishes with them."

FATHER JOSEPH FRANÇOIS LAFITAU

the dead, in which two of her daughters accompanied her," the priest later wrote. "I became aware that I was given in return for a dead man...causing the departed to become alive again in my person." She treated him affectionately as a family member, tending to his finger and giving him clothes and a blanket. Europeans did not understand the depth of this bond. When a Frenchman fled his captors after having spent more than a year with them, his two native "sisters" trailed him to Fort Orange (eventually the city of Albany, New York) where they wandered the streets weeping and crying out for him. After living with the Iroquois for five years, one priest concluded:

> Nothing is more real than the women's superiority.... It is they who really maintain the tribe, the nobility of blood, the genealogical tree, the order of generations, and conservation of the families. In them resides all the real authority: the lands, fields, and all their harvest belong to them; they are the soul of the councils, the arbiters of peace and war; they hold the taxes and the public treasure; to them the slaves are entrusted; they arrange the marriages; the children are under their authority; the order of succession is founded on their blood. The men...are isolated and limited to themselves. Their children are strangers to them. Everything perishes with them.

Spirituality suffused native life, and women—the life-givers and nurturers—took an active role in that arena. Women played prominent roles in rituals and celebrations such as the Cherokee Green Corn Ceremony, during which an old woman presented the new crop in thanksgiving for the harvest. Respected as healers, women—particularly pregnant ones—were valued in some curing rites. According to the Huron, an arrow had to be taken out in the presence of a pregnant woman for the wound to mend properly.

Even women's seemingly mundane contributions to native life could help ensure the very survival of their tribes. Some archaeological research indicates that nets woven by women in ancient times were perhaps more effective in trapping game than were spears hurled by men. A fur trader in the Great Lakes region recounted how his native wife had saved a group from starvation, as she was the only one who knew how to make and mend fishing nets. Native women were equal partners with men in a culture that valued cooperation and community, yet a few extraordinary women have come down in history largely because of their interactions with whites.

During the 1676 popular uprising known as Bacon's Rebellion, the Virginia colonial government summoned a potential ally, the chief of the Pamunkey Indians, who had been in power for 20 years. The leader, Cockacoeske, was a woman, and an eyewitness described her commanding presence as she strode into the chambers of the Governor's Council "with grave courtlike gestures and a majestick air in her face." She was dressed in a deerskin robe, and her head was adorned with a braid of wampum, the polished beads made from mollusk shells that were used as currency. When asked by the council how many warriors she could supply to the government, she took on "an earnest passionate countenance as if tears were ready to gush out and with a fervent sort of expression [she] made a harangue about a quarter of an hour, often interlacing with a high shrill voice and vehement passion these words, 'Tatapatamoi Chepiack,' i.e. Tatapatomoy dead." Her cry was for her husband, Tatapatomoy, who, with a hundred of his bowmen, had been killed while fighting for the crown in an earlier campaign. She had never been compensated for her loss. Cockacoeske grudgingly agreed to provide a dozen warriors for the current situation, though it was known she had some 150 at her disposal.

Bacon's Rebellion eventually failed, and the queen of the Pamunkey was able to make political hay out of it. She concluded a treaty with the British that expanded her sovereignty to include several other Indian nations. By order of Charles II, the queen was also presented with a silver badge engraved with the English Royal Arms. The crafty Cockacoeske died in the 1680s, but two more Pamunkey queens—Betty and Ann—would reign in the 18th century. Queen Ann stood firm against Anglo incursions into native lands, tried to stamp out drinking among her subjects, and convinced Virginia authorities to forego collecting annual payments from the Pamunkey.

As a teenage wife, Cherokee Nancy Ward (née Nanye'hi) went on a military expedition with her husband; after he was shot and killed in battle, she took his gun and fought valiantly, earning herself the title War Woman. As an exalted personage, she had the power to spare the lives of captives, which she did once when a white woman was about to be burned at the stake. (The woman gratefully taught Ward how to make butter.) A supporter of the patriot cause during the Revolutionary War—a minority viewpoint among her people—Ward warned white settlers of imminent attacks by Cherokee warriors, yet maintained a lofty status in her tribe. She served as a Cherokee diplomat and negotiated

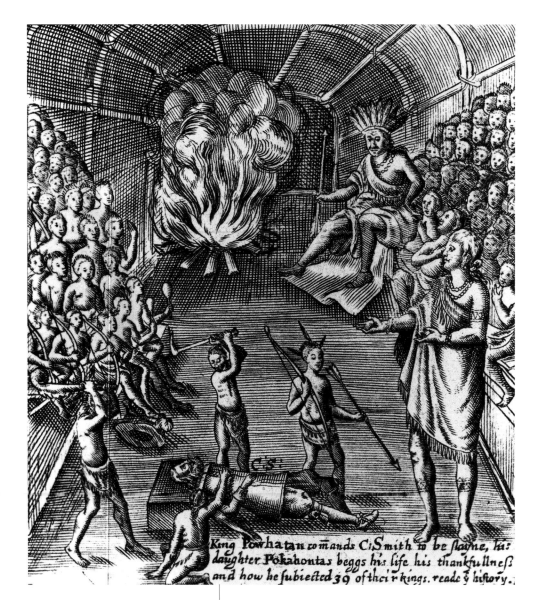

King Powhatan comands C: Smith to be slayne, his daughter Pokahontas beggs his life his thankfullnesß and how he subiected 39 of their kings. reade ý history.

In this dramatic scene, Pocahontas drapes her arm across Capt. John Smith and saves him from club-wielding Indians poised "to beate out his braines." Published in Smith's 1624 history, this image helped establish the legend of Pocahontas. Intent on creating a figure palatable to Europeans, another artist pictured Pocahontas (opposite) with pale skin and carrying an ostrich feather, a symbol of royalty.

with the new nation. "Our cry is all for peace," she declared at a treaty conference in 1781. "This peace must last forever. Let your women's sons be ours; our sons be yours. Let your women hear our words."

Another Cherokee woman made a similar appeal for peace in a letter to Benjamin Franklin: "Consider that women is the mother of All—and the Woman does not pull Children out of Trees or Stumps nor out of old Logs, but out of their Bodies, so that they ought to mind what a woman says." Ward and other Cherokee women desperately urged tribal leaders to retain the traditional communal ownership of land rather than yield to white pressure to divide the land into plots. In an 1818 petition, Cherokee women made an impassioned appeal:

> *We have heard with painful feelings that the bounds of the land we now possess are to be drawn into very narrow limits. The land was given to us by the Great Spirit above as our common right, to raise our children upon, & to make support for our rising generations. We therefore humbly petition our beloved children, the head men & warriors, to hold out...in support of our common rights, as the Cherokee nation have been the first settlers of this land; we therefore claim the right of the soil.*

Within 20 years, the Cherokee would be forcibly driven off their homeland and sent a thousand miles west in a tragic exodus called the Trail of Tears. Even the eloquent voices of native women—resonant and powerful as they were—could not hold back the tide of white expansion.

Ætatis suæ 21. Aº 1616.

Matoaks als Rebecka daughter to the mighty Prince
Powhatan Emperour of Attanoughkomouck als Virginia
converted and baptized in the Christian faith, and
Wife to the wor.ll Mr Tho: Rolff.

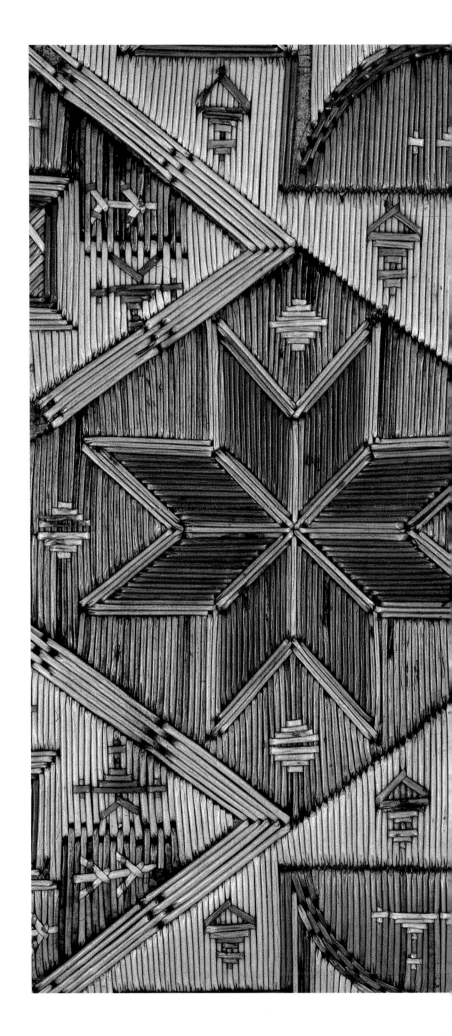

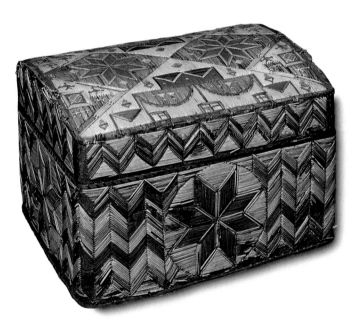

Following the ancient quillworking
techniques of her northeastern
woodlands tribe, an 1800s
Micmac woman used porcupine
quills to decorate this birchbark
box (above and right, detail). The
handsome star-shaped designs
represent eight-legged sea stars.
Finely crafted boxes such as
these were traded to Europeans.

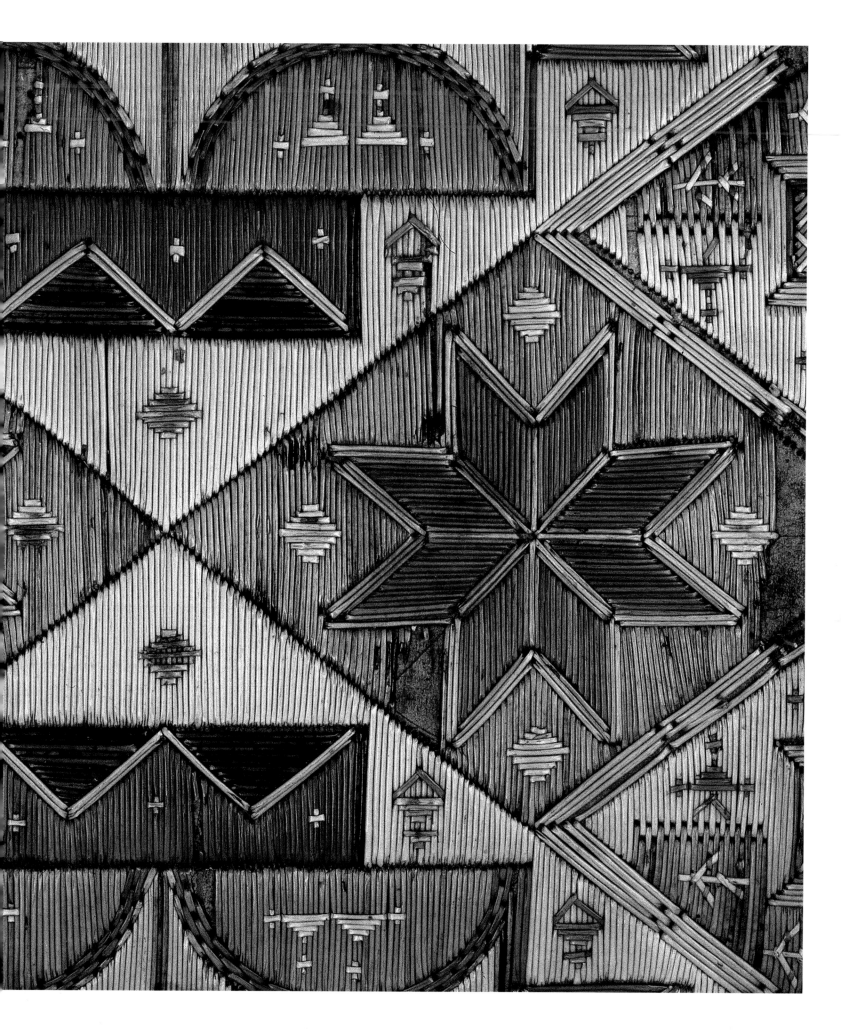

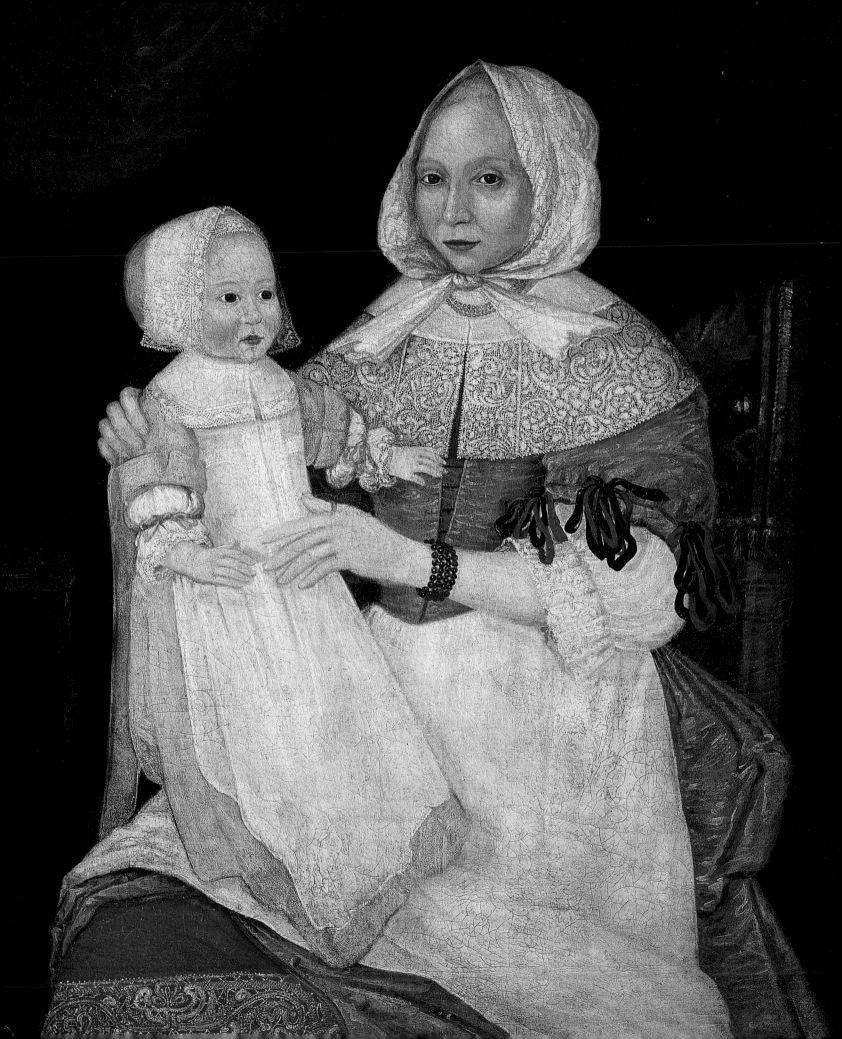

COLONIAL WOMEN

*T*HE PORTRAIT AT LEFT of Mrs. Elizabeth Freake and her baby daughter, Mary, painted in Puritan New England in the late 1600s, comes as something of a shock. The self-assured gaze of the mother, her elegant clothing and jewelry—the sheer colorfulness of the painting—surprises the viewer. Colonial-era women are often thought of as dull, mousy creatures devoid of any style or even personality, devoted "Good Wives" who dared not raise their voices against the prevailing dark religious culture. Yet here is Elizabeth Freake sporting

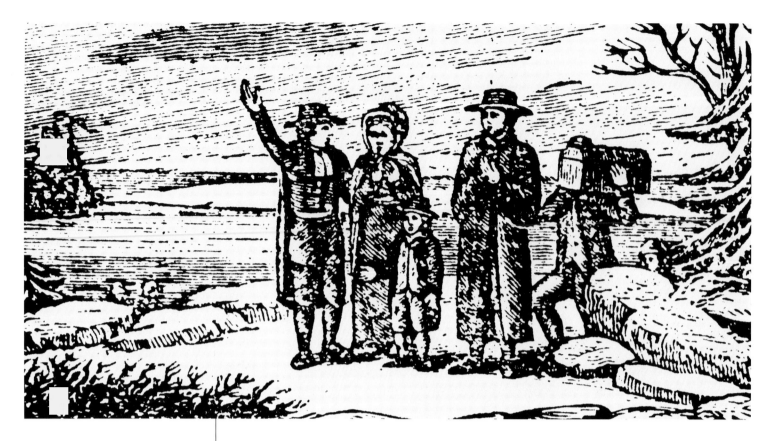

frivolous bows on her sleeve, a bright red underskirt with a beautiful band of ornate brocade or embroidery, and even jewelry—a good bit of it.

This was a woman who cared deeply about fashion, and was eager to flaunt it. Scientific evidence has confirmed that fact. Radiographs of the painting reveal that this was an updated version of a portrait made of Elizabeth, without child, some years earlier. After her baby was born, the artist added the newest addition to the family—as well as the latest fashions for her mother. Elizabeth now wears three strands of pearls around her neck, a beaded bracelet, and even a gold thumb ring. Her clothes were altered to make them more modish. This was not only a record of the family's growing prosperity in the New World, but a statement about Elizabeth's own tastes.

Colonial women indeed had a stake in the New World—and they made the most of it. Despite legal, social, and religious restrictions placed upon them, women managed to make their voices heard. In the process they were instrumental in helping to create a vibrant new culture in the wilderness—and in shaping its economic, religious, and literary life. Truly, they brought a burst of color and energy onto the scene.

One of the first ships bringing English settlers to New England carried an 18-year-old passenger who would win fame on two continents during her lifetime; her writings would break through the crust of Puritan restraint and earn a permanent place in the literature of the New World. Anne Bradstreet crossed the Atlantic in 1630 with her husband, Simon, and her parents. They came as members of John Winthrop's Massachusetts Bay Company, the Puritan band that settled Boston.

The pioneers endured appalling conditions, living in shacks with meager food and water. An epidemic swept through the colony the first summer. Of the troubles she endured and the entirely new way of life she had to take up, Bradstreet wrote stoically, "After I was convinced it was the way of God, I submitted to it." That ethic of submissiveness to divine will was an underpinning of the Puritan way of life, and she embraced it wholeheartedly. As her family moved ever farther into the Massachusetts wilderness—from Boston, to Ipswich, to Andover—Bradstreet bore eight children. Both her father and husband served as governors of the colony, which brought Bradstreet social status but also loneliness, since her husband's duties compelled long absences from home.

In one important respect, Anne Bradstreet typified the Puritan migration to the New World. Of the first wave of English settlers in New England, about 85 percent came with family members. Religion motivated the northern settlers: The pioneers of Plymouth Plantation, Massachusetts Bay Colony, Rhode Island, and New Haven, Connecticut, were Pilgrims and Puritans, religious refugees seeking the freedom to worship as they chose. (Spiritual considerations soon yielded to the profit motive in the New World—the governor of Plymouth Colony lamented that some Pilgrim families left the original settlement to acquire more land "for the enriching of themselves.") The daily lives of women were filled with work—brewing "small beer," making cheese, raising chickens and geese for sale, and performing the myriad tasks that a male observer airily described as "righting up the house."

Amidst her work, the bouts of illness that plagued her, and the periodic absences of her husband, Bradstreet drew comfort and strength from her faith, and she did something quite astonishing for a woman of her time and place—she began to write poetry. To fully understand how remarkable an achievement this was, we must realize that the great majority of colonial women could not write at all. Many colonial women were taught to read because that skill was necessary for access to the Bible, but only a small fraction of them could write, which was a male skill, taught by fathers to their sons.

Bradstreet wrote not for fame but for herself—as a result, her work has a startling intimacy, as if she had opened the pages of her diary to the world. Her verses to her husband, absent on business, lament that "My sun is gone," leaving her in the "frigid colds" of loneliness—"My chilled limbs…lie forlorn."

> *If ever two were one, then surely we.*
> *If ever man were loved by wife, then thee.*
> *If ever wife was happy in a man,*
> *Compare with me, ye women, if you can.*

One of Bradstreet's most deeply moving poems, "Before the Birth of One of Her Children," demonstrates the vast gulf between the world of the colonial woman and the modern. On such an occasion a 21st-century poet would put down thoughts of anticipation and excitement; for Bradstreet the final weeks of lying-in brought forebodings of death. As the poem progresses it becomes clear to the reader that Bradstreet has written a farewell note to her husband, expressing her deep love for him and urging him to take comfort in their children—"Look to my little babes, my dear remains." Only in the last lines is it revealed that the poem was written in secret and left in a drawer to be found by her husband in the event the poet died in childbirth:

> *And if chance to thine eyes shall bring this verse,*
> *With some sad sighs honor my absent hearse;*
> *And kiss this paper for thy love's dear sake,*
> *Who with salt tears this last farewell did take.*

Bradstreet circulated her poems informally among family and friends. In that era women were sternly discouraged from writing—in 1650 a Massachusetts minister wrote to his sister in England, who had just published a book there, "Your printing of a book, beyond the custom of your sex, doth rankly smell." But Bradstreet was fortunate that the men in her life—her husband, her father, and brother-in-law—all admired her work. Indeed, her brother-in-law, a minister named John Woodbridge, carried a sheaf of the poems to London without Bradstreet's knowledge and arranged for publication under the title, *The Tenth Muse Lately sprung up in America.* That volume became a literary landmark: Bradstreet was the first North American to publish a book of poetry.

The Tenth Muse was glowingly received—to the astonishment and embarrassment of the poet. She was dismayed she had not been given the opportunity to revise her work for publication. In a later edition she wrote good-naturedly but ruefully that her words were like children to her, and had been snatched from her side "by friends, less wise than true, Who thee abroad exposed to public view." Publication inspired Bradstreet to work even harder, and it gave her confidence in her own voice. She revised her early verses and, shedding the imitativeness of her literary apprenticeship, wrote new ones of greater sophistication. When her house burned in July 1666, she wrote melancholy lines that evoke the awful heartache of a woman who passes the site of her former beloved home and wonders what might have been:

> *Under thy roof no guest shall sit,*
> *Nor at thy table eat a bit...*
> *No candle e'er shall shine in thee,*
> *No bridegroom's voice e'er heard shall be.*
> *In silence ever shalt thou lie.*
> *Adieu, adieu; all's vanity.*

Bradstreet died in 1672 at the age of 60, esteemed as both a "gentlewoman" who did her pious, wifely duties, and as a poet. So great was the admiration for her in colonial Massachusetts that a Boston publisher brought out a new edition of her work six years after her death. That book, *Several Poems Compiled with great variety of Wit and Learning, full of Delight,* was the first volume of belles lettres printed in the British Colonies. Though Bradstreet's poems fell from favor by the 19th century, in the 20th she was rediscovered, joyfully, by readers who were astonished at the power of her voice that called from the New England wilderness of old.

Anne Bradstreet crossed a cultural boundary into a literary realm normally forbid-

A 1757 invoice (opposite) shows the amount owed to enterprising Mary Taylor for ferrying the mail in Beaufort County, North Carolina. Eking out a living in the southern colonies was particularly difficult. Since "our arrival in Carolina," one young woman wrote in 1685, "we [have] suffered all sorts of evils....sickness, pestilence, famine, poverty, and the roughest labor."

den to women, but in matters of faith and politics she remained firmly within her assigned sphere. Bradstreet's contemporary, Anne Hutchinson, went much further—she courted martyrdom by exercising a right taken for granted today: the right to speak and worship as one wishes. From the moment of her arrival in Massachusetts in 1634, Hutchinson caused suspicion among the colony's Puritan authorities. She had to undergo a special religious interrogation to ensure that her ideas were within church orthodoxy. She passed this initial test, and the authorities did not seem to mind when she began holding weekly meetings at her home to discuss sermons and the Bible. The group of hearers grew until she was attracting 50 to 80 people, and she began holding meetings twice a week. Many women came to hear her, but so did some of the colony's most powerful men, including almost all of Boston's elected officials.

It soon became apparent that Hutchinson's

A gravestone rubbing in Grafton, Vermont, dramatically illustrates the high mortality rate in early America. Rebecca Park buried 13 infants, as well as another child depicted in the center panel, before her own death at age 40. Her husband outlived two more wives, all of whom were buried in a row.

ideas were definitely not orthodox. Mainstream Puritan theology contended that good works and obedience to church laws and practices were required for salvation. Hutchinson preached that divine grace alone assured salvation and that it was not necessary to bow slavishly to church rules mandating attendance at church every Sunday, rest on the Sabbath, strict obedience to ministers and religious magistrates, and literal adherence to the Bible rather than one's own conscience. The Puritans called these heresies Antinomian, literally "opposed to law." Puritan leader John Winthrop realized the threat that Hutchinson posed not just to the church but to the state: Hutchinson's preaching, he said, "overthrows all."

Her beliefs sparked something of a women's movement. One of the Puritan leaders complained that "the weaker Sex" (a phrase he uttered without irony) "thronged" to follow Hutchinson and that they were raising a clamor that "New England men usurp over their wives, and keep them in servile subjection." Winthrop claimed that Hutchinson was creating "divisions between husband and wife…till the weaker give place to the stronger." What frightened the leaders was the breakdown of authority—in the face of Hutchinson's movement the household's religious beliefs would not necessarily be determined by the husband, but by the person with the stronger faith and the stronger will. Having to contend against strong-willed women terrified the magistrates. One minister stated the prevailing wisdom: "The woman is more subject to error than a man." Thus he forbade women to speak in church except to confess a sin or sing. If a woman had a legitimate question about faith, "she should ask her husband at home."

It was deeply unsettling for the male rulers to contend with a religious movement that was "covered with women's aprons" and attracting staunch, brave, and determined adherents. When Hutchinson walked out of a meeting house to protest a sermon, many of the women in the congregation followed her through the door. One of Hutchinson's followers was repeatedly brought before the court and punished with whippings, imprisonment, being put in the stocks, and having a cleft stick fixed on her tongue. Another disciple, Mary Dyer, found herself denounced as a woman "of a very proud spirit," who was "much addicted to revelations."

The Puritans had previously succeeded in silencing a religious dissenter by banishing him. They had sent Roger Williams to Rhode Island in 1635, and in the following year another dissenter, Thomas Hooker, had left Massachusetts for Connecticut. Next they banished a male Antinomian minister, closed the colony to Antinomian immigrants, and engineered elections to unseat religious dissenters and install orthodox Puritans. Then they moved against Hutchinson.

Massachusetts authorities brought Hutchinson before two tribunals in 1637 and 1638. Her trials have been overshadowed in American history by the notorious Salem witch trials of 1692, in which 20 innocent men and women were put to death; but Hutchinson's trials are arguably far more significant in the history of the struggle for freedom. At Hutchinson's first trial Governor Winthrop charged her with conducting a "meeting and an assembly in your house that hath been condemned by the general assembly as a thing not tolerable nor comely in the sight of God nor fitting for your sex." (Not for nothing did the Founders include freedom of assembly in the Bill of Rights.) When Hutchinson tried to answer the charges, Winthrop thundered "we do not mean to dis-

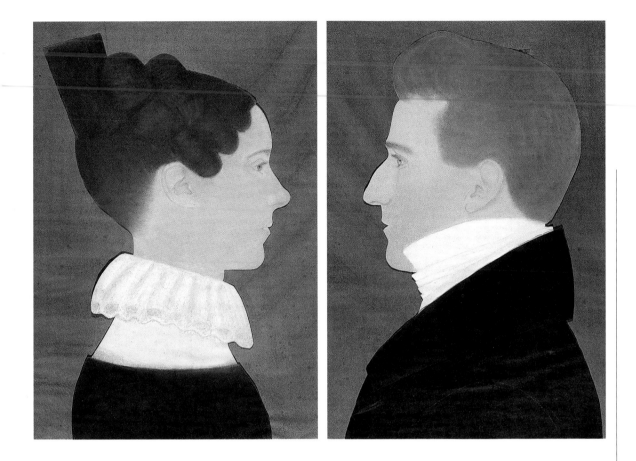

course with those of your sex." Another judge declared bluntly, "you have stept out of your place," accusing Hutchinson of wishing to be a husband instead of a wife.

But Hutchinson deferred to a higher authority, insisting that the judges cite "a rule...from God's word" to justify their commands. She matched their accusations with citations from the Bible, including the injunction that "the elder women should instruct the younger." This enraged Winthrop, who declared "We are your judges, and not you ours." At one point, overcome with emotion, Hutchinson called down a curse: "God will ruine you and your posterity, and this whole State."

Governor Winthrop intoned the judgment of the court: "Mrs. Hutchinson, the sentence of the court...is that you are banished from out of our jurisdiction as being a woman not fit for our society." When she left the room, she was not alone. Mary Dyer, at the door, offered her hand. The two walked off, hands clasped in comradeship.

Roger Williams offered refuge to Anne Hutchinson and her family in Rhode Island, where they spent four years. In 1642 Anne went into farther exile amid fears that the Massachusetts colony might annex Rhode Island, which would once again bring her within the power of her enemies. She settled in the Dutch colony of New Netherland, on the northern edge of present-day New York City. In the following year Hutchinson and five of her children were murdered in an Indian raid. Recent scholarly research suggests that the raid might not have been random: There are indications that the Puritans

Women's voices were both reviled and celebrated in colonial New England. Anne Hutchinson, shown preaching in her home in Boston, outraged Puritan leaders with her unorthodox religious views, and she was banished from the Massachusetts Bay Colony. Anne Bradstreet, on the other hand, earned praise for her deeply moving, yet pious, verses. A book of her poetry, *The Tenth Muse Lately sprung up in America,* was published in London in 1650. Eight years later it would be named one of the "most Vendible Books in England."

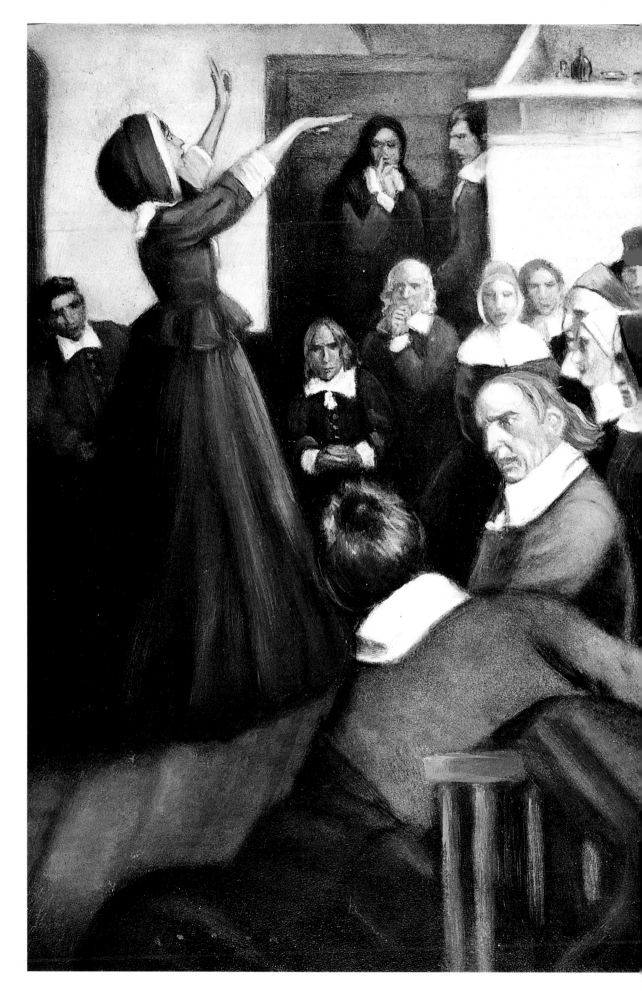

arranged the attack to erase once and for all this threat to their authority, the woman they called "the American Jesabel." What is certain is that Massachusetts officialdom rejoiced at news of the slaughter. "Thus the Lord heard our groans to heaven and freed us from this great and sore affliction." They rid themselves of another "affliction" in 1660, when Massachusetts hanged Mary Dyer for preaching Quakerism.

For the great majority of colonial women, however, activism of any kind was far from their minds—they were too busy working. Before going to sleep one night, a New York woman snatched a moment to mark her wedding anniversary in her diary. Her hasty note speaks powerfully of the realities of colonial life: "This day is forty years since I left my father's house and come here, and I have seene little else but hard labor and much sorrow....I am dirty and tired almost to death." From the South, lyrics to an old Virginia song sung by women give a glimpse of female life in the early days of the Old Dominion. It is not a hymn to female beauty, or a lusty alehouse ballad, but something less romantic and more forthright: "The Axe and Hoe have wrought my overthrow....If you do here come, You all will be weary, weary, weary, weary...."

Unlike the Good Wives of New England, most of the early female colonists to the Chesapeake Bay colonies of Maryland and Virginia came as indentured servants—young single women bound to work for a master for four to seven years. Life in the tobacco colonies was exceptionally hard in the 1600s. Virginia court records tell of two seamstresses whipped for turning in shirts that were too short, and of one servant forced to work even though she was ill—she died in the field, a tobacco hoe in her hand.

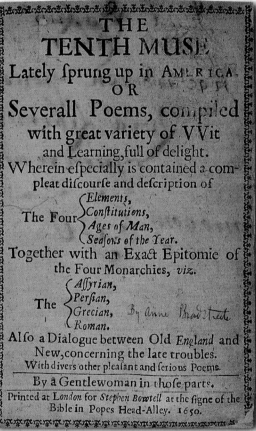

Nearly all women had to perform arduous field labor—distinctions between men's work and women's work did not really exist because all hands were needed in the fields. Tobacco required backbreaking toil in planting the delicate seedlings, plucking worms from stalks, and cutting the ripe plants. Working in the heat and humidity of the Chesapeake region took a heavy toll—it was said that newcomers needed six months of "seasoning" to get used to the southern climate, which seemed torrid to the English. Malaria, dysentery, "agues and fevers," childbirth, and accidents carried off most women before the age of 40 (men managed to last, on average, until their mid-40s). One quarter of the infants in the Chesapeake area died in their first year; 40 to 55 percent of all white children born in the Chesapeake died before their 20th birthday. Because early death was so common, most people married two or three times and the peculiar phrase "now-wife" entered the colonial lexicon, meaning "the wife I have now but not the ones I had before." Mixed families became common, as did orphans, who were typically "bound out" to work for a planter until they reached adulthood.

One Maryland planter called his colony a "paradise for women" because there were so few of them and they supposedly had their pick of husbands from hordes of suitors. Indeed the sex ratio stood at about six men for every woman in the early decades of settlement and didn't reach parity until the early 1700s. This gender gap might have been enjoyable for a young unattached woman living in a town with a lively social scene, but this was not the scenario in the colonial Chesapeake. "Thinly inhabited; the Living solitary and unsociable," one inhabitant described Virginia in the 1680s. To make matters worse, indentured servants, male and female, were forbidden to marry during their term of service. A female servant would have to share a cramped house with her master's family and a gang of male laborers of doubtful character. A woman who yielded to romance or fell victim to rape faced harsh consequences for bearing a child. Since a newborn added to a master's expenses, he was allowed to take the mother to court and have her term of indenture extended; her labor would compensate the master for the cost of feeding and housing her child. The law reserved its worst fury for a woman who bore a mixed-race child. Not only could she be heavily fined or whipped; she would also see her infant bound to serve her master for 30 years, a sentence bordering on enslavement.

In all the English Colonies, women had to contend with the prevailing social convention that women were subservient first to their fathers and then to their husbands. Indeed, the rule of the husband was enshrined in law: "The very being or legal existence of the woman is suspended during the marriage," famed English jurist, William Blackstone, wrote. (In the Dutch colony an entirely different climate prevailed. Women enjoyed much more economic and social independence; they could acquire real estate on their own and conduct business transactions without their husbands' consent.)

The English legal system allowed husbands to disavow debts incurred by their wives by posting a legal notice in a newspaper. These notices open a window onto the intimate domestic life of the colonial era, offering up fragments of stories sometimes humorous, sometimes

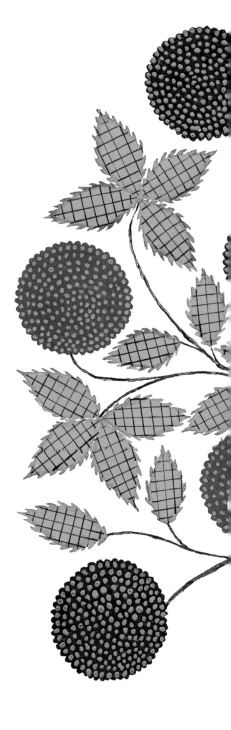

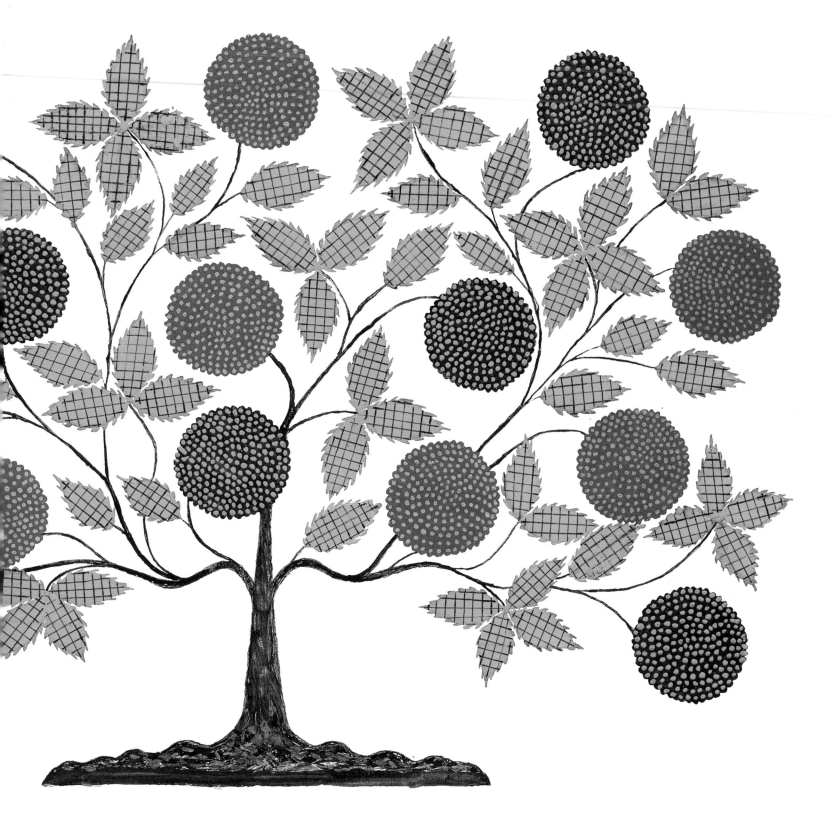

After experiencing a vision in 1854, Shaker member Hannah Cohoon painted "The Tree of Life," a symbol of unity for that utopian religious community. Eighty years earlier, Ann Lee, founder of the Shakers, had led a small group of persecuted English followers to New York State and founded a society based on faith, communal property, and celibacy. Though the movement eventually withered and died, the Shakers left a legacy of art, furniture, and household objects now much admired for their fine craftsmanship and powerful simplicity.

heartbreaking. Notices in *The Connecticut Courant* were most often posted by husbands, but there were also rejoinders from the wives forcefully stating their cases in an attempt to rescue their reputations as harridans, spendthrifts, and layabouts. Richard Smith posted a notice about his wife, Hannah, claiming that she "makes it her steady business to pass from house to house, with her buisey news, in tattling and bawling and lying, and carrying out things of my house...therefore [I] forbid all persons of having any trade or commerce with the said Hannah." Three weeks later Hannah launched a counterattack on Richard, who "keeps himself...intoxicated ten degrees below the level of a beast, and allows some of his children to treat a step mother with the most abusive, ignominious language, not sparing to kick her."

Richard's notice, beyond insulting his wife, had the purpose of cutting off her sources of income—he effectively prevented anyone from hiring her, or from buying anything from her. In similar fashion, another husband declared in an advertisement that he "forbid all persons. . .to employ her as a midwife, or in any other business." Swallowing their pride, husbands publicly accused their wives of infidelity in order to escape liability for their wives' debts. One man wrote that his wife had "taken her lodgings at Stephen Whites"; and another admitted that his wife and a man "were found late in the night in a tight room, partly undressed, with the bed clothes turned down."

Gravestones reveal that for some couples, marital strife ceased only when the Grim Reaper visited the household, giving the surviving mate the chance to get in the last word—permanently. One long-suffering woman ordered the epitaph:

> *Stranger, call this not a place of fear and gloom*
> *To me it is a pleasant spot—It is my husband's tomb.*

Another woman went to her reward under the inscription:

> *She lived with her husband fifty years*
> *And died in a confident hope of a better life.*

Obviously, some colonial women were not afraid to speak their mind for all posterity. Others broke from the conventional day-to-day roles assigned to them through sheer determination and talent. Eliza Lucas was of the latter school.

In 1739 at the tender age of 17, Eliza Lucas took charge of three South Carolina plantations covering some 5,000 acres. She would run them by herself for the next five years. Her father, Lt. Col. George Lucas of the British Army, had been summoned to Antigua, and he would never return to the Carolinas. He offered advice from afar, but mail service was erratic: "It was near 6 months since we had the pleasure of a line from you," Eliza wrote to her father in 1741. Some of his advice she ignored altogether. When he suggested that she marry—and had, conveniently, two prospects lined up—she did not mince words. Of the first candidate, whom she referred to as "the old Gentleman," Eliza wrote: "The riches of Peru and Chili if he had them put together could not purchase a sufficient Esteem for him to make him my husband." As for the second choice, "I have so slight a knowledge of him I can form no judgment of him, and a Case of such consiquence requires the Nicest distinction of humours and Sentiments." She made her own preference clear: "A single life is my only Choice and...as I am yet but Eighteen, hope you will [put] aside the thoughts of my marrying yet these 2 or 3 years at least."

In the meantime she would tend to business. She experimented with various West Indian seeds sent from her father, and had the greatest success with the gold-leafed indigo plant. English merchants enthused over the quality of the blue dye cakes produced from Eliza's crop, comparing them favorably to the best samples from France. Indigo proved so profitable to Carolina planters that within a few years the French declared it a capital crime to send indigo seeds out of their colonial islands. Eliza's success paved the way for other planters and helped transform the local economy. Eventually over a million pounds of dye cakes would be exported annually from South Carolina.

Eliza hatched a number of other moneymaking schemes—she planted an orchard of figs, to dry and export the fruit; inspired by reading Virgil, she established a cedar grove; and, since she looked "upon an old oak with the reverencial Esteem of a Druid," she invested heavily in oaks with a shrewd eye to the future. "I am so busey in providing for Posterity I hardly allow my self time to Eat or sleep," she wrote to a friend. "I am making a large plantation of Oaks which I look upon as my own property, whether my father gives me the land or not; and therefore I design many years hence when oaks are more valueable than they are now—which you know they will be when we come to build fleets."

Her interests were wide ranging. Studying law on her own, the teenaged Eliza drew up wills for neighbors and was named a trustee for a local widow's estate. On her own

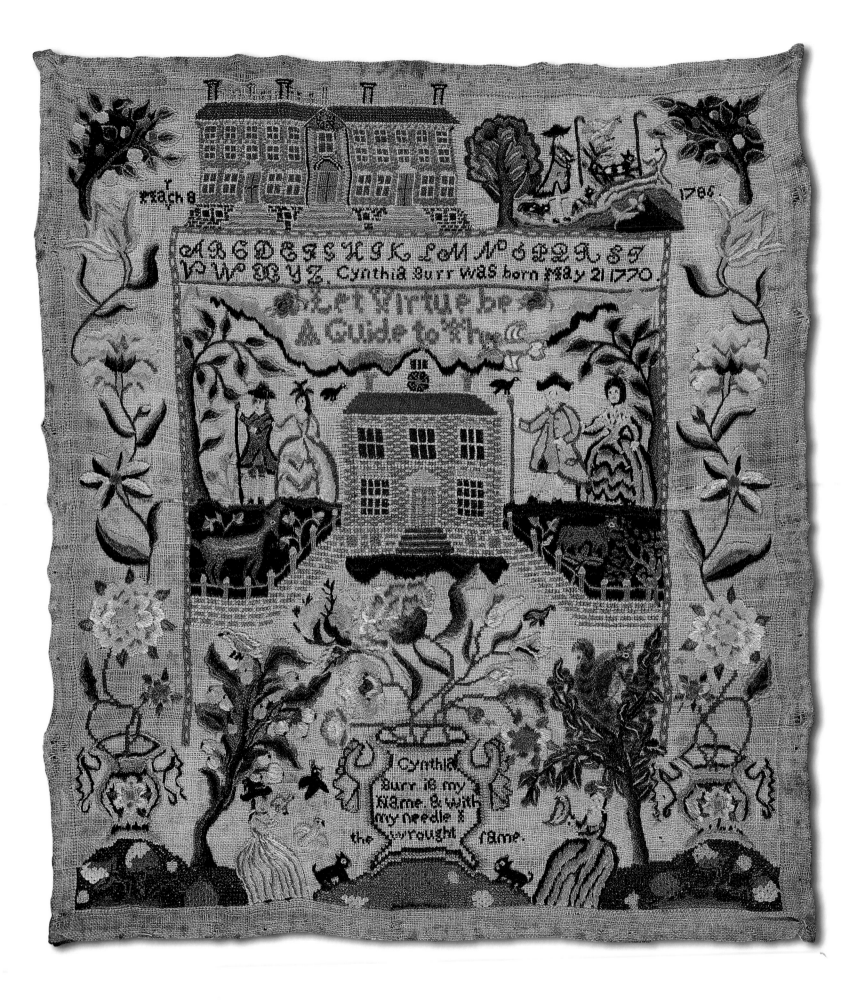

plantation she taught several slaves to read so that they could in turn teach the black children—a plan certainly not embraced by most slaveholders. In the midst of all of these duties, Eliza also devoted herself to the gentle arts so esteemed by her father, promising him that she would make herself "mistress of the Harpsicord."

In 1744 she married (undoubtedly to her father's relief) the wealthy South Carolina lawyer and landowner Charles Pinckney. Within a decade she and her husband and three children moved to England. In 1758 Pinckney, fearing a collapse of land values, returned to the Carolinas to dispose of his property. Eliza and their daughter accompanied him. Within two months of arriving home Pinckney contracted malaria and died.

Once more Eliza stepped into the breach. The 36-year-old widow took over the management of the Pinckney plantations and other landholdings, noting: "I find it requires great care, attention and activity to attend properly to a Carolina Estate...and make it turn to account." In a way, Eliza was grateful for the distraction; her grief over the loss of her "dear husband" was compounded by the pain of having left her two sons behind in England. "My heart bleeds at our separation," she wrote plaintively.

Her British-educated sons would eventually return to the Colonies and help lead the fight against the crown. After the war they would take on important political roles—one as the governor of South Carolina, the other as a delegate to the Constitutional Convention. Eliza did her part as well, lending the new state of South Carolina a large sum of money in 1779—money she had earned from her skillful land management. Even George Washington recognized her contribution to the new nation; after her death in 1793, he asked if he could serve as one of her pallbearers.

Self-possessed, accomplished, and proud of her achievements, Eliza Lucas Pinckney represented the new spirit of American womanhood that took root in the 18th century. She sat atop the social and economic ladder, but even on lower rungs the rising prosperity of the American Colonies allowed many women to move beyond "housewifery" into a realm of more genteel femininity, more sophisticated social interactions, and broader achievement. To be sure, drudgery filled many a day, and the boundaries of a woman's world were still irksome, but a measure of independence, even defiance, came into being. When a 1760s Rhode Island woman was upbraided for "moving beyond my line," as she put it, she shot back at her male critics: "Would you advise me to shut up my Mouth...and creep into obscurity?" That time had passed.

Just shy of her 16th birthday, Cynthia Burr showcased her talent in a detailed sampler she embroidered at school in 1786. Among the earliest depictions of Providence, Rhode Island, her scene includes the State House (center), as well as Brown University's first building (top). She also proudly stitched the sentiment: "Cynthia Burr is my Name & with my needle I wrought the same." Offering proof of a young woman's needle skills, such samplers became cherished heirlooms in colonial society.

Around 1780 Prudence Punderson of Connecticut embroidered
this self-portrait showing three
stages of her life: as an infant
being rocked by a black servant,
as a young woman sketching a
floral design, and in her own
closed coffin that bears the initials
"P.P." She entitled her silk-on-silk
needlework masterpiece "The
First, Second, and Last Scene
of Mortality." The artist would die
at the age of 26.

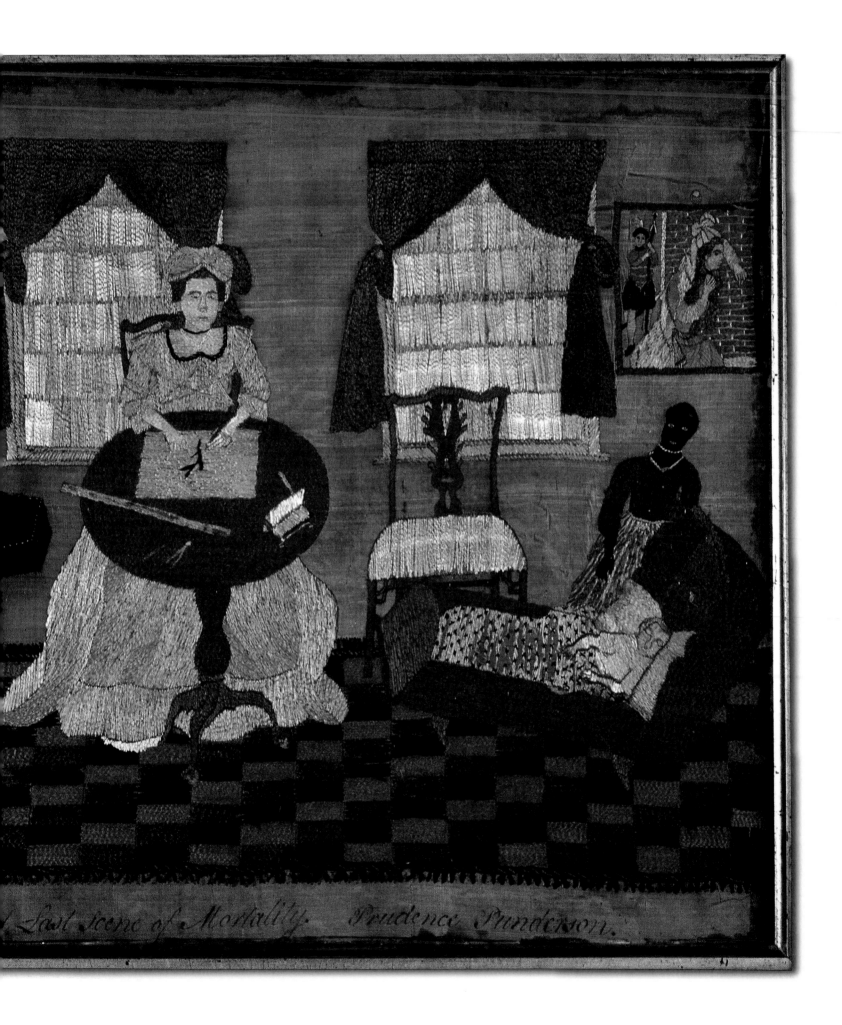

Last Scene of Mortality. Prudence Punderson.

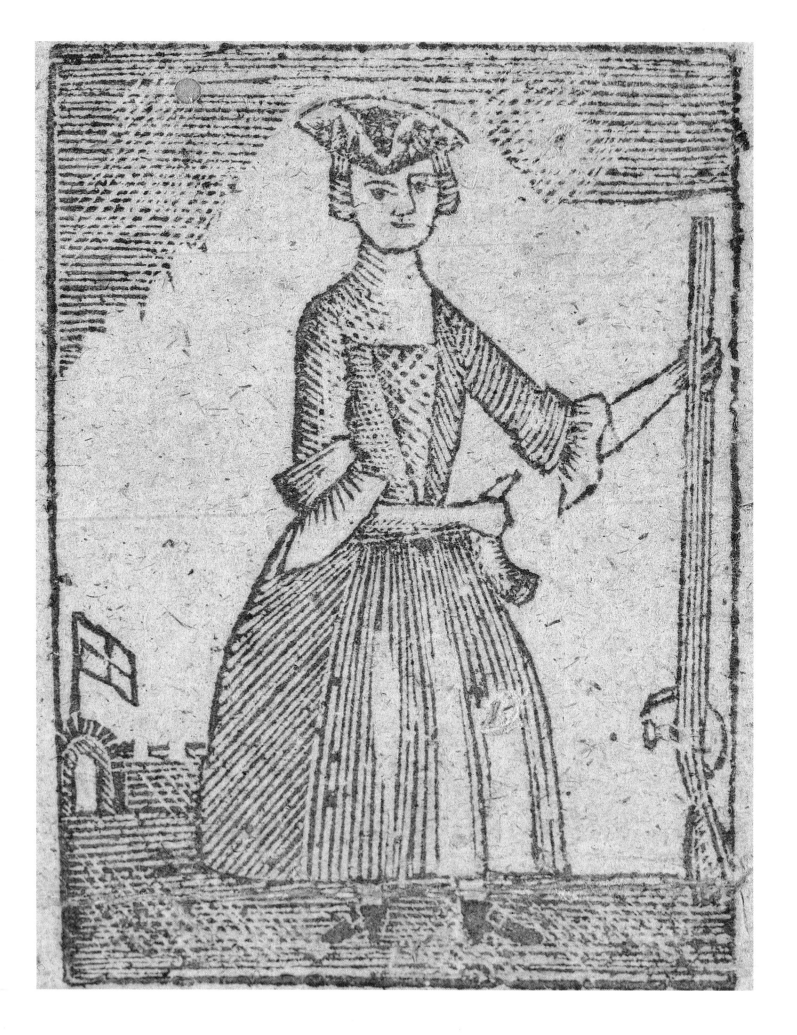

REVOLUTIONARY WOMEN

"**B**E IT KNOWN unto Britain," declared one Massachusetts woman in defiance, as the Revolution was unfolding, "even American daughters are politicians and patriots, and will aid the good work." For a very few daughters of America, exemplified by this anonymous, stern-faced patriot grasping a musket and powder horn, doing the good work meant taking up arms. Others boycotted tea and melted their own pewter to make ammunition. And the fiery Massachusetts patriot, Mercy Otis Warren, who wrote the warning to Britain to beware American daughters, took up her pen in defense of liberty. Warren became one of the key combatants in the nasty propaganda war before the Revolution, joining the fray with three satiric plays, *The Adulateur, The Defeat,* and *The Group,* which skewered Royal Governor Thomas Hutchinson and his coterie. Careful to avoid outright libel, Warren dubbed the villainous governor "Rapatio," a stage name that caught on with Boston's radicals. After reading one of Warren's plays, which were published anonymously in pamphlet form, Abigail Adams wrote an admiring letter to Warren, saying that the playwright had "thoroughly looked thro the Deeds of Men, and Developped the Dark designs of a Rapatio."

Mercy Otis Warren was the sister of one famous patriot, James Otis; the wife of another, James Warren; and an early convert to the Revolutionary cause. Her home in Plymouth was a gathering place for strategy sessions by Massachusetts patriots, and the launching pad for her own brand of scathing political satire. In December 1773, Abigail Adams wrote to Mercy about the arrival in Boston Harbor of a controversial cargo—"the Tea, that bainfull weed is arrived." A new tax on tea had enraged local citizens who were determined to prevent the cargo from reaching shore; in the ensuing Boston Tea Party, raiders heaved some 60 tons of English tea into the water.

Eager to celebrate the revolutionary event in verse, but lacking the skill to do so himself, patriot John Adams called upon Mercy's talent. In a letter to Mercy's husband, Adams outlined what he had in mind: "I want a poetical genius to describe a late frolic among the Sea Nymphs and Goddesses." She complied, producing an allegorical poem that appeared on the front page of the *Boston Gazette*. The verse set up a dispute between Neptune's two wives—the envious Amphytrite and the fair Salacia—over which type of tea was best; barely disguised Bostonians stepped in to settle the argument. [They]

> *Pour'd a profusion of delicious teas*
> *Which, wafted by a soft favonian breeze,*
> *Supply'd the watry deities, in spite*
> *Of all the rage of jealous Amphytrite.*

After the tea had been hurled into the waters,

The fair Salacia victory, victory sings,
In spite of heroes, demi-gods or kings;
She bids defiance to the servile train,
The pimps and sycophants of George's reign.

Though Warren won admiration and respect for her work, she still labored under the handicap of being a woman in 18th-century society. At that time it was considered unseemly for women to take an active interest in politics. Warren grudgingly accepted what she called women's "appointed subordination" in the scheme of things "for the sake of order in families." But she urged women not to submit to "such an inferiority as would check the ardour of our endeavors to equal in all mental accomplishments the most masculine heights."

After the Revolution, Warren drew upon her extensive contacts among patriot leaders (notably the Adams family) for the material that went into a monumental, three-volume history of the Revolution and its aftermath. Her friendship with John Adams enabled her to write a particularly detailed and useful account of diplomacy. But Adams hated Warren's account of his career, and he wrote her a string of cranky letters, including one insisting that her history should have ended with the Revolution, as everything beyond that was, as the French would say, "mustard after dinner." Ironically, Adams himself had urged Mercy Warren to write the history, as had his wife Abigail.

Mercy Warren's friend Abigail Adams also provided a vivid window onto the birth and formative early years of the nation, though she never composed a formal history. A compulsive letter writer, Abigail left behind an epistolary chronicle of the era. In her chatty letters she commented on the small and great matters of the day: the creation of the new government, the conduct of the war, the economy, religion, education, and the latest styles in dress and manners. Abigail directed her missives to many of the most important political figures of the day, but especially to her beloved husband, John.

Married in 1764, their partnership was a near-perfect match of wit, intelligence, and passion that lasted for over half a century. A country lawyer turned patriot and leader, John spent long periods away from their Braintree, Massachusetts, farm. For most of a decade—part of it while the Revolutionary War raged within sight—the young Abigail was left alone to manage their farm and raise their four young children. She did both

"These were times…which tried women's souls as well as men's."

JOHN ADAMS

LIBERTY TEA AND HOMESPUN

"We cannot be indifferent on any occasion that appears...to affect the peace and happiness of our country...."

THE EDENTON RESOLVES, SIGNED BY 51 LADIES, OCTOBER 1774

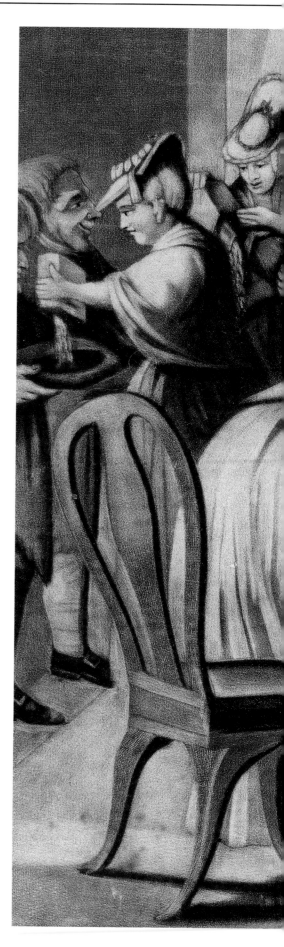

Women in late-18th-century America turned the spinning wheel and tea table into effective political weapons and, in the process, helped defeat the most powerful empire on Earth. When the English imposed taxes on treasured items such as silk, linen, and tea in the 1760s and 1770s, the "Daughters of Liberty" switched to homespun dresses—and wore them proudly; similarly, anti-tea leagues spurned "the pestilent British herb" in favor of "liberty teas" concocted from native plants.

In Edenton, North Carolina, a group of 51 women signed a petition announcing their intention to boycott tea and cloth, only to be lampooned in this British cartoon (right). Stunned that women would organize a political entity, one Englishman mocked, "Is there a Female Congress at Edenton too? I hope not, for...the Ladies... have ever, since the Amazonian Era, been esteemd the most formidable Enemies." American women would have the last laugh. Their political voice—proclaimed even on their teapots and in their mode of dress—would indeed be formidable.

"Let the Daughters of Liberty, nobly arise," Milcah Moore inscribed in her commonplace book in 1768:

Stand firmly resolved and bid Grenville to see/That rather

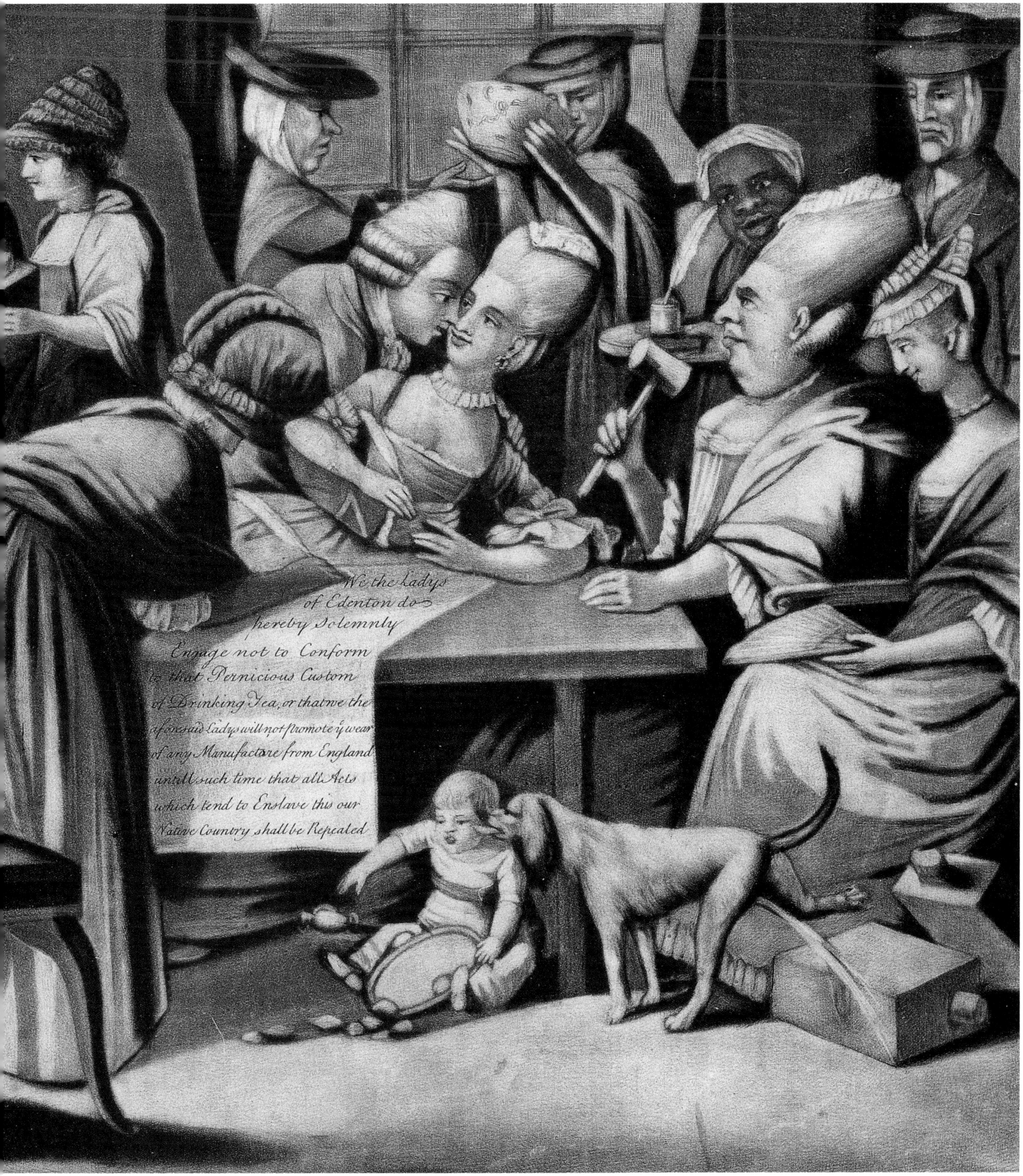

We the Ladys
of Edenton do
hereby Solemnly
Engage not to Conform
to that Pernicious Custom
of Drinking Tea, or that we the
aforesaid Ladys will not promote y.e wear
of any Manufactore from England
untill such time that all Acts
which tend to Enslave this our
Native Country shall be Repealed

than Freedom, we'll part with our Tea. And well as we love the dear Draught when adry/As American Patriots,—our Taste we deny.

Women sacrificed for the cause—and some did it with dramatic flourish. When nine-year-old Susan Boudinot was offered a cup of tea at the home of the Tory governor of New Jersey, she accepted it politely, curtsied, raised the cup to her lips, then threw the tea out the window. Women made alternative brews out of sassafras, strawberry, raspberry, sage, and currant leaves. One English aficionado was not impressed; after sampling a "liberty tea" he declared it had "a very physical taste." Patriot John Adams got an earful from his landlady who lectured him on the need to drink coffee—a

drink few people cared for at the time—rather than tea. And woe unto the merchants who stocked imported goods; when William Jackson of Boston did so, the Sons and Daughters of Liberty published the broadside below that urged a boycott of his shop.

Defying the dictates of both fashion and the English economy, women foreswore fine British cloth and made their own homespun. England depended on exporting textiles to the Colonies; an effective boycott would be a crippling blow to its economy. Spinning and weaving became acts of patriotism. Women gathered en masse for public spinning bees. In Newport, Rhode Island, Daughters of Liberty arrived at Minister Ezra Stiles's doorstep, where they "spun and reeled, respiting and assisting one another" until they had completed 170 skeins.

Patriot leaders pointedly wore homespun at public appearances, as did Harvard's entire graduating class one commencement. Tape looms like the one at right, adorned with a heart and a pair of young girls in profile and inscribed with "R. Lee," were used to make narrow strips of trimming. In the hands of determined patriots, such ancient weaving tools became instruments of rebellion. Abigail Foote of Colchester, Connecticut, created this handsome bed rug (left). She wrote in her diary on the eve of the Battle of Lexington, "I carded two pounds of whole wool and felt

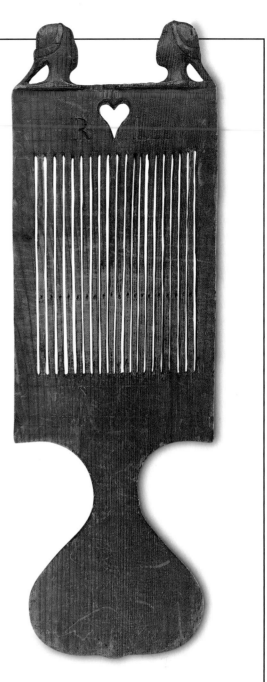

Nationly." She was right to take such pride in her work. Indeed, the activities of women like her would help wrest freedom from England. A Revolutionary-era New England minister recognized the importance of the patriotic spinners and declared his hope that "the women might recover to the Country the full free Enjoyment of all our rights, Properties & Priveleges (which is more than the Men have been able to do)." ∎

[January, 1770]
[1776 (?)]

WILLIAM JACKSON,

an IMPORTER; at the

BRAZEN HEAD,

North Side of the TOWN-HOUSE,

and *Oppofite the* Town-Pump, *in*

Corn-hill, BOSTON.

It is defired that the SONS and DAUGHTERS of LIBERTY, would not buy any one thing of him, for in fo doing they will bring Difgrace upon *themfelves*, and their *Pofterity*, for *ever* and *ever*, AMEN.

ably. Abigail traded livestock, hired farmers, oversaw the planting and harvesting, dealt with tenants, and even bought land (in her husband's name since as a woman she was legally barred from owning property). "I hope in time to have the reputation of being as good a Farmeress as my partner has of being a good Statesman," she wrote. With the wartime economy in disarray, Abigail instructed her husband, who was then posted in France, to send home luxury goods which she could sell at a profit. Similarly, she shrewdly speculated in currency. Abigail's sound management of their money and property rescued the family from the financial ruin that many other Revolutionary leaders, including Jefferson, suffered.

Finances were not her only concern; dealing with the vicissitudes of war became a daily reality. Shortly after the fighting began, John left for the Continental Congress in Philadelphia; though she tried to be "very sensible and heroic," Abigail admitted that her heart "felt like a heart of lead" at his departure. On a clear June day in 1775, Abigail awoke to a thunderous noise. She rushed to the top of nearby Penn's Hill with her seven-year-old son, Johnny (John Quincy Adams, the future President of the United States). Looking across Boston Harbor, she saw smoke rising from Charlestown as it was being bombarded by the British during the Battle of Bunker Hill. A sense of panic gripped local citizens: The English Army might march south en masse toward Braintree, as the Redcoats were already making forays into the area. "They delight in molesting us upon the Sabbath," Abigail wrote with disgust.

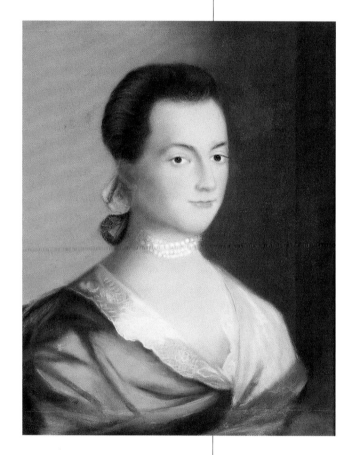

Abigail Adams deeply admired Mercy Otis Warren (opposite, in a painting by John Singleton Copley) for her literary flair in penning anti-British tracts. A voluminous letter writer herself, Abigail was embarrassed by her lack of formal education and urged her husband to burn her correspondence. Fortunately, he refused.

Over the spring and summer months, the Adams's farm often became a temporary refuge for patriots fleeing Boston, and a way station for militiamen in need of food, drink, or a night's rest. Their house was "a Scene of Confusion...you can hardly imagine how we live," she wrote to her husband. An entire company of militia encamped there one night, some soldiers sleeping in the attic, others in the barn. Young Johnny was delighted; he joined the militia as they marched up and down the field behind their house. For Abigail, however, the arrival of the soldiers meant more work and more anxiety.

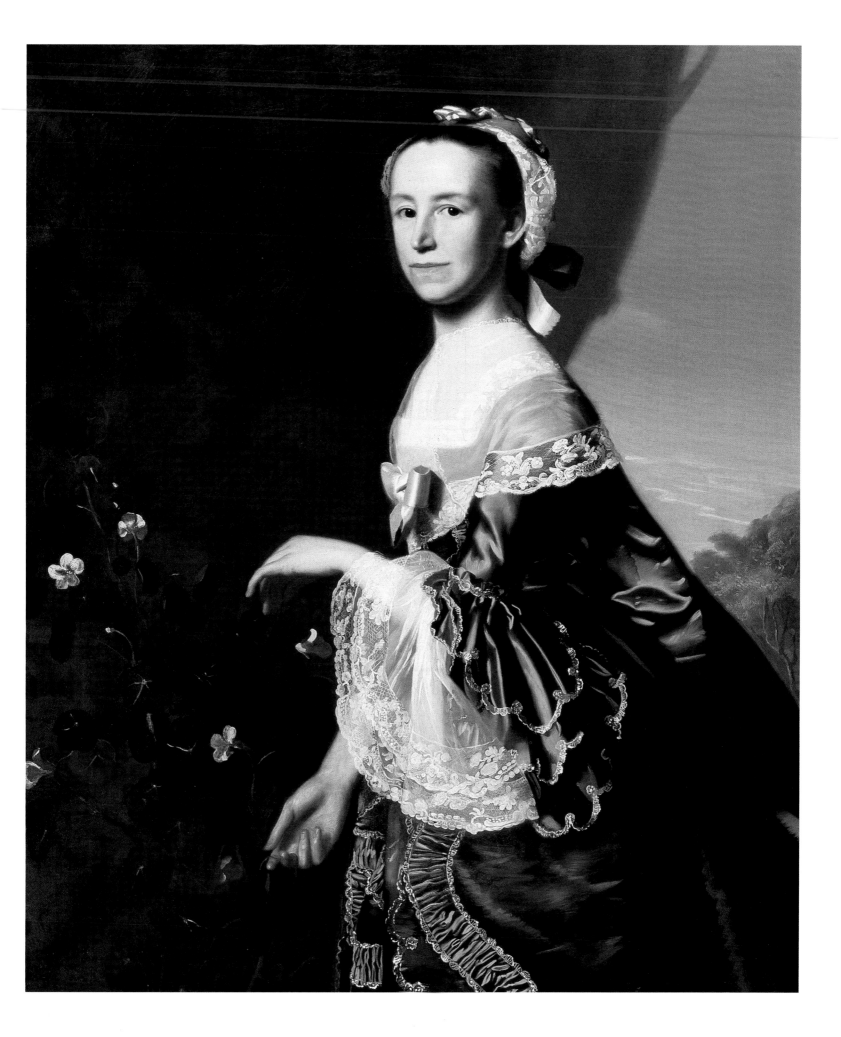

By the fall of 1775 an epidemic of dysentery had spread through Braintree and surrounding towns. Nearly everyone in the Adams's household came down with the disease—including Abigail and her youngest son, Tommy. Abigail recovered quickly, then took on the role of nurse. Abigail's son survived, but her mother contracted the disease and succumbed. The loss nearly overwhelmed Abigail. "At times I almost am ready to faint under this severe and heavy Stroke," she confided in a letter to her husband. Nonetheless, she soldiered on.

John Adams marveled at her bravery from afar, writing to her from Philadelphia in July of 1775, "It gives me more Pleasure than I can express to learn that you sustain with so much Fortitude, the Shocks and Terrors of the Times. You are really brave, my dear, you are an Heroine." John depended on Abigail's letters not only for family news, but also for an accurate account of events unfolding in New England. This was not an insignificant achievement, considering the limited means of communication in that day. Her letters provided "clearer and fuller Intelligence, than I can get from a whole Committee of Gentlemen," he boasted. In fact, John sometimes passed her informative letters around to his fellow delegates in Philadelphia.

Though her correspondence was filled with creative spelling and grammar, it also bristled with passion, love, and ideas. Beginning many of her letters with "Dearest Friend," and signing them with her pen name "Portia" (the virtuous wife and learned jurist of Shakespeare's *The Merchant of Venice*), Abigail was not afraid to express her emotions as well as her forceful opinions. "My pen is always freer than my tongue," she admitted to her husband. "I have wrote many things to you that I suppose I never could have talk'd." As members of the Continental Congress began to draw up a new code of laws in 1776, Abigail dashed off a note to her delegate husband, offering a famous bit of advice:

> *Remember the Ladies, and be more generous and favourable to them than your ancestors. Do not put such unlimited power into the hands of the Husbands. Remember all Men would be tyrants if they could. If perticular care and attention is not paid to the Laidies we are determined to foment a Rebelion, and will not hold ourselves bound by any Laws in which we have no voice, or Representation.*

Husband John responded with tongue firmly in cheek:

Depend upon it, We know better than to repeal our Masculine systems. Altho they are in full Force, you know they are little more than Theory.... We have only the Name of Masters, and rather than give up this, which would compleatly subject Us to the Despotism of the Peticoat, I hope General Washington, and all our heroes would fight.

But Abigail would have the last word, pointing out the hypocrisy of his position: "I can not say that I think you very generous to the Ladies, for whilst you are proclaiming peace and good will to Men, Emancipating all nations, you insist upon retaining an absolute power over Wives." Similarly, Abigail (despite the fact that she had grown up in a household with two slaves) was deeply troubled by the perpetuation of slavery in a new nation based on the principle of freedom. She distrusted the patriotism of Southerners, believing that "the passion for Liberty cannot be Eaquelly Strong in the Breasts of those who have been accustomed to deprive their fellow Creatures of theirs."

Throughout her life, Abigail remained an impassioned advocate of education for women, regretting her own deficiencies in that regard. When the time came to educate her daughter, Abigail insisted that she study Latin—the bedrock of a boy's classical education. Her husband, John, might not have entirely approved, but he was gone and Abigail was firmly in charge. Learning about the range of his daughter's studies, John warned the girl: "You must not tell many people of it, for it is scarcely reputable for young ladies to understand Latin and Greek."

John Adams was acutely aware of the great personal sacrifices and struggles that his wife and other women endured during the Revolutionary era. When he committed himself to the radical cause, he knew that the burden would fall on his wife. Years later, he recounted the scene in 1770 when he announced his decision to Abigail: "I said to my wife, 'I have accepted a seat in the House of Representatives, and thereby have consented to my own ruin, to your ruin, and to the ruin of our children....' She burst into tears, but instantly cried in a transport of magnanimity, 'Well, I am willing in this cause to run all risks with you, and be ruined with you, if you are ruined.'" Amazed and gratified by her spirit and resolve, John Adams went on to sum up the turbulent era: "These were times...which tried women's souls as well as men's."

The times were difficult; but for some women, the revolutionary spirit in the air was intoxicating—and liberating. While serving refreshments to Massachusetts men debat-

"*If perticular care and attention is not paid to the Laidies we are determined to foment a Rebelion, and will not hold ourselves bound by any Laws in which we have no voice, or Representation.*"

ABIGAIL ADAMS TO HER HUSBAND

An unknown artist depicts the brutal murder of Jane McCrae, an event in July 1777 that enraged colonists and led many to join the patriot cause. While traveling to meet her fiancé—ironically, a Tory officer—the beautiful 23-year-old woman was attacked and scalped by native warriors friendly to the English. The Indians presented her long tresses to British general Burgoyne. Patriot leaders played up the sensational story and won many new converts; the ranks of the Continental Army and local militias swelled.

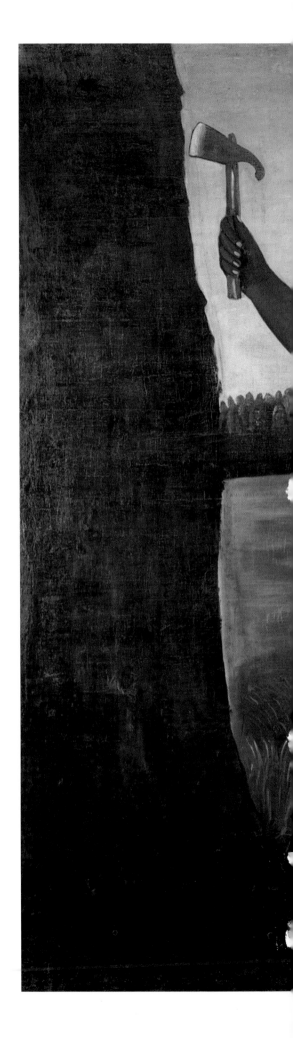

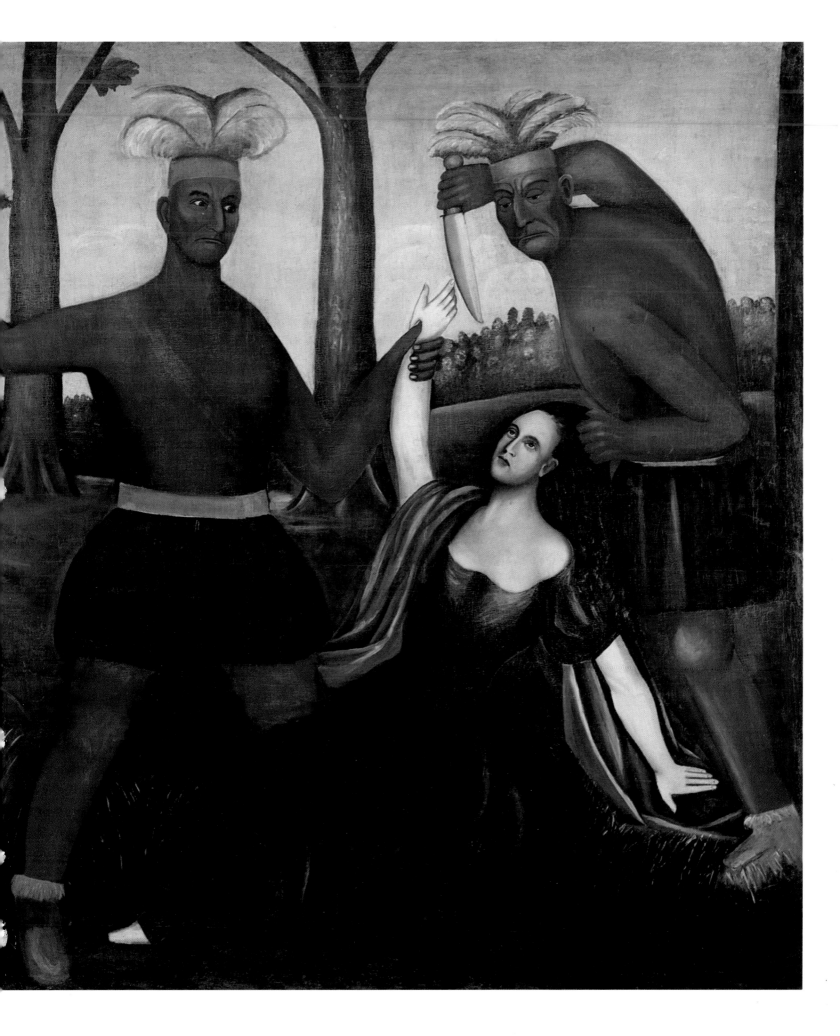

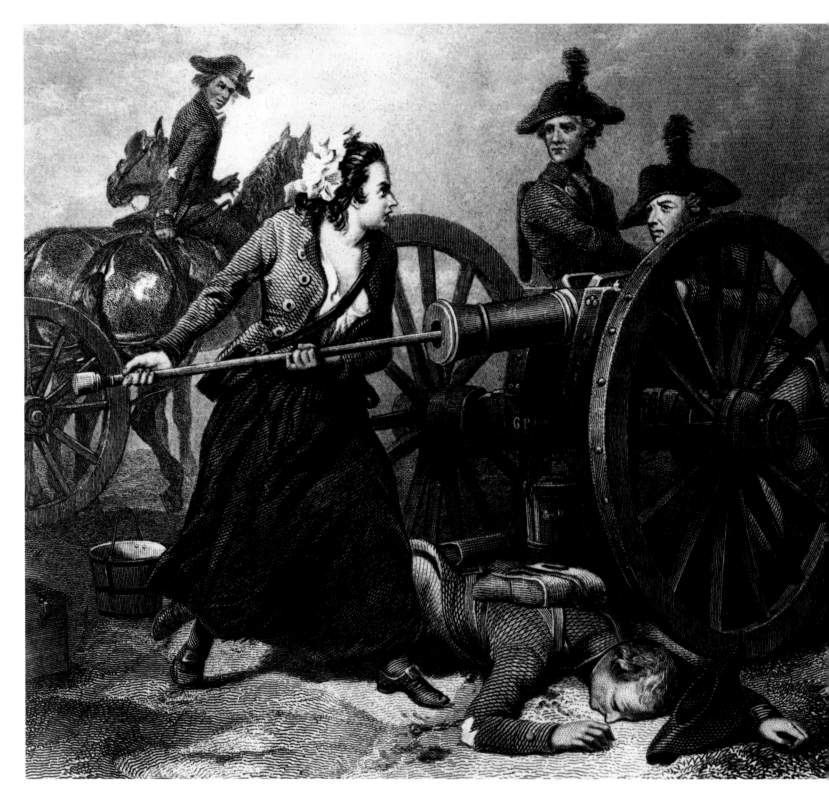

In this romantic engraving, Mary Hays, better known in legend as Molly Pitcher, bravely takes over her husband's artillery post after he fell wounded during the Battle of Monmouth, New Jersey. Nearly half a century after the battle, the Pennsylvania legislature awarded Hays a lifetime pension of $40 per year for her valor on the battlefield.

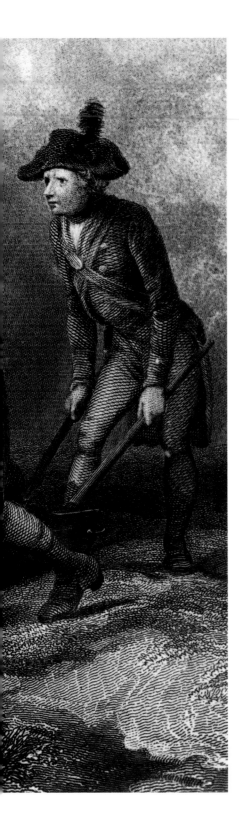

ing the rights of freedom, an illiterate slave nicknamed Mumbet overheard the discussion and was inspired by it: If all men were free and equal, then so was she. She kept her own counsel for some time on the subject, but when her mistress, in a fit of anger, hit her with a heated kitchen shovel, Mumbet had had enough. She stalked out of the house and went to a lawyer—she was determined to win her freedom and she would go to court to sue for it. She later told the lawyer's daughter that "if one minute's freedom had been offered to me, and I had been told I must die at the end of that minute, I would have taken it just to stand one minute on God's earth a free woman."

Arguing before court in the summer of 1781, Mumbet's lawyer, Theodore Sedgwick, Sr., alleged that she was being illegally held in bondage, in light of the new Massachusetts constitution. The jury found for Mumbet, and ordered her ex-master to pay 30 shillings in damages as well as court costs. She relished freedom and flaunted it, renaming herself Elizabeth Freeman. She seized upon the revolutionary sentiments of the time and made them a reality in her own life. During Freeman's final illness, Sedgwick's daughter visited every day: "I felt as awed as if I had entered the presence of Washington. Even protracted suffering and mortal sickness...could not break down her spirit."

Another woman who eloquently championed the cause of freedom wrote directly to George Washington in October 1775, shortly after he had been named commander in chief of the army.

> Sir,
>
> *I Have taken the freedom to address your Excellency in the enclosed poem, and entreat your acceptance, though I am not insensible of its inaccuracies. Your being appointed by the Grand Continental Congress to be Generalissimo of the armies of North America, together with the fame of your virtues, excite sensations not easy to suppress....Wishing your Excellency all possible success in the great cause you are so generously engaged in. I am,*
>
> *Your Excellency's most obedient humble servant,*
> *Phillis Wheatley*

The author of the letter and accompanying heroic verse was an extraordinary young woman who was already the darling of Boston intellectuals. An African, Wheatley had been abducted from her village at age seven or eight by slave traders and transported to Boston on the slave galley *Phillis* (from which she got her first name). Though a slave in a merchant's household and unable to speak English, the child quickly proved herself a

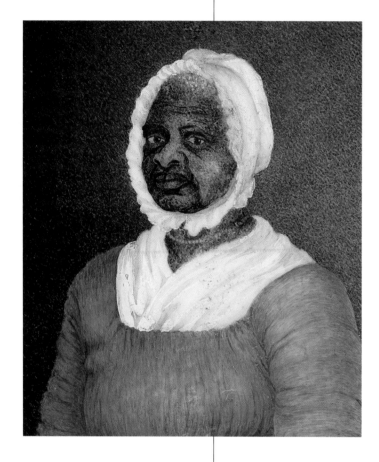

prodigy. She mastered English, then Latin; she took up pen and began writing poetry. In 1770, when only a teenager, Wheatley had her first poem published in pamphlet form in Boston. It was an immediate sensation. The literary set in Boston beat a path to her doorway to hear her read her verses or engage in conversation.

Her fame spread to England, where the Countess of Huntingdon sponsored publication of a book of her poems. In 1773 Wheatley arrived in London to great fanfare; English aristocrats sought her out. Her triumph was to be capped with her presentation to the royal court, but Wheatley cut her trip short when news came that her mistress was gravely ill. Back in Boston, Wheatley was set free by her dying mistress.

Both before and after receiving her freedom, Wheatley wrote influential verses lashing out against British tyranny and in favor of the Revolutionary struggle. Her ode to Washington was, in fact, published by Thomas Paine in *The Pennsylvania Magazine.* The commander in chief himself invited the poet to his headquarters in Cambridge, Massachusetts, where he met with her for half an hour. Washington recognized her as an eloquent—and stirring—voice for freedom. Yet her own story was a tragic one. She endured an unhappy marriage and the death of two of her children. In her early 30s she died, along with her last child, in a cheap boardinghouse where she worked as a servant. She and her child were buried in an unmarked grave. Despite her personal suffering and disappointments, Wheatley remained an impassioned supporter of the Revolutionary cause. One of her final poems celebrated the end of the Revolutionary War. It was entitled simply, "Liberty and Peace"—the very commodities Wheatley had sought, with only limited success, her entire life.

Voices such as Wheatley's were invaluable to the cause; they helped create an Amer-

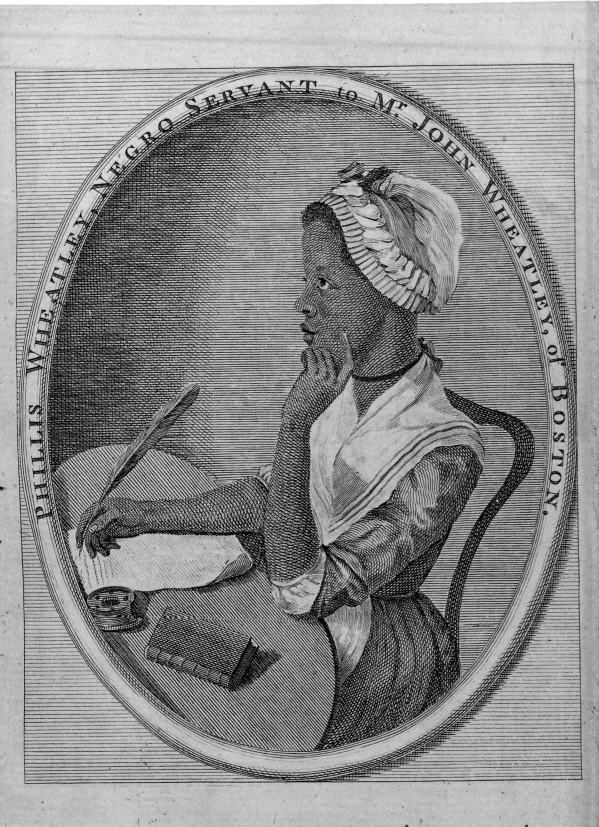

PHILLIS WHEATLEY, NEGRO SERVANT to Mʳ JOHN WHEATLEY, of BOSTON.

Publiſhed according to Act of Parliament, Septʳ. 1, 1773 by Archᵈ. Bell, Bookſeller Nº 8 near the Saracens Head Aldgate.

Poet Phillis Wheatley strikes a thoughtful pose in a frontispiece engraving that appeared in a collection of her verses published in London in 1773. An African-born slave in a Boston household, Wheatley stunned the literary world with her poetic achievement and became an eloquent champion of liberty during the Revolution. Similarly, during the war an enslaved woman named Mumbet would go to a Massachusetts courtroom, sue for her own freedom—and win. Years later, a miniature watercolor portrait of Mumbet (opposite) was painted on ivory. Though free, she still bears the mark of slavery; the scar above her left eye was inflicted by her cruel master.

ican spirit. The Revolutionary War not only pitted patriots against the British, but against Loyalist neighbors as well. The idea of independence was hardly embraced by all; in fact, more than half the population either actively supported Britain or remained neutral. Neighbors and acquaintances might suddenly turn up as enemies. Mary Silliman of Fairfield County, Connecticut, learned this the hard way.

As she and her husband, Gold Selleck Silliman, brigadier general of the local militia, were sleeping one spring night in 1779, loud banging awakened them. A group of men burst in and seized the general. Mary Silliman, then six months pregnant, cowered in bed as the kidnappers seized valuables and smashed all the windows. And then they vanished—dragging with them her husband and eldest son. Mary rushed to the rooftop and spied the raiders and their captives heading to a whaleboat on Long Island Sound.

Mary was certain the family would be attacked again, surrounded as they were by British sympathizers. In fact, she had known several of the men who had absconded with her husband and son; one of them had built a cider mill at the Silliman farm, another had made shoes for the family. For three weeks she heard nothing about her loved ones. Then one day her kidnapped son appeared at the door. Ill, he had been sent home on parole—meaning he remained a pawn, along with his father, in any prisoner exchange. Mary wrote to patriot officials urging them to arrange some kind of swap, but her pleas were met with indifference. General Washington had made it clear that he would never exchange British generals for militia officers.

While her husband languished as a prisoner, Mary had to bear the burdens of war alone. From her rooftop one day she spied enemy ships landing on the shore nearby and had to flee immediately with her family and their possessions. Mary remained outwardly calm, though panic must have gripped her when the carriage they were fleeing in broke down. Her nearly two-year-old son, Selleck, loved it. "The Cannon began to roar" from the enemy ships, Mary wrote, "which pleased Selleck, and he would mimic them by saying bang, bang. But they were doleful sounds in our ears." In the attack, the town of Fairfield was reduced to ashes. Mary returned home three days later and found it "full of distressed people who had lost their habitations"; rather than displace them, she retreated again to her refuge farther inland. There, she gave birth, at the age of 44, to her last child. That fall she returned to the family house.

A plan was hatched to free her husband. With the blessing of the governor of Connecticut as well as Mary, family members and friends arranged the kidnapping of a wealthy Tory named Thomas Jones, Chief Justice of New York's Superior Court. He lived in a splendid but isolated mansion on Long Island. On a November night in 1779, a band of 25 rowed across the Long Island Sound. Hiding the boat in the woods, the raiders stealthily approached the judge's house, from which they heard the sounds of music and dancing; the place was full of guests. The raiding party came upon the judge and one of his guests alone in the hallway; pouncing on them, they managed to kidnap them without alerting the other guests. Judge Jones would share breakfast the next morning with Mary Silliman at her home in Connecticut. Though he was grumpy, Mary was quite gracious to her unwelcome guest. In fact, the wife of the kidnapped judge would later write to Mary, expressing gratitude for her kindness to Mr. Jones and begging her to accept a pound of green tea.

An exchange of prisoners was finally negotiated after a torturous five months. Mary hired a boat to transport the judge and retrieve her beloved husband. She also sent along a fat turkey, and the kidnapped men, though officially enemies, shared a dinner at sea (it turned out that Gold Silliman and Thomas Jones had been students together at Yale) before returning to their respective homes. Mary and her husband were joyfully reunited. The war had literally burst into her home and turned it upside down, but she had persevered. Her son later remarked that she always cheerfully travelled "up instead of down the hill of life."

Mary Silliman was not alone in her uphill struggles. The Revolutionary War disrupted the lives of women throughout the Colonies, and forced many of them to take strong political stands and actions. Some, like Peggy Shippen, a young Philadelphia aristocrat, fervently supported the British. As an 18-year-old, Shippen married the ambitious—and embattled—general of the Continental army, Benedict Arnold. Arnold

The color of Martha Washington's pink satin shoe (below) has faded with time, but captures her understated elegance, as does her miniature portrait (opposite). A watercolor on ivory, the graceful portrait by Charles Willson Peale depicts a stylish Martha with a swag of pearls in her hair complementing her pearl necklace. The artist completed this, as well as a matching miniature of George Washington, just weeks after the adoption of the Declaration of Independence in 1776.

was fighting charges of profiteering that had been leveled against him, and when Washington failed to support him, Arnold turned his back on the patriot cause—at the urging of his new wife. She became deeply enmeshed in a plot that, if successful, would have resulted in the surrender of West Point and the capture of Washington himself. When a British spy was caught with papers outlining the treasonous plot, Arnold's fate seemed sealed, but Peggy staged a dramatic fit of hysteria; in the confusion, Arnold made his escape. Her feigned madness convinced Washington, who had her sent back to her family in Philadelphia. Peggy, along with her husband, would eventually be exiled from her native country—and reviled forever.

Other women fought just as doggedly for the patriot cause. They sewed uniforms and bandages for the soldiers and donated their pewter dishes, cutlery, and candlesticks to be melted into cannonballs and shot. One New England woman was so eager to supply bullets for the troops that she even pilfered from her ancestors—melting down the nameplates accompanying her family's graves. A women's group in Litchfield, Connecticut, managed to obtain most of the monumental equestrian statue of King George III that had been torn down by angry patriots on Bowling Green in New York City. Ingeniously, they melted the hated statue down for its lead, which they poured into molds to make musket cartridges (over 42,000 of them) for use by patriot troops.

Individual women stepped to the fore in a time of crisis. Sybil Ludington of Fredericksburg, New York, was the female equivalent of Paul Revere. The 16-year-old daughter of a militia commander, Sybil raced to her horse when word came that 2,000 British and Loyalist troops were then besieging the town of Danbury, across the border in Connecticut. Riding 40 miles through the night, she woke the scattered members of the militia, banging on their doors with a stick and calling them to arms.

On the battlefield, women carried ammunition and water to the troops—both to slake the thirst of the soldiers and to swab out the blisteringly hot cannon after each firing. For their work hauling water, these women were referred to as "Molly Pitchers." Mary Ludwig Hays won lasting fame as Molly Pitcher for her role in the Battle of Monmouth, New Jersey, on June 28, 1778, an exceedingly hot day when the temperature rose to over 100 degrees. Hays carried water from a nearby well to the wounded and exhausted soldiers—including her own husband who was manning the artillery. Legend has it that when her husband was wounded at his post, she stepped in and took over. Another soldier, however, described seeing the two of them working together during the battle, and he was struck by her courage under fire: "a cannon shot from the enemy passed directly between her legs without doing any other damage than carrying away all the lower part of her petticoat," he noted. "Looking at it with apparent unconcern, she observed that it was lucky it did not pass a little higher, for in that case it might have carried away something else." She continued on with her work.

Margaret Corbin also won fame as another Molly Pitcher. When her artilleryman husband was mortally wounded during the defense of Fort Washington in Manhattan, she bravely took over at his cannon even though it was in an exposed position. Shortly thereafter, she, too, was felled by grapeshot—one of her arms was nearly torn off and her breast pierced. Her wounds left her disabled for the rest of her life. In 1780 Congress appointed her (the only woman thus named) to the Invalid Regiment, a unit posted at West Point. She was awarded a lifelong monthly Congressional pension, and she later petitioned and won an increase in rations—including the portion of rum or whiskey that had been denied her because she was a woman. A hard-drinking eccentric known in her later years as "Captain Molly," Corbin died and was buried in an unmarked grave. Over a century after her death, however, she was reinterred at West Point and honored with a monument for her remarkable sacrifice in battle.

Women rose up to defend their home ground, and at times, that included taking up arms—or destroying them. In 1781 the Shell family in upstate New York had been under attack by Loyalist forces and their Indian allies from early afternoon until twilight. Elizabeth Shell had spent the day feverishly reloading guns for her husband and sons. Suddenly five of the enemy poked their muskets right through the walls. In a flash, Elizabeth grabbed an ax and smashed at the gun barrels, ruining them. The invaders melted back into the forest, clutching their mangled rifles.

When news reached the residents of Groton, Massachusetts, that the British were en route, local women promptly organized a female militia. Wielding muskets and pitchforks, the women successfully dispersed a detachment of British soldiers. A handful of women actually joined up with the regular army, drawn perhaps by economic need. They bound their breasts and disguised themselves as men to do so. At least one, a young Creole woman named Sally St. Clair, was killed in battle; another woman rose to the rank of sergeant before her sex was discovered and she was discharged.

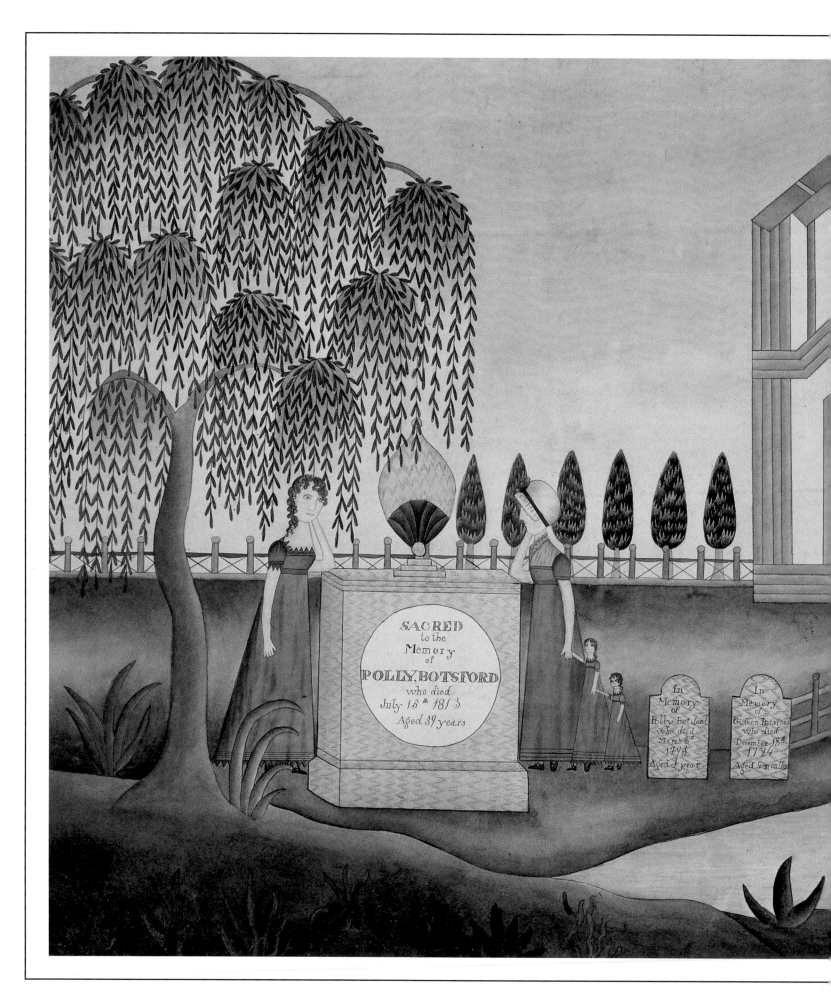

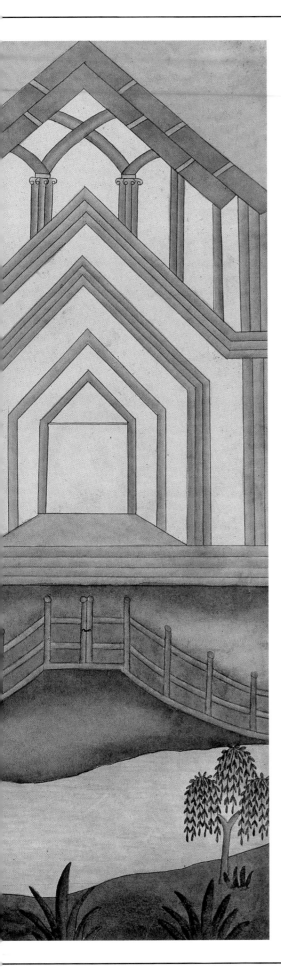

SOMBER MASTERPIECES

*"Here let the orphan drop the filial tear
O'er the frail casket of a mother dear!"*

ANONYMOUS ARTIST, CIRCA 1822

The early 1800s saw the flowering of a remarkable art form practiced by young American women, mainly schoolgirls between the ages of 10 and 20. Mourning art—fed more by fashion than by a morbid fascination with death—became the rage. Highly stylized pictures commemorating the deceased were produced in great numbers in female academies. Many of the recurring motifs and designs were drawn directly from widely circulated memorial prints dedicated to George Washington.

The earliest mourning scenes were embroidered, and the skill required to create detailed scenes by stitching silk threads onto a silk background (with some figures having real hair) made memorial pieces prized samples of a student's needlework. In fact, some young women specifically enrolled in embroidery schools to create one of these intricate mourning scenes.

In *Oldtown Folks*, Harriet Beecher Stowe harked back to the days when "female accomplishments consisted largely of embroidering mourning pieces, with a family monument in the centre, a green ground worked in chenille and floss silk, with an exuberant willow tree, and a number of weeping mourners, whose faces were often concealed by flowing pocket handkerchiefs."

Though the design elements remained the same, mourning scenes were soon painted rather than stitched. The ink and watercolor painting at left entitled "Memorial Picture for Polly Botsford and her Children," was probably made by a young woman around 1815. Its spare, simple quality and the austere, geometric evocation of the church seem to presage modern painting.

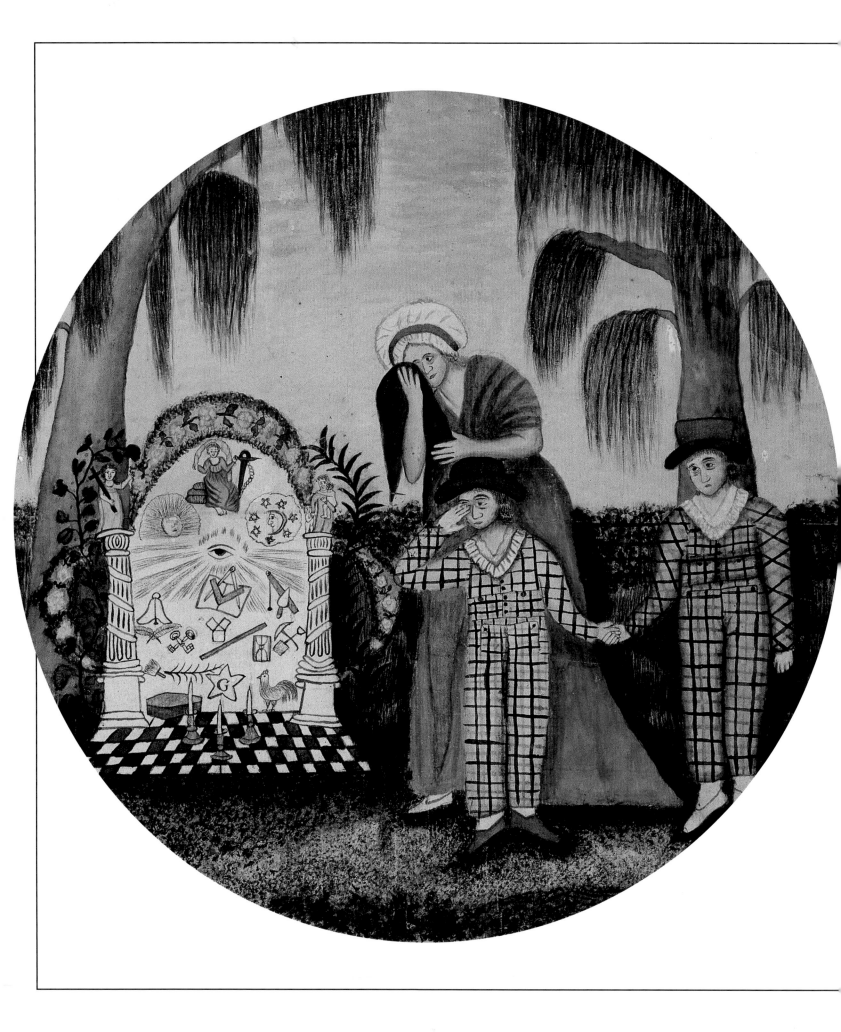

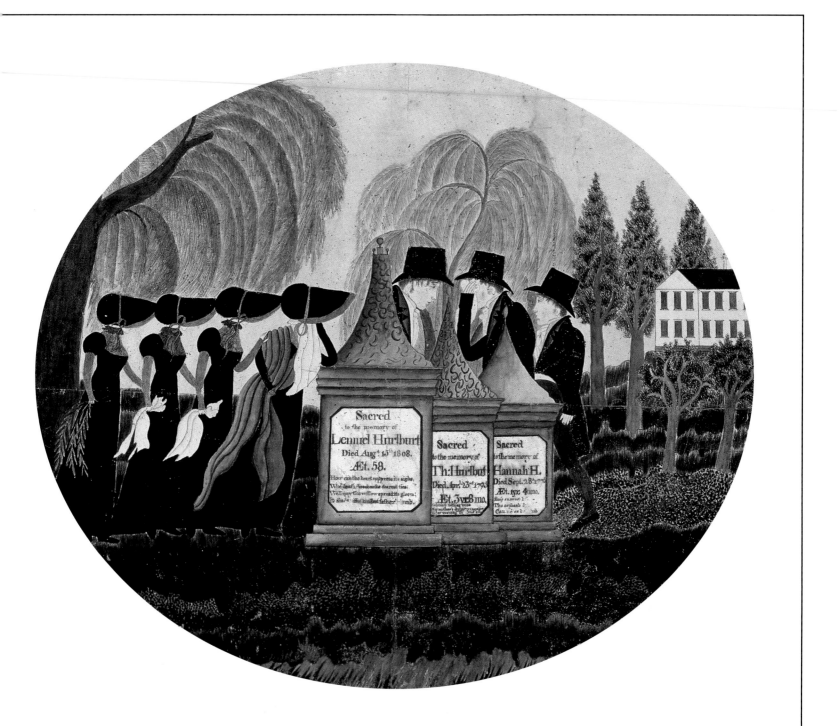

In 1809 Eunice Pinney painted the watercolor at left to memorialize the death of her friend, Rev. Ambrose Todd, the 41-year-old rector of the Episcopal church in Simsbury, Connecticut. Todd was obviously a member of the Masons — as evidenced by the masonic symbols that adorn his tombstone.

Artist Elizabeth Hurlburt chose to paint her grieving family members (above) in profile as they gathered at a grave site. The outline of the figures in their identical black bonnets and top hats, dresses, and frock coats lends a strikingly original element to the watercolor.

Though marvels of early American art, mourning art was not appreciated by everyone. Around 1800, one gentleman visiting an academy scribbled this verse:

In useless labors all their hours are spent
They murder Time,
then work his monument. ∎

Deborah Sampson cut her hair, put on men's clothing, and signed on with the Continental Army as "Robert Shurtliff." During a skirmish near Tarrytown, New York, she took a bullet in the leg and a saber blow to her forehead. Carried to a military hospital, she somehow eluded detection (legend has it that she removed the bullet herself before the doctor could get to her). Her secret was discovered, however, during another hospital stay when she was ill with fever. Honorably discharged, she eventually used her adventures to help support herself and her family: She appeared on the lecture circuit in full military regalia and gave a narration of her army days, along with a stirring performance of military drills.

Though few actually donned the uniform of the Continental Army, women swarmed to the encampments, where they cooked, sewed, washed, and nursed the soldiers. Usually the wives, daughters, or mothers—or in the South, often the slaves—of the enlisted men, these camp followers were critical in sustaining the troops; in semi-official recognition of that fact, they received half rations for themselves and quarter rations for each of their children. They also suffered the consequences if they failed to uphold their duties. During the desperate winter at Valley Forge in 1778, Mary Johnson and a number of other men and women were charged with planning to desert the army. For her crime Johnson was sentenced to receive a hundred lashes; she was also "drummed out of the army by all the fifes and drums of the division."

Officers' wives also joined the encampments, including the Virginia aristocrat Martha Washington, who spent the infamous winter at Valley Forge with her husband. Martha and George were deeply devoted to one another (throughout their married lives George wore a miniature portrait of his wife around his neck); and each winter, between campaigns, she would join her husband in camp. "I was," she later recalled, "a kind of perambulator during eight or nine years of War." Though she disliked traveling great distances and being away from Mount Vernon, she felt bound to duty: "If he does [call me], I must go," she explained to her brother-in-law.

Her presence in camp brought solace—as well as nursing skills—to both her husband and his men. "Mrs. Washington combines in an uncommon degree great dignity of manner with the most pleasing affability," one soldier confided in his diary. An aide to Baron Steuben was mightily impressed by her: "She reminded me of the Roman matrons of whom I had read so much, I thought that she well deserved to be the companion and friend of the greatest man of the age." Though life in camp was not nearly as spartan for her as it was for regular camp followers (she and her husband generally stayed in a private residence), she had her share of anxious moments. When alarms roused the headquarters at Morristown, New Jersey, Martha and the woman who owned the house "were obliged to lie in bed, sometimes for hours, with their room full of soldiers, and the keen winter air from the open windows piercing through their drawn curtains."

Though she was treated with deference and referred to as Lady Washington in camp, she was a model of humility and hard work. When a trio of women visited her at Morristown, they dressed in elegant silks, expecting to meet a grand lady. "Don't you think we found her knitting *and with a (check) apron on!*...General Washington's lady with her own hands was knitting stockings for herself and husband! And that was not all. In the afternoon her ladyship took occasion to say....'We must become independent by our determination to do without what we cannot make ourselves. Whilst our husbands and brothers are examples of patriotism, we must be patterns of industry.'"

Martha Washington would bring that same modesty, lack of pretense, and sense of duty to her role as First Lady. In turn, she helped shape the nature of the Republic itself. After Washington had been elected President, there was great controversy over his role and even how he should be addressed: His Elective Highness and Majesty were among the titles considered. As for Martha's title, some suggested Marquise or Lady. The couple could have easily affected a kind of royal presence. But Martha remained Mrs. Washington (the term "First Lady" would not be used for another century), thus setting a precedent and a tone for succeeding wives. Abigail Adams, wife of the Vice President and an apt judge of character, had this to say of Martha: "Her manners are modest and unassuming, dignified and femenine, not a tincture of ha[u]ture about her."

Though she intensely disliked public life, Martha accepted her lot for the good of the country. "I live a very dull life hear and know nothing that passes in the town," she complained of her situation in New York, the nation's first capital. "I never goe to any publik place.... I think I am more like a state prisoner than anything else, there is certain bounds set for me which I must not depart from—and as I can not doe as I like I am obstinate and stay at home a great deal." But her very presence and manner helped establish a dignified yet democratic presidency, the hallmarks of the new nation.

> *"Whilst our husbands and brothers are examples of patriotism, we must be patterns of industry."*
>
> MARTHA WASHINGTON

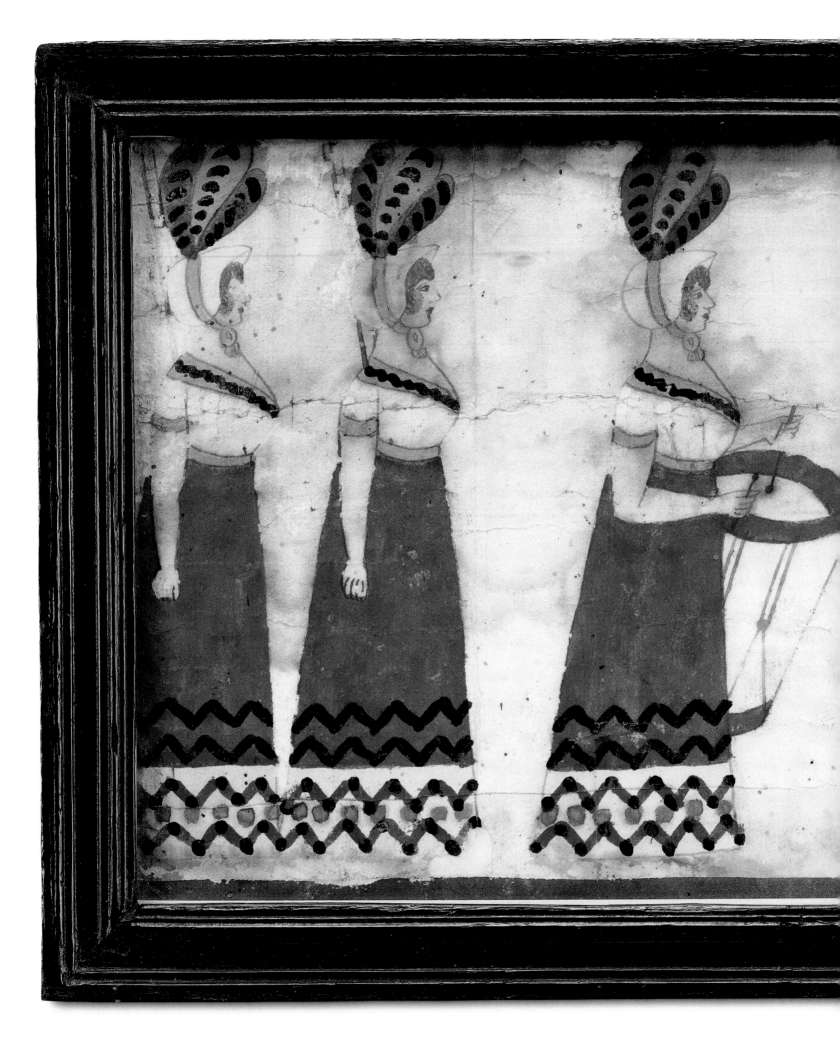

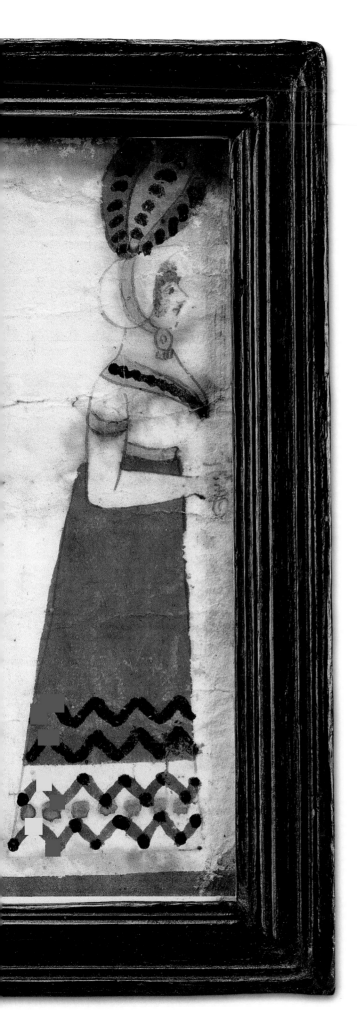

Four women march to the beat of a drum in this charming watercolor dating from the early 1800s. Having battled both behind the scenes and on the front lines during the Revolutionary War, women had helped wrest freedom from England and took pride in the new nation.

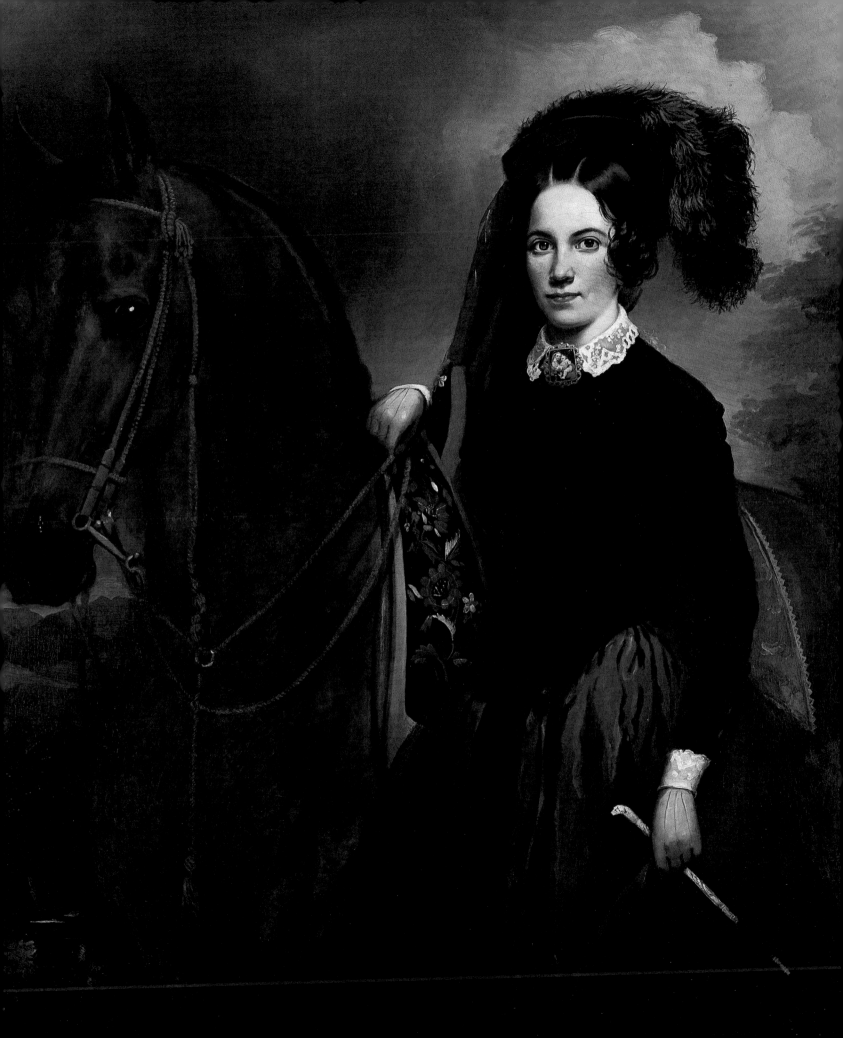

PLANTATION MISTRESSES

*T*HE SOUTHERN BELLE. Dressed in a hoop skirt, she oozes charm and a deep drawl. She's sweeter than a mint julep, yet more seductive—and dangerous—than the bourbon in it. Think Scarlett O'Hara. Or worse yet, the flip side of the coin—the treacly, long-suffering and noble Melanie in *Gone With the Wind.* These Hollywood-fed stereotypes persist in the American imagination.

The reality, of course, was infinitely more complicated and interesting. The portrait of Adelicia Acklen at left barely hints at the reserves of strength, financial acumen, and sheer audacity she would exhibit in her lifetime. In fact, aristocratic Southern women were not mere baubles; they were essential to the very creation and development of the plantation economy. Even the Virginia House of Burgesses recognized that reality, declaring in 1619: "In a newer plantation it is not knowen whether man or woman be the most necessary."

Women literally held the keys to the plantation ("I keep all the keys and if anything is wanted they are obliged to come to me," wrote one plantation wife), and that domain included the Big House, the mansion where the planter and his family lived, as well as the barns, stables, warehouses, smokehouses, and slave quarters. She was undisputed ruler of the household, a task which the 18th-century Virginian Molly Randolph claimed "bears a Lilliputian resemblance to the government of a nation.... The contents of the Treasury must be known, and great care taken to keep the expenditures from being equal to the receipts." While the husband usually oversaw the production and sale of the crops, the woman of the house had to manage and organize everything else. The female half of the team often kept detailed records of the day-to-day expenses involved in running the household—and in the process, outlined the complexity of her job. She had to feed, clothe, and nurse everyone on the plantation, which included her own family and perhaps scores (or even hundreds) of slaves. She was in effect the chief executive officer of a domestic corporation.

Ann Hairston of the Beaver Creek plantation in Virginia painstakingly kept an account book for 37 years, from 1831 to 1868. Not a penny was spent on household goods or a bundle of raw cotton given to a slave without its being noted. (Ann would subsequently record how much thread had been produced from that cotton, to make certain that her slaves were not stealing from her.) The plantation was largely self-sufficient, and the quantity of textiles produced at Beaver Creek was prodigious. Rugs, tablecloths, fine linens, bed ticking, and curtains for the Big House; bonnets and frocks for the mistress of the house and diapers for her children; coarse winter and summer clothing for the slaves; blankets for newborn slaves—Ann shrewdly oversaw the production of all of these textiles. With an eye to saving money one season, Ann directed her slaves to spin cow's hair with wool in making coarse carpets for the main house—and blankets for the black children. Chillingly, Ann also kept an annual tally of the number of slaves between ages 12 and 50 that they owned, along with the number of horses—both being taxable assets.

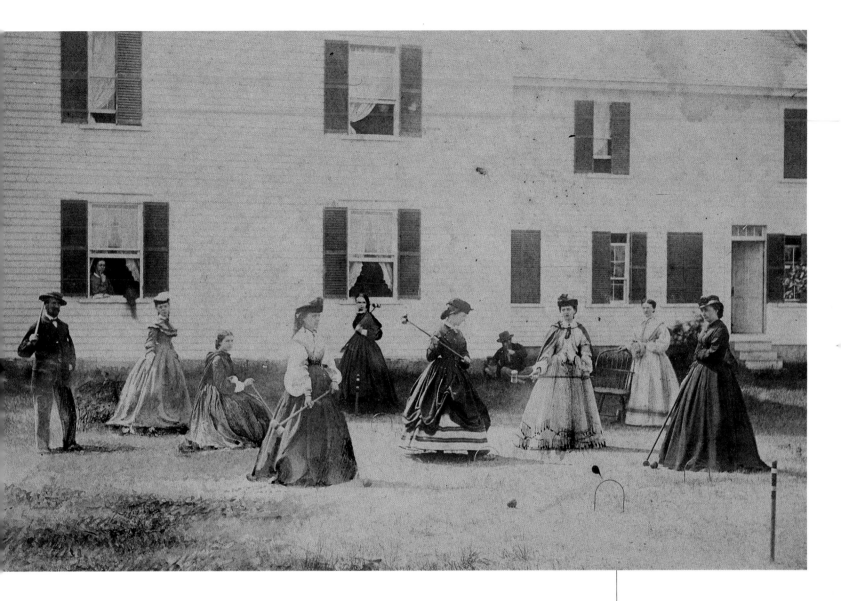

As caretakers of the slaves who lived and worked on their plantations, white plantation mistresses often wrestled with conflicting emotions about their role. One young wife expressed horror over slavery's violence. "Awakened this morning by the screeching of a female slave who was fleeing from the whip of her enraged master. I never witnessed such a scene...her neck torn and bloody, her eyes swollen." Over time, however, her own views would shift dramatically. Seventeen years later she would mention matter-of-factly that she "had her little servant Jim whipped for fighting." .

Some women were so disgusted by the evils of the "peculiar institution" that they decided to do something about it. Landonia Randolph, one of Virginia's slave-holding elite, spent over 30 years battling with cousins over the ownership of slaves she wanted to free and send to Africa. In 1830 she tried to gather scattered members of an enslaved family, some from nearly a hundred miles distant. She even offered to purchase one woman's husband, who worked on a different plantation, for $500 so that the couple could go to Africa reunited. Landonia tried to free a slave woman named

The unknown, well-heeled southern matron (opposite) stares
intently at the camera in this mid-
19th-century daguerreotype.
Dark circles ring her eyes and her
tight-lipped expression bears not
an ounce of lightheartedness or
flirtatiousness, the supposed hallmarks of the southern woman.
She is surrounded by her young
children. Looming behind her is
the shadowy figure of her slave,
a woman whose features have
been lost over time. Scratched
and murky, this enigmatic image
dispels the clichéd notion of the
romantic southern belle and
gives a hint of the complexity
of her world.

Sarah Ann whose mistresses, Ann and Nancy Kincaid, had kept a "secret" from their slave. The Kincaids asked Landonia not to let Sarah Ann know that she would be legally free upon their deaths, a fact that "might cause some impatience in her to see that day arrive" even earlier.

The newly widowed Martha Washington found herself in a similar position in 1800. According to the provisions of her husband's will, Washington's slaves were to be freed upon the death of Martha, a situation fraught with tension. Surrounded by what she considered potential assassins, Martha prudently freed the slaves early. Some mistresses feared being poisoned—or suffering even worse fates—at the hands of their slaves. Keziah Brevard, a middle-age South Carolina widow, lived in perpetual fear of her large labor force, admitting in 1861 that "we know not what moment we may be hacked to death in the most cruel manner by our slaves."

Many plantation mistresses viewed slavery as a curse—and viewed themselves as the victims of that curse. In detailing the "evils of slavery," one white southern woman complained that "slaves are a continual source of more trouble to housekeepers than all other things, vexing them, and causing much sin." The sin that was most feared—and yet most consciously ignored—was one that Mary Chesnut, the South Carolina aristocrat and renowned diarist, spoke about openly:

> God forgive us, but ours is a monstrous system, a wrong and iniquity. Like the patriarchs of old, our men live all in one house with their wives and their concubines; and the mulattoes one sees in every family partly resemble the white children. Any lady is ready to tell you who is the father of all the mulatto children in everybody's household but her own. Those, she seems to think, drop from the clouds.... A magnate who runs a hideous black harem with its consequences under the same roof with his lovely white wife, and his beautiful and accomplished daughters? He holds his head as high and poses as a model of all human virtues to these poor women whom God and laws have given him.

Indeed, miscegenation was widespread on plantations, and the white mistress was expected to look the other way. Naturally, there were exceptions to the rule. One wife became so enraged that she "slipped in a colored gal's room and cut her baby's head clean

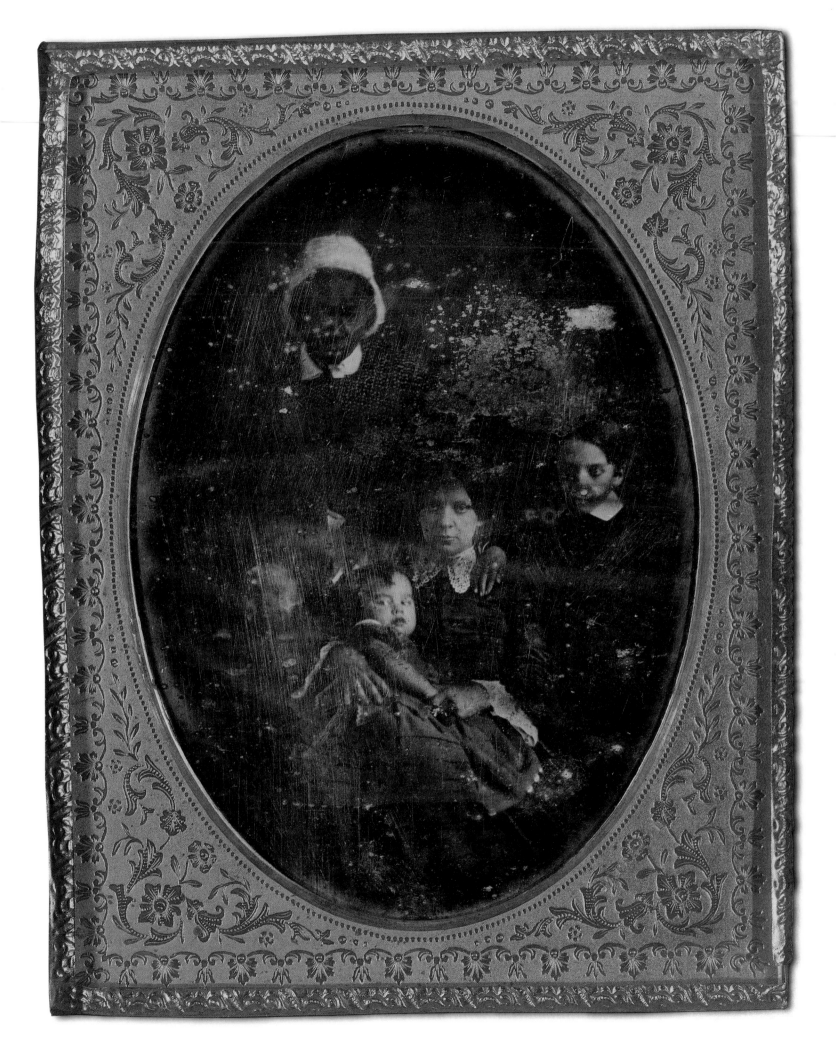

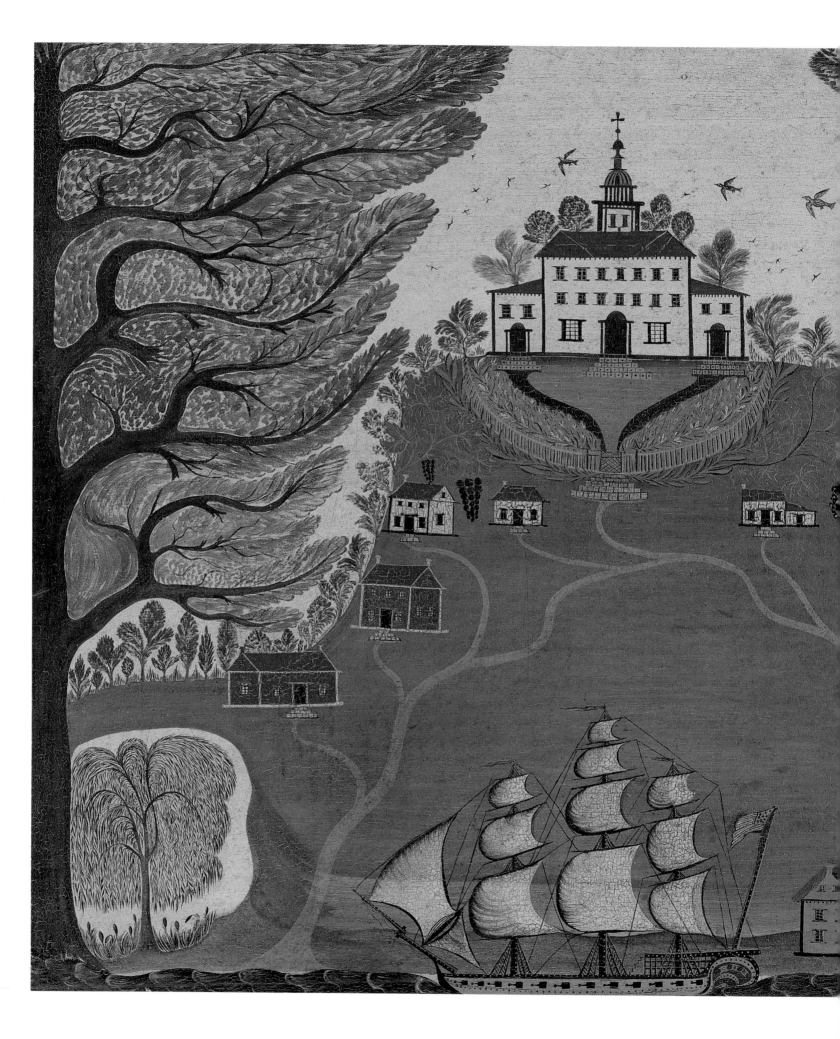

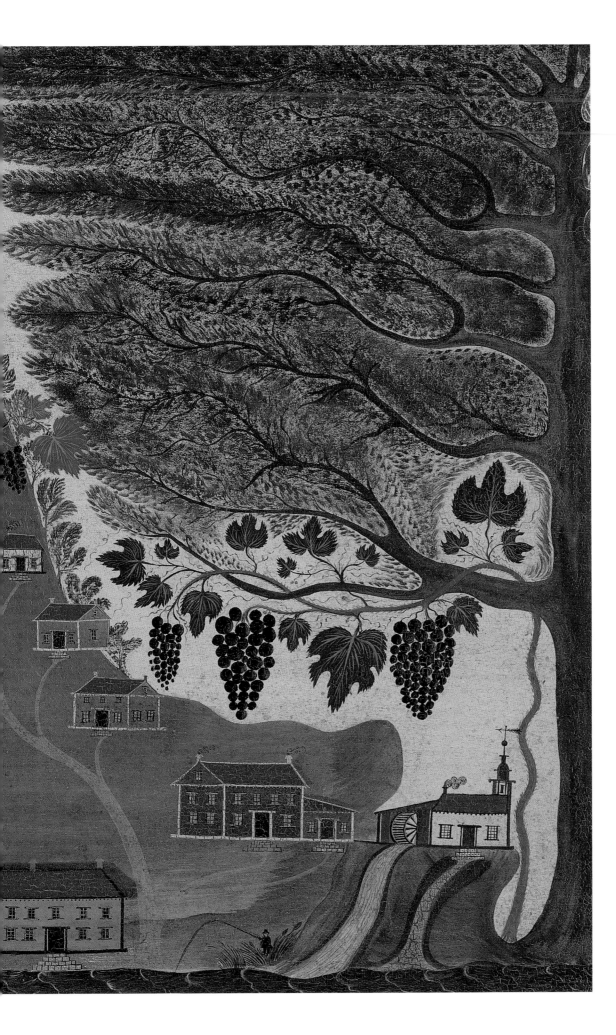

The Big House sits atop the hill, with outbuildings spilling down to the water, in this early 19th-century folk painting of a southern plantation. Though grand, plantations could be lonesome places for women. One wealthy mistress sat forlornly in her mansion at Christmastime, entirely alone except for her black cat. She complained bitterly to a relative that she "remained there ten days at a time without seeing a single white person."

off 'cause it belonged to her husband." More often, however, white women had to endure the reality of their husbands and sons making nocturnal visits to the slave quarters.

In the 1840s Mary B. Carter, mistress of 18th-century Shirley Plantation in Virginia, sought advice from a minister as to whether she should sell a slave woman "for committing adultery." In response, the Reverend Okeson came down firmly on the side of the status quo: "By the will, or if you prefer the expression, by the permission of God slavery *exists*....He chose that you should be born in Virginia—that you should grow up under the peculiar influences of slavery—that you should live at Shirley, *be what you are*; and have to *suffer* and *do* whatever may be peculiar to your position. In all these things it is your duty...to cheerfully acquiesce in the will of God." The reverend admitted that as a slave mistress she had "*peculiar trials* as well as *peculiar privileges*"; but it was her job to advance "*the salvation* of the *souls* of *your negroes*." Finally, he compared her banishing of the adulterous slave woman as an act akin to cutting "a man's head off in order, the more conveniently, to extract a tooth!" Mary Carter thought over his arguments carefully. Weeks later she wrote again. If indeed she had to keep the slave woman, could she then dispense with the adulterous man? Could she divorce her husband? The idea itself must have struck the minister like a thunderbolt. A woman of her high social status divorcing? He assured her that she was stuck with her unfaithful husband.

The rebellious voice of Mary Carter, crying out amidst the madness of slavery, is compelling. White slave mistresses were not immune from the horrors of the institution (though they certainly did not suffer as greatly as the people they enslaved). Regardless of the reality of their lives, social dictates demanded that aristocratic southern women maintain the veneer of gentility. Even their skin color was open to criticism: Tanned skin and freckles were frowned upon for well-bred women. Only slaves or lower-class women who worked in the fields were expected to be exposed to strong sunlight. Upper-class husbands and fathers were blunt on the subject. Thomas Jefferson wrote to his daughter, Maria, in 1786: "Remember too as a constant charge not to go out without your bon-

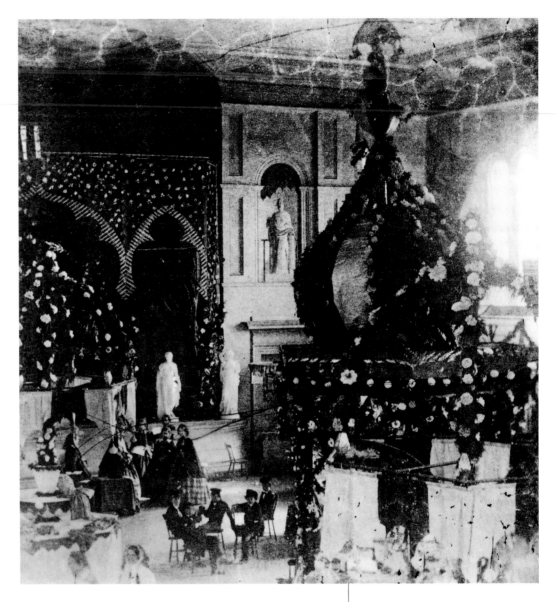

net because it will make you very ugly and then we should not love you so much."

On remote plantations, women often suffered through long stretches of isolation and loneliness. Men frequently traveled on business, while women stayed behind. The governor of Virginia, David Campbell, remained in Richmond at Christmas in 1822. His wife, Maria, was not pleased. "You have it in your power to enjoy company when you please," she wrote to him. "But here I am shut up like a canary bird." The governor replied, "I know you are shut up like the canary bird, but you sing so sweetly that to make you sing seems mere justification for the tyranny exercised."

Yet southern white women could also make their voices heard more stridently—and even reach out beyond their cages and into the political arena. South Carolina's decision to secede from the Union in December 1860 reverberated throughout the south and plunged everyone, both male and female, into heated public debate.

Maria Valentine of Richmond detested all things Yankee. They were, in her words, "the vilest of Creation." In January 1861 she proudly declared to her brother-in-law, "I am a real secessionist and wear constantly the blue Cockade," (the symbol of that cause). Maria and other women flocked to the Virginia Convention that winter, some arriving an hour early to assure themselves a good seat in the ladies' gallery. Fiery secession debates ensued. Maria was particularly taken with the arguments of South Carolinian John S. Preston. "I can't tell you how perfectly delighted I was with him, his oratory sur-

South Carolinians—both men and women—gather inside Charleston's Secession Hall, site where state delegates formally agreed to break with the Union. Mary Chesnut (opposite), a plantation aristocrat from that state, wanted to "let the fire-eaters have it out." On the eve of secession, her husband resigned as U.S. senator. Said one wag, "Mrs. Chesnut does not look at all resigned."

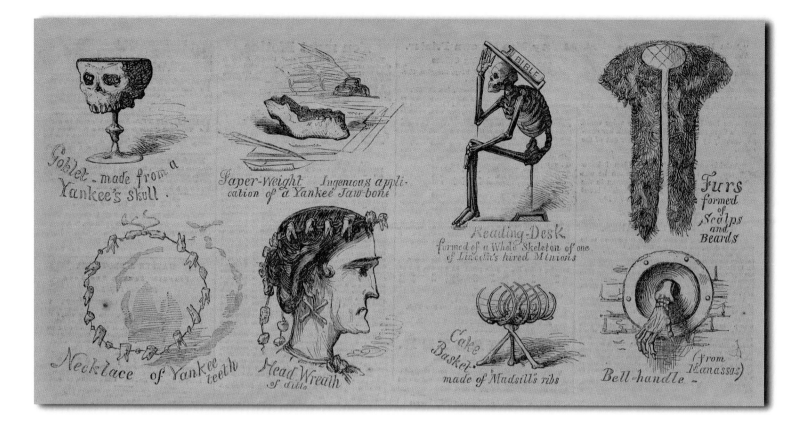

Goblet - made from a Yankee's skull.

Paper-weight. Ingenious application of a Yankee Jaw-bone.

Reading-Desk formed of a Whole Skeleton of one of Lincoln's hired Minions.

Furs formed of Scalps and Beards

Necklace of Yankee teeth

Head Wreath of ditto

Cake Basket made of Madsill's ribs

Bell-handle. (from Manassas)

passed anything I ever heard, and if he did not convince the people that S Carolina's position is right nothing in human shape or intellect can." Maria was ready to shout from the rooftop—in fact, her father jokingly threatened to rent a nearby empty office so that she could speechify to her heart's content from its front porch—in order to push reluctant Virginians into the secessionist fold.

When war came, women mobilized into volunteer groups throughout the South, sewing uniforms, knitting socks (one rebel woman made socks from unraveled Union Army tents), and raising huge sums of money to build gunboats for local defense. One Alabama woman, who signed herself "Delilah, a Niece of James Madison," urged every southern female over 12 to cut off her hair and sell it to European wigmakers: "Let every patriotic woman's head be shingled...and even the vilest foe will stand abashed in her presence." When word spread that Confederate Gen. James Longstreet needed silk to construct a surveillance balloon during the Seven Days battles in Virginia, local women rushed to their closets and donated enough gowns to construct a balloon that the general dubbed "the last silk dress in the Confederacy."

Many women wanted to join in the battle themselves. "O if I was only a man!" wrote Louisianan Sarah Morgan in her diary. "Then I could don the breeches and slay them with a will!" Indeed, a number of women—perhaps as many as 250—disguised themselves as men and fought for the Confederacy. At least one woman soldier died at Shiloh and another at Gettysburg, probably as part of Pickett's ill-fated charge. In a letter to his father, a Union soldier described an 1864 battle near Dallas, Georgia:

> One Secesh woman charged....waving the traitor flag and screaming vulgarities at us. She was shot three times but still on she came....Another She-Devil shot her way to our breastworks with two large revolvers dealing death to all in her path....If Gen. Lee were to field a brigade of such fighters, I think the Union prospects would be very gloomy indeed for it would be hard to equal their ferocity and pluck.

Despite her hard-core secessionist views, Maria Valentine fled Richmond for the safety of the country when war approached "The Sacred City," as she referred to the Confederate capital. She feared anything less than victory: "If Richmond goes what will we do? I can't think of living with them [the Yankees], and home is the sweetest place in the world." Yet as details of suffering and dying reached her, her bellicose tone alternated with genuine sorrow and concern. "It makes me shudder at this moment to think of our brave and noble sons weltering in blood as they must be now, the fight commenced last evening at four oclock and was terrific I hear until eight last night.... My faith is strong as to our success, but oh, the streams of blood that will flow before our fate is decided." She would soon report that one acquaintance had suffered ten deaths in his family in less than a year. She feared for her own family members who were fighting. "What has become of dear Brother?" was a cry she repeated over and over again in her letters. "I am so anxious about Richmond and Brother and the whole South," she wrote in June of 1862. Yet, like many southern women, she was determined to thwart the Northern troops, no matter what the cost. Rather than capitulate to the hated Yankees she preferred that "poor Richmond...be buried in ashes by our own people...New Orleans Memphis and all the rest of our cities ought to have been burned before the tyrants got possession of them."

Though Maria Valentine's bravado came at a safe distance from the fighting, other women were not so fortunate; for them, the war came directly to their homes and plantations. For over a month and a half, the city of Vicksburg was surrounded and under siege. Round-the-clock shelling by Union artillery forced terrified families to take refuge

The northern press skewered the warmongering—and ghoulish—spirit of southern women in cartoons (opposite). Entitled "Secesh Industry," this illustration from an 1862 *Harper's Weekly* jokingly shows how rebel women made use of Yankee corpses. In fact, one southern diarist admitted that she kept a Union soldier's skull on her dressing table. Union Gen. Benjamin Butler had such trouble subduing the female population of New Orleans that he issued an order (opposite) stating that any woman who showed contempt for a Union soldier would be treated as if she were a prostitute. Though vilified as "Beast Butler," the general later justified his action: "I did not carry on war with rose-water."

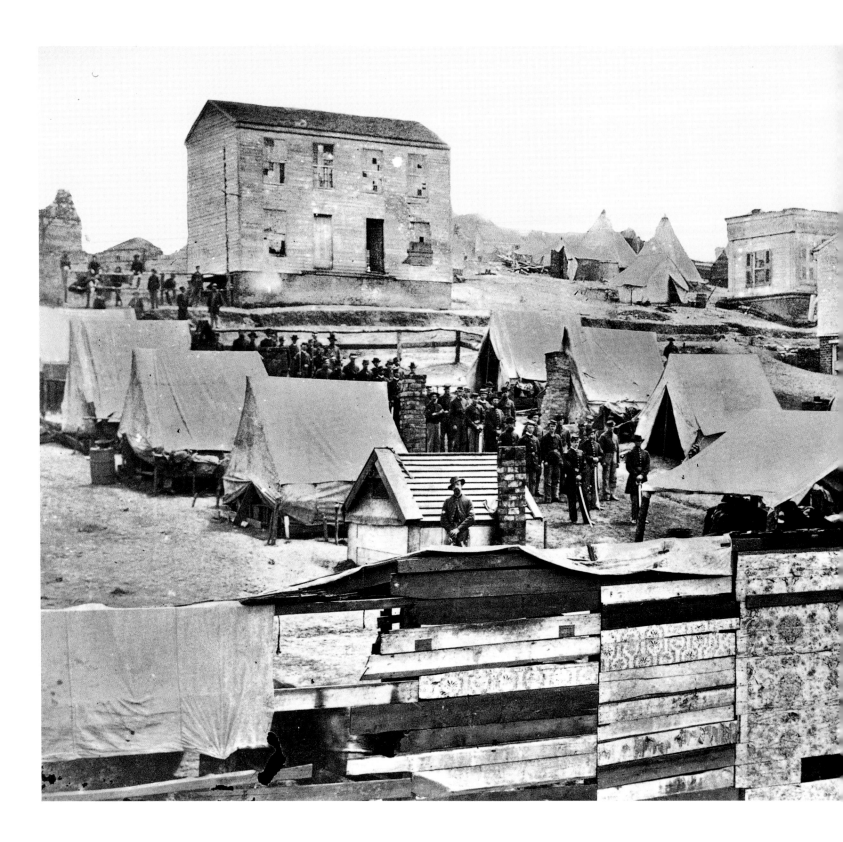

Setting up their winter camp, Union soldiers used wallpapered planks (foreground) obviously torn from the parlors of nearby houses. The war literally came into the households of southern women, who suffered a great deal at the hands of the enemy. One Alabama woman listened nervously for the "tramp of the mighty Northern host" as she prepared to flee her home.

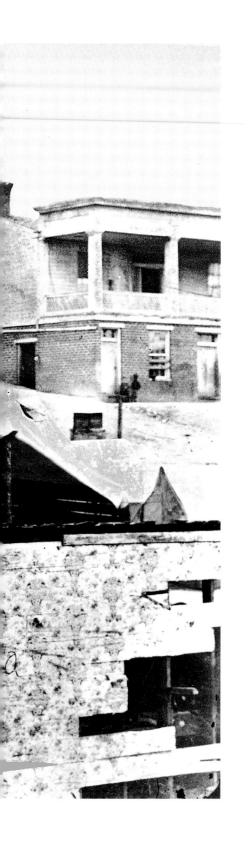

in nearby caves. Roughly 500 caves were dug out of the clay hillsides of Vicksburg, one woman noting that the area was "so honeycombed with caves that the streets look like avenues in a cemetery." Confederate soldiers and families trapped during the siege saw their food supplies dwindle, and they eventually resorted to eating horses, rats, and dogs.

Even when under the thumb of an occupying force, many women maintained their feisty, combative spirit. Laura Lee, a young woman in her 20s, kept a diary of her days in wartime Winchester, Virginia, a strategic border town that changed hands 97 times during the war. Her feelings about the Yankee invaders, whom she referred to as "hordes of robbers and murderers who come here to destroy all we hold most dear," were obviously shared by most of her compatriots. In some occupied towns, women spit on the soldiers and emptied chamber pots on their heads. One Arkansas woman angrily covered the dining table with ashes from the hearth when a group of Union soldiers walked in and demanded dinner.

Women expressed their contempt even through their clothing. Winchester women took to wearing "secession bonnets...adopted for their cheapness and for their defense against staring soldiers." When Federals banned women from wearing miniature Confederate flags, the response was just as rebellious; women put on black mourning bands in protest.

Fashionable 19th-century dresses became effective conveyances for smuggling critical goods, particularly medicine that was needed desperately by Confederate troops. Union soldiers nicknamed Alicia Buckner the "Fair Apothocary" when they discovered that she had secreted 127 ounces of quinine beneath her voluminous hoop skirt. Other, more extravagant goods were hidden as well. Susan Leigh Blackford of Virginia tried to hang her silver sugar dish, creamer, bowl, forks, and spoons around her waist in an attempt to keep them out of the clutches of Yankee soldiers. The results were mixed: "It did well while I sat still, but as I walked and when I sat down the clanking destroyed all hope of concealment."

A handful of southern women gained notoriety by passing along military secrets. Belle Boyd—a gently bred Virginian, who was educated in a refined female seminary—launched her career as a Confederate spy shortly after she shot and killed an invading Yankee soldier who cursed her mother "in language as offensive as it is possible to conceive." Eavesdropping on Union troops while nursing the wounded, she passed on

For Confederate Grey.
White and blue, a little more white
than blue, when these are well
mixed together put ⅙ black.
        Blue Grey
3 lbs o blue to 1 oz of black white.
        Black Grey
⅔ Black wool, + ⅓ cotton or white wool.

Rice Bread. "Secession bread"
1/1 lb of rice boiled very soft, when
cold mix in ¾ lb of wheat, 1 teacup of yeast, 1 teacup of milk,
salt to taste. Mix and let it
stand 3 hours, then it must
be kneaded in flour enough to
render the outside hard enough
for the oven. In an hour & a
quarter after bake it

Corn Bread
Take 2 pts of corn meal and
mix with warm water a thick
batter adding a little salt,
put it in a vessel in which
it will easily rise (do this in

invaluable information to Gen. Stonewall Jackson, earning herself a commission as a captain and an honorary aide-de-camp. The northern press, which vilified her for her flirtatious manipulations, dubbed her The Secesh Cleopatra.

Rose O'Neal Greenhow, a longtime fixture of Washington, D.C., society and intimate of some of the most powerful political figures in town (she allegedly had an affair with an abolitionist senator from Massachusetts), became part of a southern spy ring. After the war broke out, hired detectives kept the 44-year-old Confederate sympathizer under surveillance. Their efforts were rewarded when they discovered that the widow had passed on vital information about Union troop movements before the Battle of Bull Run. Rose and her eight-year-old daughter were placed under house arrest for nearly five months (during which time she and her cohorts still managed to pass information to couriers). Mother and daughter were then clapped into the Old Capitol Prison, where Rose became alarmed about her child's health. Locked in a war of wills with the Federal government, the Union blinked first and released Rose and her daughter to Virginia in June 1862. "If the tyrant has released her," the *Richmond Dispatch* opined, "it was because that even he quailed before the might of her power as representative of the feelings of every true Southern lady."

The following year Greenhow traveled to Europe as an emissary for President Jefferson Davis, and was received by both Napoleon III and Queen Victoria. Smuggling back gold and official documents for the Confederate president, Rose abandoned ship when a Federal patrol spotted the vessel off the North Carolina coast. She set off in a rowboat with two other Rebel agents, but never made it to shore. A wave capsized the small boat, and Rose, weighted down with a bag of gold around her neck and more gold sewn into her dress, was drowned. Her body was retrieved and brought to Wilmington, North Carolina, where she was buried with full military honors.

In contrast to the encomiums southerners heaped upon Rose Greenhow, only the worst epithets were reserved for Elizabeth Van Lew, when it was discovered that she had secretly worked for the Union. Viewed as a wealthy eccentric and harmless sympathizer of the northern cause by her Richmond neighbors, it turned out that Van Lew had been successfully relaying sensitive information from the Confederate White House to General Grant throughout the war. She cunningly placed an informer—one of her former slaves, a woman named Mary Elizabeth Bowser—inside the Confederate president's home. Bowser bravely gathered information and passed it on to Van Lew. Grant was so grateful for Van Lew's wartime intelligence, and so worried for her safety, that he posted guards outside her house when Richmond fell.

No southern woman was immune from the horrors of the war. The sheer scope of the conflict—almost all of which was waged on southern soil—was staggering. Several million soldiers fought, and over 600,000 were killed. The landscape itself was littered with the dead. The carnage was on such a vast scale that the armies were unable to properly bury all of the bodies. Shallow mass graves opened up after a hard rain or from the force of gases generated by decaying corpses. "The dead were strewed on every side" and "the most horrible sights" were seen, Fanny Tinsley wrote of an 1862 trip to Richmond. Along many roads the stench of dead horses was sickening.

Overnight, houses and entire towns turned into hospitals. Elizabeth Neely felt "crazed" as she watched the yard to her home filling up with amputated arms and legs. Casualties from Antietam poured into and overwhelmed the town of Winchester, Virginia. On September 20, 1862, Laura Lee reported in her diary: "This has been the most awful day

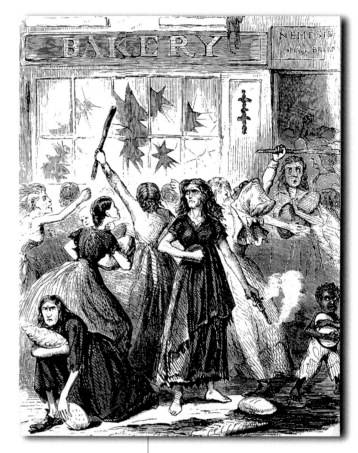

Desperate women break into a Richmond bakery in April 1863 to get bread for their starving families. Food shortages and price-gouging drove nearly a thousand women and children to storm the Confederate capital's stores. Scant food supplies also forced women to improvise. The South Carolina recipe book (opposite) includes "Secession bread," made in part from rice, a local crop still in ample supply.

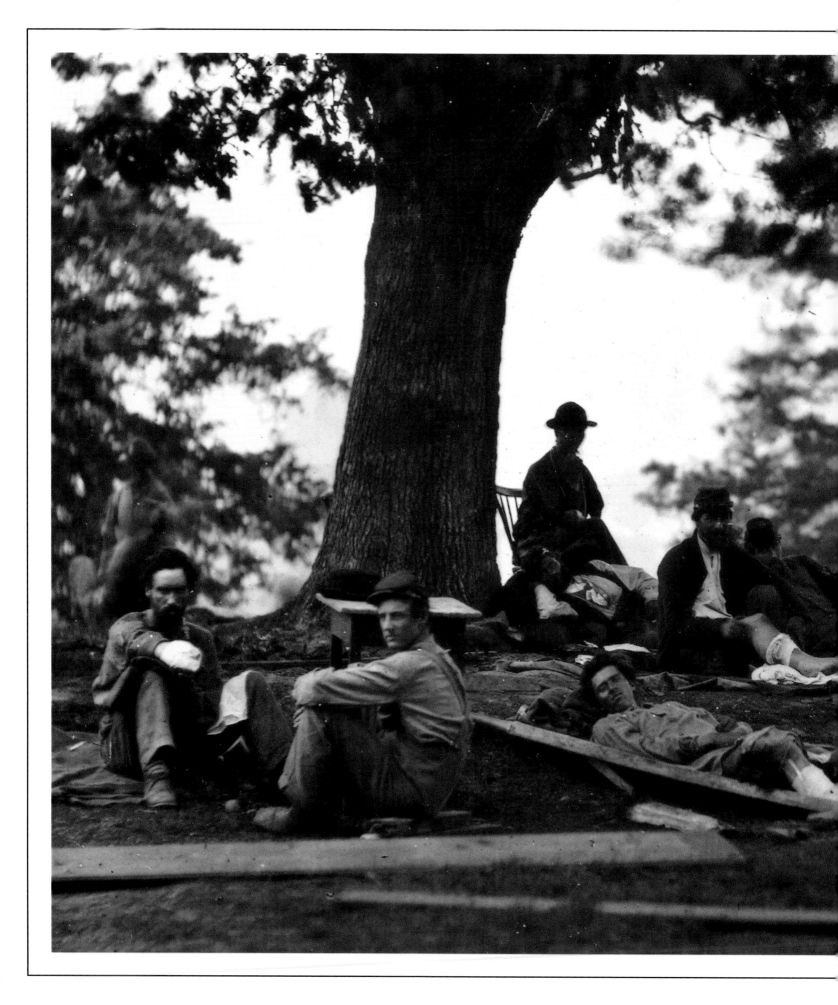

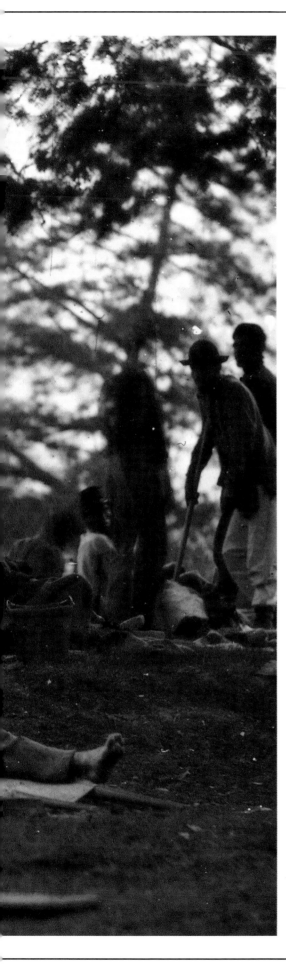

"The battle draws near, and I must catch one hour's sleep for tomorrow's labor."

CLARA BARTON AT FREDERICKSBURG

Early reports from Civil War battlefields described Union soldiers with "bare feet, tattered and unchanged shirts, blanketless limbs, and untold destitution." Northern women—as fiercely loyal as southern women were to their cause—flew into action. They tirelessly raised funds, gathered supplies, and even distributed more than half a million Bibles to the soldiers for moral uplift.

Dorothea Dix arrived in Washington, D.C., the day Fort Sumter was attacked, and went directly to the White House to offer her services as a nurse, gratis, wherever needed. She was appointed Superintendent of Women Nurses, choosing only volunteers between the ages of 30 and 45 who were "plain in appearance," attributes that would curtail bedside romance.

Clara Barton, barely five feet tall but an incredible force of nature, went by mule-drawn wagon to personally deliver supplies to the front lines. She believed that her place was "anywhere between the bullet and the hospital." Her devotion to the troops nearly cost her own life. At the Battle of Antietam, a bullet pierced her dress and killed a wounded soldier she was caring for. She never mended the dress.

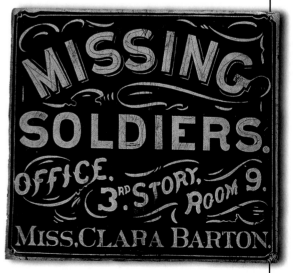

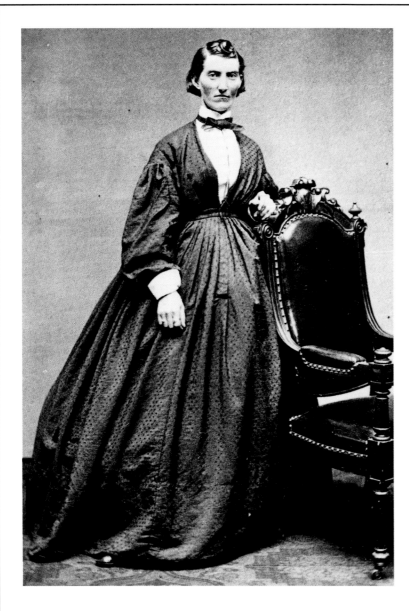

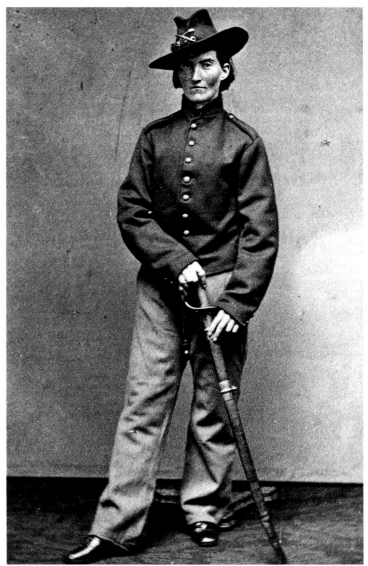

Dubbed the Angel of the Battlefield by Union soldiers, Barton did whatever was necessary—including supplying the men with tobacco and whiskey—to relieve their suffering. After kneeling and comforting a dying soldier, she recalled that she had to wring "the blood from the bottom of my clothing before I could step, for the weight about my feet." At Antietam, Barton discovered that one soft-faced wounded "boy" she was nursing was actually a woman, and she succeeded in convincing her to go home.

Other northern women passed as fighting men, including Frances Clalin, above, shown as she looked before and after she went into battle. Mary Scaberry took the alias of Charles Freeman and fought with the 52nd Ohio Infantry. Stricken with fever, her "sextual incompatability" was discovered and she was discharged.

Family members, like the ones at right, followed soldiers to wartime camps. Many others, however, lost touch with their loved ones. As the war came to an end, Barton was deluged with more than 60,000 letters from frantic families seeking missing soldiers. In the summer of 1865 she went, in her words, to "not the gate of hell, but hell itself"—the infamous prisoner-of-war camp in Andersonville, Georgia, to help identify the graves of nearly 13,000 who had died there. ■

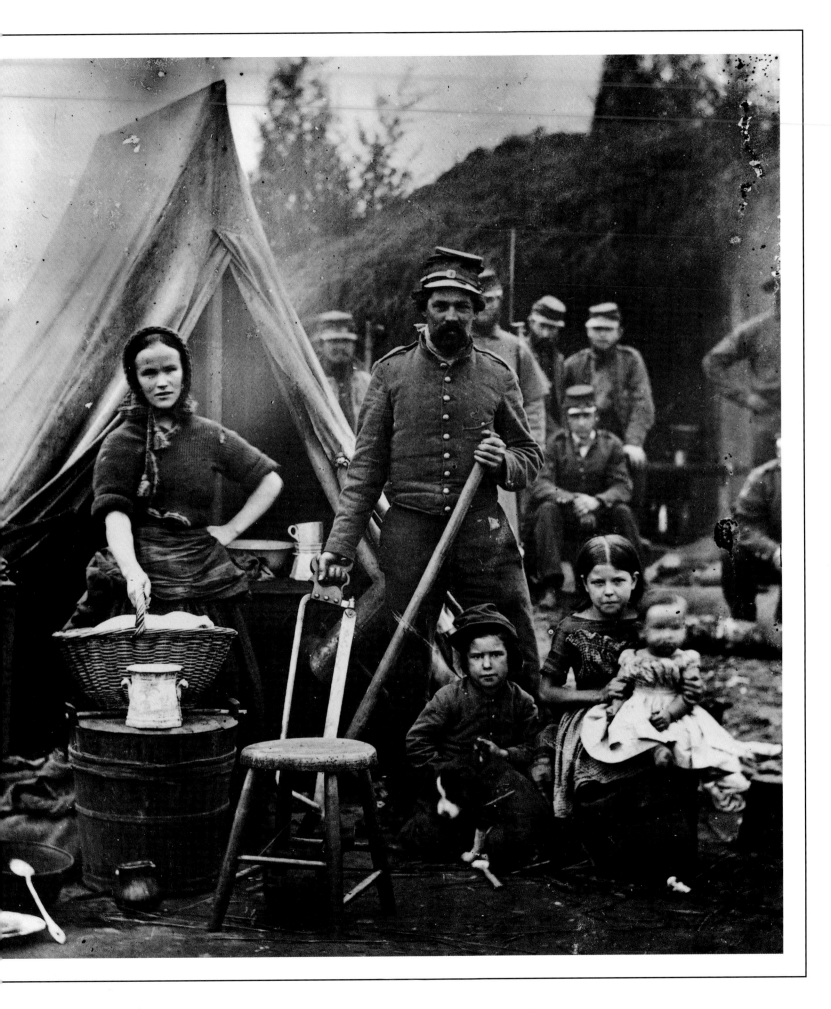

we have ever spent. Directly after breakfast the lines of ambulances began to come in, and since then it has been an incessant stream. 3,000 wounded men have been brought in. Every place is crowded with them, and it is perfectly heartrending to know how much suffering and misery there is around us." Within a week the number of wounded needing assistance would more than double.

Although nursing was considered indelicate for upper-class women in the 19th century (after all, it involved touching the bodies of men), as the war expanded women ignored social niceties. Ladies visited hospital wards—and had to be warned not to brush their hoop skirts against the patients' injured limbs—to help out in any way they could. They fed and washed the men, wrote letters home for the soldiers, read to them, fanned away flies, and even bandaged their wounds.

Women steeled themselves and grew accustomed to the awful suffering and dying that surrounded them. On her first day as a volunteer in a Richmond hospital, Sara Agnes Pryor fainted at the sight of a freshly amputated arm; yet she returned the next day and began serving 12-hour shifts. Hospital matron Phoebe Pember wrote to her sister in 1863: "After the Battle of Fredericksburg I stood by and saw men's fingers and arms cut off and held the brandy to their lips, washing the wounds myself.... I sometimes wonder if I am the same person who was afraid to look at a dead person for I have no timidity and hardly any sensibility left."

Compassion led women to comfort the sick and dying, no matter what color uniform the soldier was wearing. Kate Kern of Tennessee sent a lock of hair to a grieving mother in the North and particulars about her Union son's death: "He died during the night, and was buried the next day in a large double white blanket, as coffins were not then furnished." She closed the letter, "Write to me if you can. And love me, for I am your sympathising friend."

In July 1862, the six Carter women then living at Shirley Plantation on the James River looked out their windows and witnessed first-hand the horrors of war. Row upon row of Union soldiers wounded at the nearby battle of Malvern Hill "lay all about on this lawn and all up and down the river bank." The Carters represented the elite of the southern aristocracy, and their world lay at the heart of the Confederacy—Robert E. Lee's own mother was a Carter and had grown up and been married at Shirley Plantation—but even they could not ignore the suffering of the enemy at their doorstep. They were horrified by the shoddy medical treatment that the Union wounded received: "Surgeons treated the wounded soldiers like dogs," Louise Carter later wrote in a memoir. "We saw one turn a man over with his foot and tell him it was not worth doing anything for him. He would be in Hell in ten minutes." The Carter women sprang to action, tearing up sheets and pillowcases for bandages and making the wounded men soup and bread "every day until they died or were carried away." In recognition of their kindness to those men "whom you probably regard as bitter foes," the Union Gen. George B. McClellan issued an official Safeguard to protect the Carter family and property from attack.

Sixty-six-year-old Hill Carter, master of Shirley Plantation, invoked this special protection earned by the women in his family when he wanted to send some corn to the mill "as we are really suffering for bread, & must starve unless we can have meal ground." He went on to outline the losses they had suffered at the hands of the enemy:

> My crops were nearly all trampled down, my stock nearly all killed, or driven off & we are left very destitute. Twenty five of my mules, & one of my riding horses, & 18 of my slaves were taken off, & in their stead some 10 or 12 lame & wounded horses & mules left.... Out of 100 head of cattle your army left me 14, out of 120 sheep they left me 20, out of 140 hogs, & 150 pigs they left me 30 or 40.

Such was the devastation wrought on the property of Hill Carter, a man whose status was so exalted that in the middle of the Civil War Abraham Lincoln's own son paid a courtesy call to him while gathering flowers for his sick mother.

Even worse depredations greeted many women who tried valiantly to run households and plantations by themselves. (Three out of every four white men of military age were off fighting, leaving the home front largely in the hands of women.) "But like demons they rush in!" Dolly Lunt of Georgia recalled of the invading Yankees. "To my smoke house, my dairy, pantry, kitchen, and cellar, like famished wolves they come, breaking locks and whatever is in their way."

Complying with the Yankees' demands did not necessarily translate into gentle treatment by the enemy. After housing some Union officers for the night, one southern woman was greeted with arson the next morning. Finishing his breakfast, Captain Berry calmly informed his hostess that he was going to set her house on fire. He poured flam-

"Like demons they rush in! To my smoke house, my dairy, pantry, kitchen, and cellar, like famished wolves they come, breaking locks and whatever is in their way."

DOLLY LUNT OF GEORGIA

mable fluid onto the sofas and curtains and applied a match to them. Frantic, the woman ran upstairs, snatched her sleeping baby from its cradle, and rushed from the house. Everything went up in flames.

With houses and crops destroyed, many women and children fled to cities that teemed with homeless beggars. Lower-class women found work in factories, but sometimes at great cost. A March 1863 explosion killed more than 40 women ordnance workers in Richmond.

The factory women of Roswell, Georgia, became the victims of Gen. William T. Sherman's vindictive campaign to "make Georgia howl." In July 1864, hundreds of women workers wept as they watched Union soldiers torch their textile mills and their homes. Sherman next sent an astounding message to the commanding officer: "Arrest all people, male and female, connected with those factories, no matter what the clamor, and let them foot it, under guard, to Marietta, where I will send them by cars to the North." Even the correspondent for the *New York Tribune* was taken aback by the severity of the punishment: "Only think of it! Four hundred weeping and terrified Ellens, Susans, and Maggies transported in the seatless and springless army wagons, away from their lovers and brothers of the sunny South; and all this for the offense of weaving tent cloth and spinning stocking yarn!"

But before being expelled from town, the rounded-up women may have been raped by the Federal soldiers—at the instigation, it seems, of their officers. One Union soldier noted in a letter that "it was a very fine sight to see four hundred girls all at once, a sight we do not often see in the army." Right after breakfast, the commanding officer issued whiskey to all of the men, an almost unheard of event. A soldier in the regiment wrote that "this was the second time we ever had...whiskey issued to us since we entered the service and we think 'this' was a mistake." Some of the men got "foolishly drunk. Upon this occasion their delirium took the form of making love to the women." The out of control soldiers had to be marched away from the scene.

The terrified women of Roswell were eventually sent North and "set adrift in Indiana." One of the deported women, a pregnant seamstress named Adeline Bagley Buice, made it as far as Chicago. Five years later, she and her daughter walked more than 700 miles back to Roswell, only to find that her husband-soldier, thinking her dead, had already remarried.

Steely-eyed Washington, D.C., socialite turned Confederate spy, Rose Greenhow (opposite) poses with her daughter in a portrait made by the renowned Mathew Brady photographic studio. Placed under house arrest for passing government secrets, Rose was eventually charged with espionage and, with her daughter, was sent to prison. She garnered sympathy for her child and publicity for herself: "I but claim the right which our fathers did in '76—to protest against tyranny and oppression," she wrote from her cell. Her northern jailers soon gave up and released her. Greenhow later died while on a diplomatic mission for the Confederacy and became a celebrated martyr to the cause.

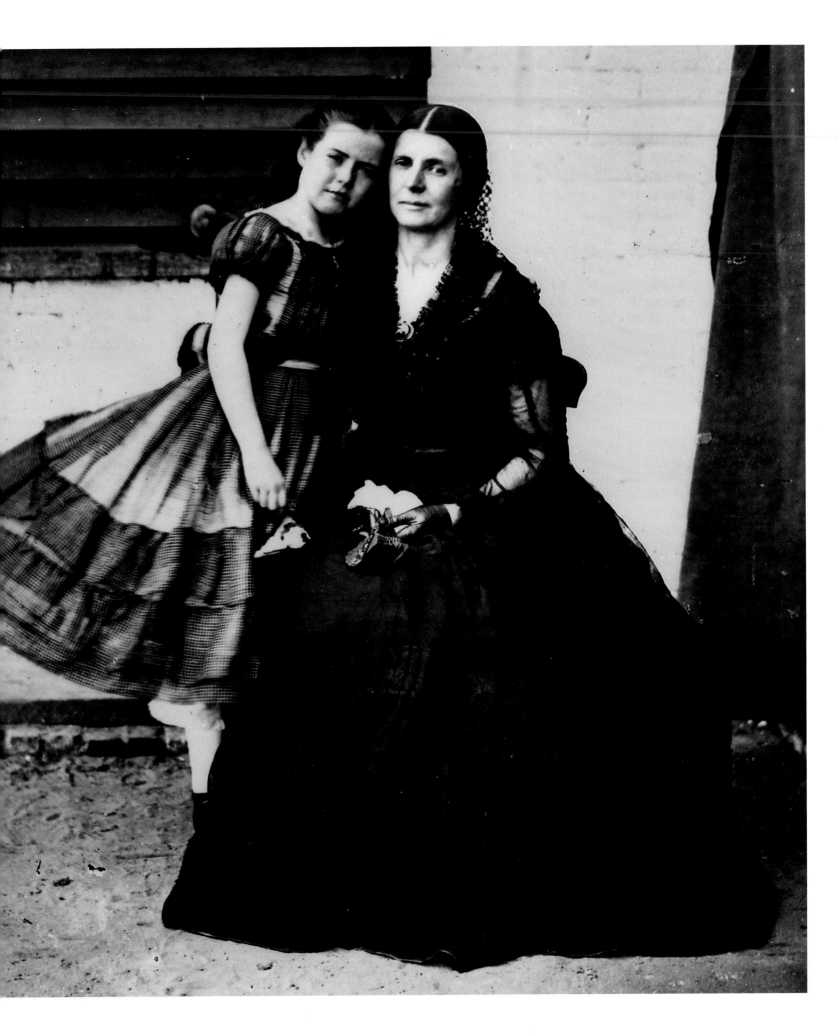

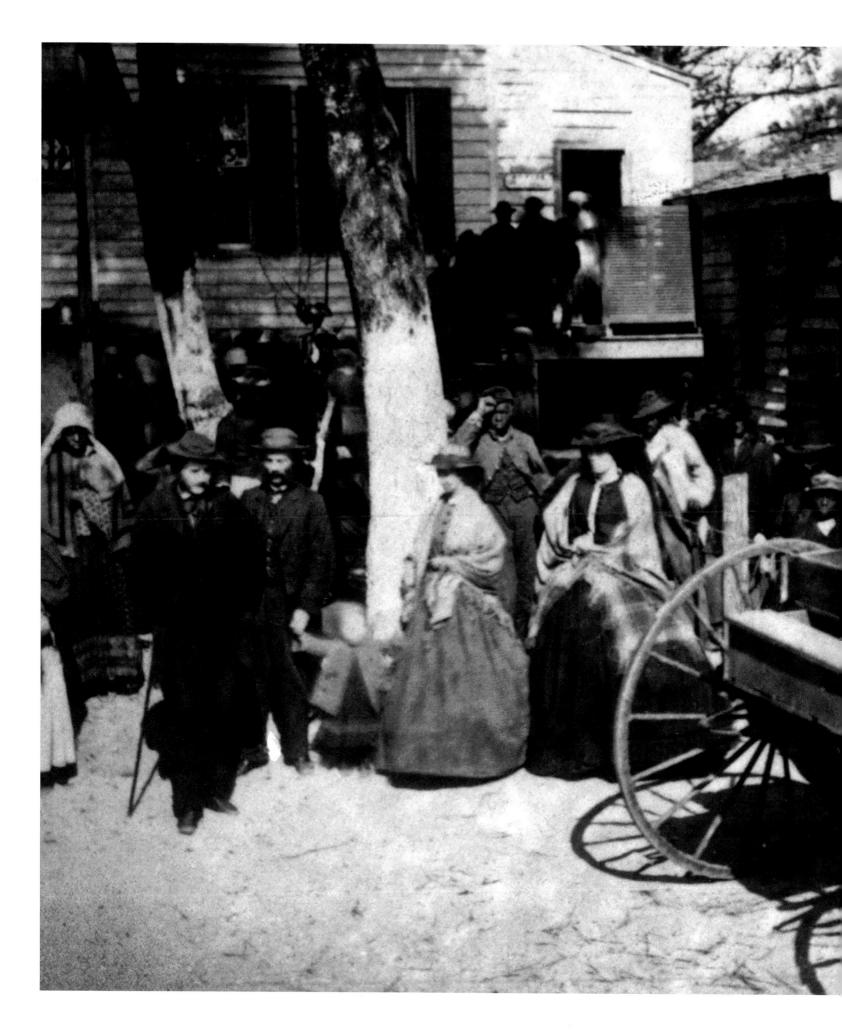

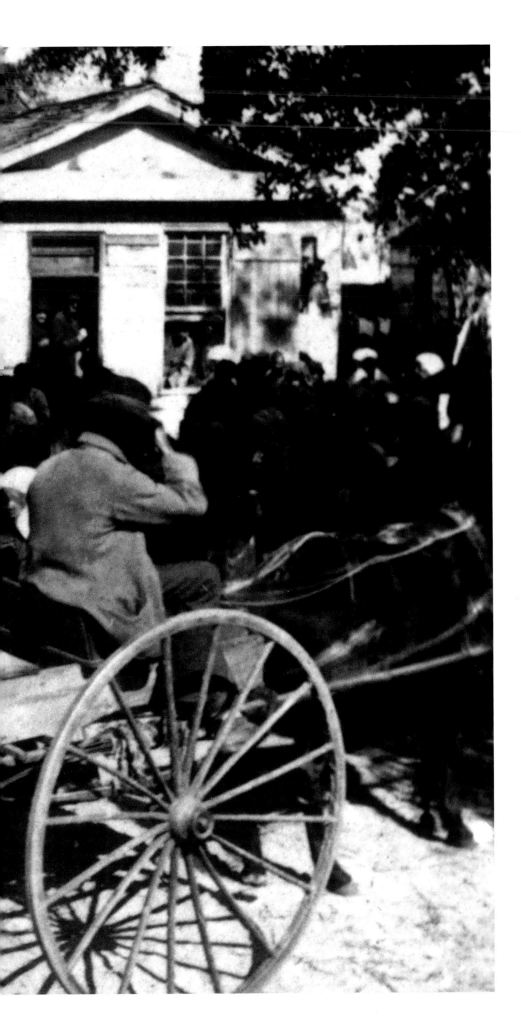

Humbled plantation mistresses in hoop skirts get rations from their Union occupiers in Beaufort, South Carolina. By war's end, plantation women desperately needed northern provisions. To get them, however, they had to swallow a bitter pill: a loyalty oath renouncing the Confederacy and pledging allegiance to the Union. "Half crying I covered my face," Sarah Morgan wrote of the hated oath, "and prayed breathlessly for the boys and the Confederacy, so that I heard not a word he was saying until the question 'So help you God?'"

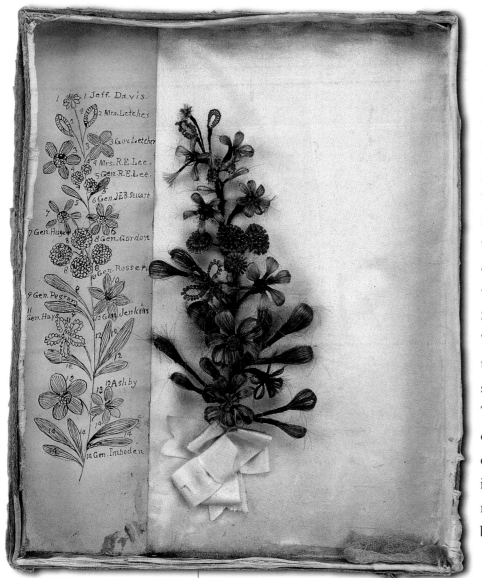

In some cases, the war's heavy toll on women proved too much. Even feisty Mary Lee, who chronicled the ever changing fortunes of Winchester, Virginia, felt as if she were "completely broken down mentally" in 1865. She noted that a number of new patients "made insane by the War—all women" had been admitted to an asylum in Staunton, Virginia. In defeat, some women remained defiant. Emma LeConte described her disgust in February 1865 when she saw the U.S. flag raised over the South Carolina State House in Columbia: "O what a horrid sight! What a degradation! After four long bitter years of bloodshed and hatred, now to float there at last! That hateful symbol of despotism!" The city had been destroyed: "The place is literally in ruins. The entire heart of the city is in ashes," she wrote. Yet her resolve remained firm: "We have lost everything, but...I would rather endure any poverty than live under Yankee rule."

One amazing woman plucked fortune from the ashes of defeat. Adelicia Franklin Acklen—to pay homage to two of the three husbands she ruled in her lifetime—was the archetype of the steely and powerful plantation mistress. Married at 22 to Isaac Franklin, one of the wealthiest men in Tennessee, who had parlayed a slave-trading fortune into plantation holdings in Louisiana and Texas, she was widowed seven years later. Much of his estate had been left to endow a school, but Adelicia contested his will and won. She and her children inherited his vast landholdings, and she began to buy up other properties. Deciding to marry again, she shrewdly insisted upon a prenuptial agreement that kept control of her property in her hands.

Her new husband, Joseph Acklen, managed her Louisiana cotton plantations so successfully that by 1860 they reported assets of real estate worth two million dollars and personal property valued at another million. Adelicia set about building and then rebuilding Belmont, her grand estate near Nashville that would match her ambition. Boasting 30-odd rooms, the Italianate mansion looked out upon extensive grounds that included fountains, formal gardens, an art gallery in the shape of a Greek temple, an octagonal bear house, an artificial lake stocked with Louisiana alligators, and three greenhouses. A brick water tower rose 105 feet above the ground, offering magnificent views of the estate. Littered with statuary of all kinds, the grounds were dismissed by one Union army official as resembling "a fashionable first-class cemetery."

When the Civil War armies approached Nashville, Adelicia sent her husband off to Louisiana to save their crops. She fended for herself at Belmont even as "the 'screws' tighten every day," in her words. Acklen, meanwhile, was caught between the Union Army, which wanted to confiscate their cotton, and the Confedcrates, who wanted to destroy it rather than have it fall into the hands of the enemy. Joseph Acklen wrote to Adelicia in despair: "I have nothing left now but my cotton and it is uncertain if I shall be permitted to dispose of it. I am in constant dread of its being burned. My mules and horses have all been taken and stole by the Confederates and my neighbours. The places are all in ruins the crops and all waisted and waisting." Less than three weeks later he died.

With the war raging all around her, Adelicia set off to Louisiana to take matters into her own hands. Her youngest sister once remarked that Adelicia could "talk a bird out of a tree." She proceeded to do just that. Confederate soldiers in Louisiana were then under orders to destroy all cotton; yet Adelicia managed to convince them that her crop was being sold to buy munitions for the southern cause. About a dozen Confederate soldiers guarded her prize; but without wagons and horses to transport it, she was stuck. Adelicia then turned her charm on a Union admiral who was on an inspection tour nearby. He gave her permission to ship her cotton—reportedly in U.S. Army wagons—to New Orleans. Having thus hoodwinked both sides, she made off with her booty to England, where she cashed it in for nearly a million dollars, probably in gold. Adelicia Franklin Acklen emerged from the Civil War as one of the richest women in the United States, and left both the Union and the Confederacy scratching their heads. So much for wilting southern belles.

In the "National relic" (opposite), one southern zealot created an intricate floral pattern with strands of hair from important Confederate leaders, including President Jefferson Davis and the generals Robert E. Lee and J.E.B. Stuart. Mrs. Robert E. Lee helped the artist, Jeannetta Conrad of Harrisonburg, Virginia, collect the hair. In the Victorian era women frequently made such relics to honor loved ones or famous people, though the ornaments were usually memorials for the dead.

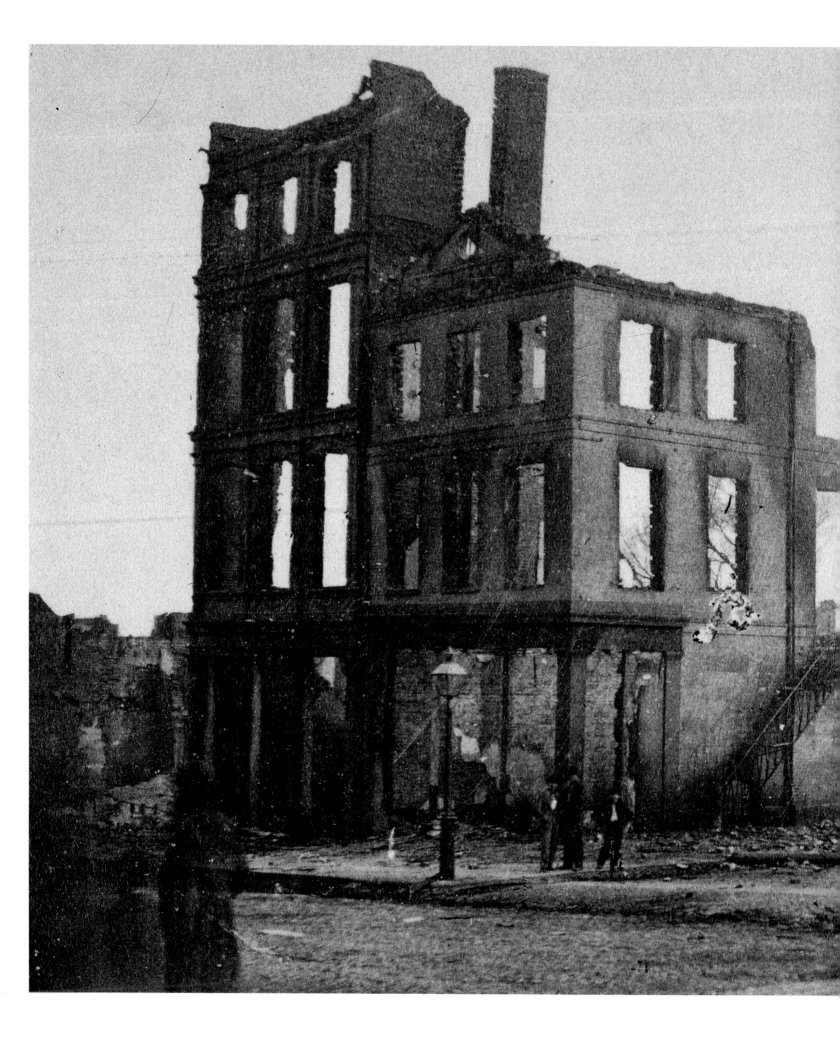

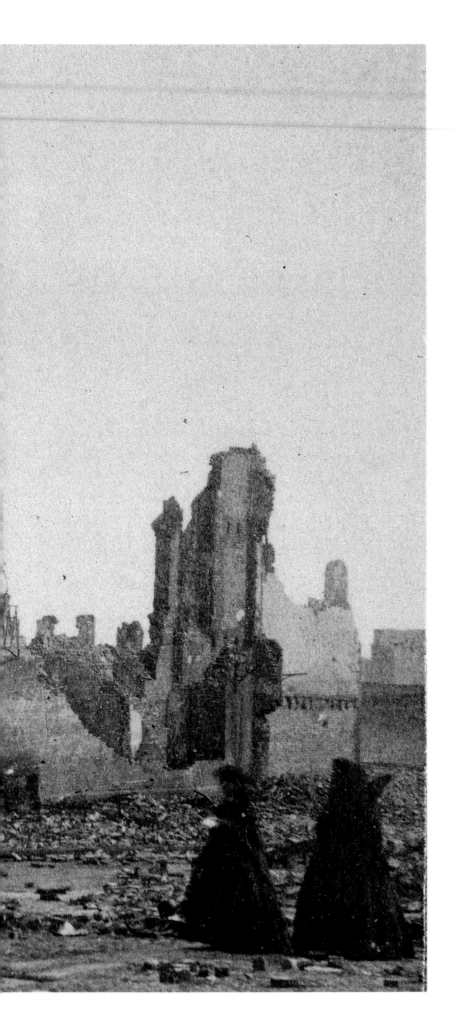

Appearing like ghostly specters, two women in black walk through the ruins of Richmond, Virginia, once proud capital of the Confederacy, in April 1865. "There is nothing for us to do but bow our heads in the dust and let the hateful conquerors trample us under their feet," one southern woman wrote in defeat. But soon they would raise their heads back up. Still devoted to the "Lost Cause," women erected statues and monuments throughout the South and carefully maintained cemeteries to keep the memory of the Confederacy alive. In fact, the federal Memorial Day holiday was inspired by the poignant sight of young girls decorating soldiers' graves in Petersburg, Virginia in 1866.

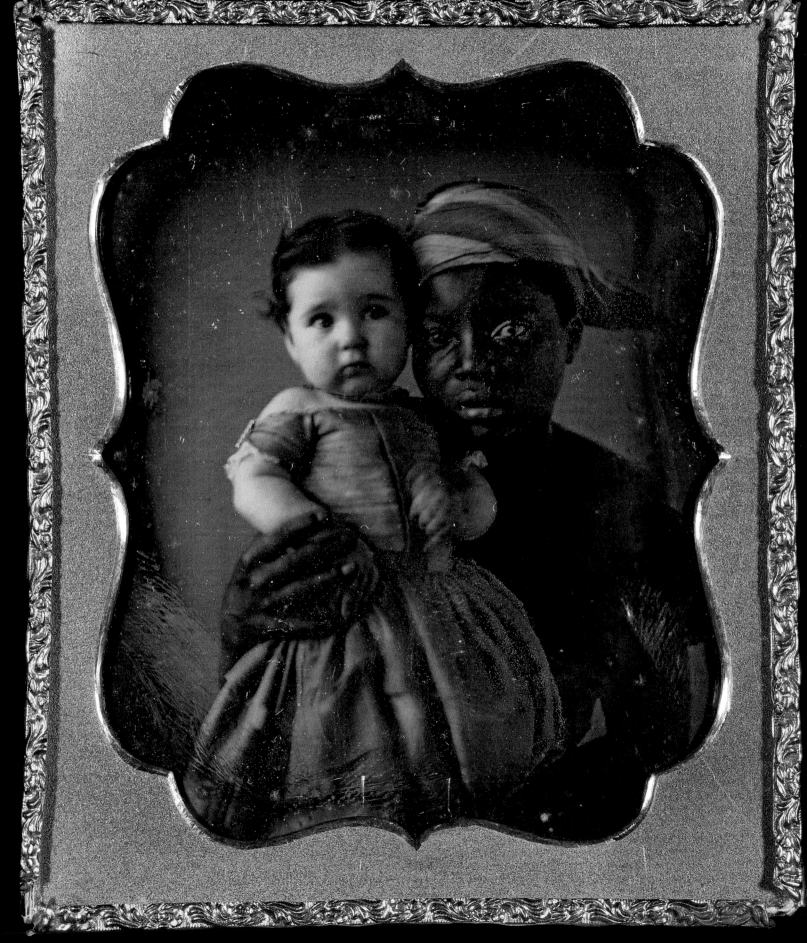

ENSLAVED WOMEN

AN AFRICAN-AMERICAN woman peers out from a mid-19th-century daguerreotype, her long fingers firmly gripping her white charge. She was trapped in a system of racial slavery that had begun in the 16th century when African men and women were forcibly taken from their own shores and brought to the Americas. The "peculiar institution" had grown ever more onerous over time with the enactment of rigid laws codifying the slaves' inferior status—laws that were designed to ease whites' fears over the rising black

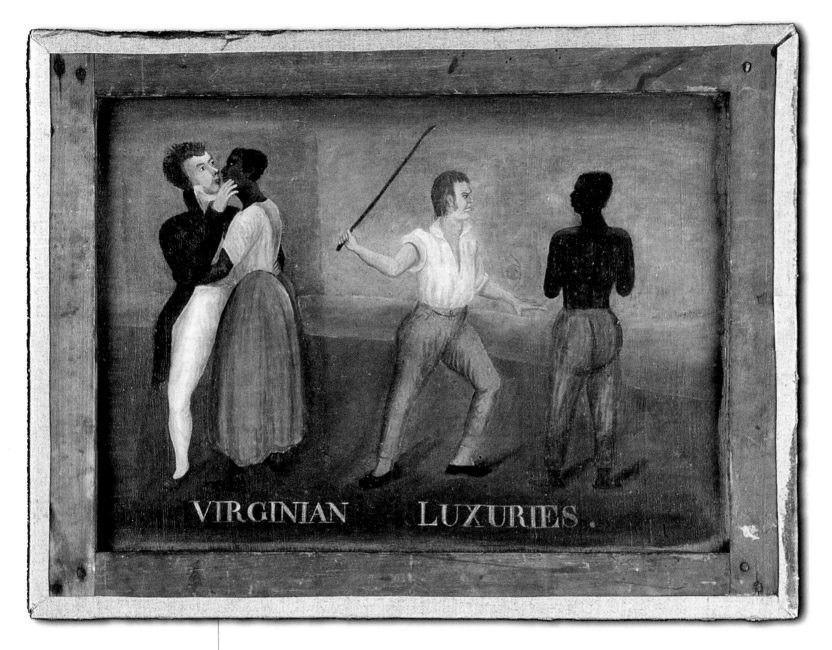

VIRGINIAN LUXURIES.

population. (For instance, by the 1700s blacks outnumbered whites by as much as five to one in South Carolina's low country.) By 1820 there were roughly two million African Americans, and more than 85 percent of them were enslaved.

Slave women were highly valued not only for their work, but for the children they produced, who in turn became the owner's property. A new name on the slave rolls meant a new asset for the master, who referred to the annual growth of the African-American population on his plantation as the "increase." Some masters prided themselves on keeping slave families intact, but others auctioned off family members to the highest bidders, brutally tearing children from their mothers. An ex-slave recalled the heartbreaking aftermath of one auction: "There was young gals an' dey were marched down to the train— baby, baby! I can recollect it—a terrible time too, it wuz. Dar was a great crying and carrying on mongst the slaves who had been sold. Two or three of dem gals had young babies...with 'em. Poor little things. As soon as dey got on de train dis ol' new master had [the] train stopped an' made dem poor gal mothers take [the] babies off and laid dem precious things on de groun' and left dem behind to live or die."

In 1856 Caroline Seabury, a white newcomer to the South, was introduced firsthand to the horrors of a "negro hiring," when slaves were hired out to other plantation owners for the coming year. She set the scene in her diary: "A large block was brought & placed on the highest spot. Around it gathered the crowd of tobacco chewers, now & then I saw a black bottle passed round among them, their voices soon telling of its virtues. The [slaves]...stood in the background dressed in their best clothes...There were about 35 in all varying from the real unmistakable Africans to the pale blue eyed mulatto."

Seabury's eyes came to rest on a "tall slender, well-formed light mulatto woman" named Suey who had a baby in her arms and two other children around seven and nine years old. The "lady of the house" explained that Suey and her husband, Jack, had been hired out on plantations ten miles apart, and "he would run away every two or three months to see her." When the husband, a skilled carpenter, refused to work, "they made him build a coffin, then made him git into it, and nailed it up to scare him—he was a'most white, a mighty smart feller, could read an write, they said, an so they was afraid to whip him...Well, they kep Jack in a leetle too long, for when they come to knock on the lid, he didn't speak, an when they opened it, he'd just done breathin." Suey "went a'most crazy." She ran off and hid in the forest for weeks, "an was nigh to bein perished." Suey had just recently returned to the plantation and now faced the auction block.

The auctioneer began his patter: "Here's Suey, got no husband to bother her, what'll you give...50-75-85-100-without the children." Suey "fixed her black eyes on the man bidding." Seabury was told that he was "a rich old bachelor, mighty rich from cross the river, but hard on niggers." The bid went to $175, and she was "struck off" to the hard-hearted man. Seabury watched Suey's reaction: "She said not a word, but her looks told what was in her heart, as she gave up the two older children, she sobbed bitterly—Any other expression of feeling would I suppose have been punished—Here was one of my own sex almost as light in color—with a poor shabby dress of mourning for her husband still on her. I could not keep back my own tears."

Enslaved Virginia Boyd, though pregnant and facing the auction block, still did not give up hope. While awaiting her fate in the slave pens of Houston, Texas, in 1853, she

With the disturbing title "Virginian Luxuries," this 19th-century painting (opposite) depicts the abuses enslaved men and women endured. "I now entered on my fifteenth year—a sad epoch in the life of a slave girl," Harriet Jacobs, escaped slave, wrote. "My master began to whisper foul words in my ear...." Following pages: A raffle poster and an 1850 daguerreotype graphically show how enslaved women were considered nothing more than commodities. Enslaved Delia, stripped bare to the waist and treated as a mere object for scientific research, looks at the camera with no expression. The portrait was made in South Carolina for celebrated Harvard scientist, Louis Agassiz, who tried to prove that Africans were a distinct species. His theory would soon be overturned by Charles Darwin.

RAFFLE.

Mr. Joseph Jennings respectfully informs his friends and the public that, at the request of many acquaintances, he has been induced to purchase from Mr. Osborne, of Missouri, the celebrated

DARK BAY HORSE, "STAR,"

Aged five years, square trotter and warranted sound; with a new light Trotting Buggy and Harness; also, the dark, stout

MULATTO GIRL, "SARAH,"

Aged about twenty years, general house servant, valued at *nine hundred dollars*, and guaranteed, and

Will be Raffled for

At 4 o'clock P. M., February first, at the selection [...]tel of the subscribers. The above is as represented, and those persons who may wish to engage in the usual practice of raffling, will, I assure them, be perfectly satisfied with their destiny in this affair.

The whole is valued at its just worth, fifteen hundred dollars; fifteen hundred

CHANCES AT ONE DOLLAR EACH.

The Raffle will be conducted by gentlemen sele[...] interested subscribers present. Five nights will be allowed to complete the Raffle. BOTH [...] HE ABOVE DESCRIBED CAN BE SEEN AT MY STORE, No. 78 Common St., secon[...] [fl]oor from Camp, at from 9 o'clock [A]. M. to 2 P. M.

Highest throw to take the first choice: [...] lowest throw the remaining prize, and the fortunate winners will pay twenty dollars each fo[...] [ref]reshments furnished on the occasion.

N. B. No chances recognized unles[...] [...]r previous to the commencement.

JOSEPH JENNINGS.

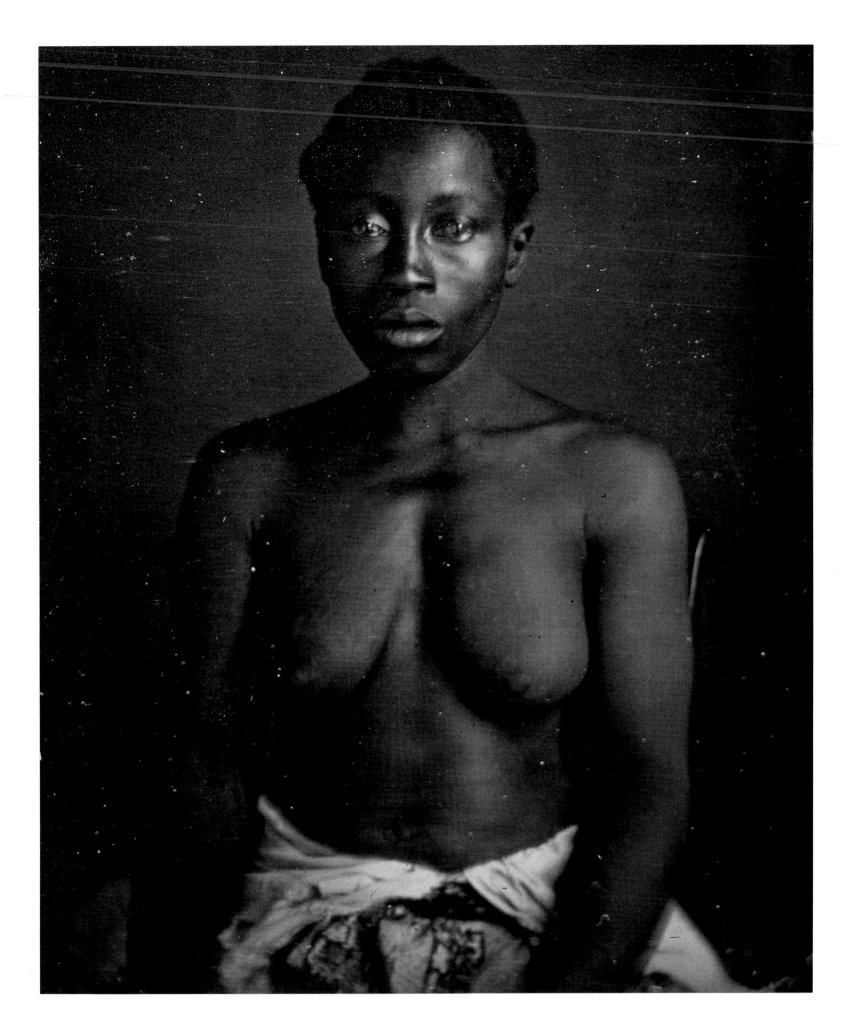

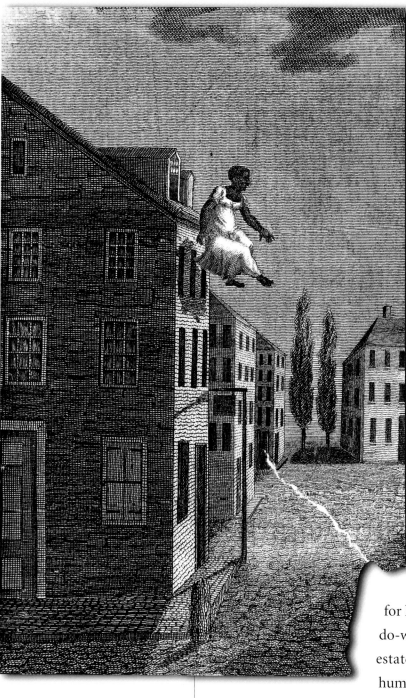

composed a courageous letter in which she accused her master of selling his own children—"Yes his own flesh & blood." She continued, "My God is it possible that any free born American would brand his character with such a stigma as that, but I hope before this he will relent & see his error." She pleaded to keep her family together and for some say about her future. "Do you think after all that has transpired between me & the old man...that its treating me well to send me off among strangers without even my having an opportunity of choosing for my self." Boyd threatened her master with exposure if she were not "dealt with fairly," but her letter was ignored, and her family broken up.

Another enslaved mother had the courage to beg a former First Lady for mercy. Dolly Madison was nearly bankrupt in the 1840s due to her taste for high living and gambling debts incurred by her ne'er-do-well son. In 1844, Montpelier, the Madisons' country estate in Virginia, was about to be sold—including its human property. The human cost would be high. The impecunious Madisons had jeopardized the lives of all of their slaves, including Sarah Stewart, who wrote eloquently to Dolly Madison for help:

My Mistress,

I don't like to send you bad news but the condition of all of us your servants is very bad, and we do not know whether you are acquainted with it. The sheriff has taken all of us and says he will sell us at next court unless something is done before to prevent it—We are afraid we shall be bought by what are called negro buyers and sent away from our husbands and wives. If we are obliged to be sold perhaps you could get neighbors to buy us...so as to save us some misery...at being separated from you as well as from one another. We are very sure that you are sorry for this state of things and we do not like to trouble you with it but think my dear mistress what our sorrow will be. The sale is only a fortnight from next monday but perhaps you could make some bargain with somebody by which we could be kept together.

—*Sarah*

Sarah's plea prompted an almost immediate response. Fearing that her son might try to sell off the slaves piecemeal and scatter them, Dolly quickly sold the entire estate, and all of its slaves, to a single person. Thus the slave families remained united at Montpelier, thanks in large measure to Sarah's intercession.

A small percentage of women worked in the Big House as maids or cooks, and though they might enjoy a higher social status in the slave community than field hands, they often suffered under the ceaseless scrutiny and demands of their mistress. Most enslaved women, however, worked side by side with men, hoeing, weeding, planting, and picking cotton and tobacco—indeed the entire economy of the South was built on their backbreaking work. When asked about her days as a slave on a tobacco plantation, Henrietta Perry bitterly recalled, "Use to wuk fum sun to sun in dat old terbaccy field. Wuk till my back felt lak it ready to pop in two....us black people had to look arter dat 'baccy lak it was gold. Us women had to pin our dresses up roundst our necks fo' we stepped in dat ole 'baccy fiel', else we'd git a lashin'...Marse ain' cared what we do in de wheat an' corn fiel', cause dat warn't nothin' but food for us niggers, but you better not do nothin' to dem 'baccy leaves."

Among blacks there was an adage: "Slave young, slave long," and it proved to be true. By age five or six young children worked in the fields. With their tiny fingers, they were particularly adept at picking worms off tobacco plants. One ex-slave recalled what happened when she missed a few. The master stuffed her mouth full of worms. "Lordy knows how many of dem shiny things I done swallered."

Rainy days did not mean a respite from labor; the type of work merely changed. Instead of going to the fields, enslaved women went to the "loom room," where they spun thread and wove and dyed cloth. In addition, after a day of work, the master gave them extra chores to do at night. The head spinner on one plantation portioned out the cotton to be spun in the evening and would sing a song to her fellow slaves urging them to work faster to avoid the wrath of their mistress:

Sold away from her husband and about to be marched to Georgia in a procession of slaves chained to one another, this mother jumps —in desperation—out a window in Washington, D.C., in 1815. She failed in her attempt to escape, and in the process broke her back and both arms. Her children, meanwhile, were carried off to Carolina. This heartbreaking engraving appeared in an 1817 book entitled *A Portraiture of Domestic Slavery*.

Keep yo' eye on de sun,
See how she run,
Don't let her catch you with your
work undone,
I'm a trouble, I'm a trouble,
Trouble don' las' always.

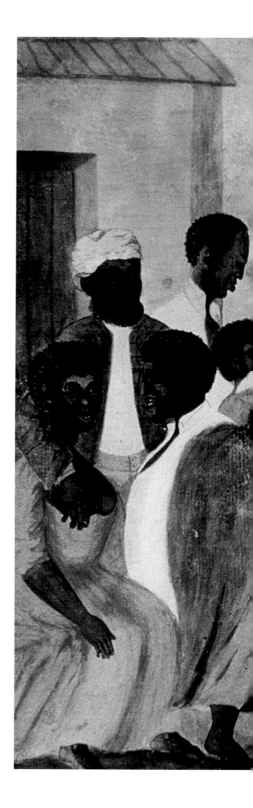

On a daily basis enslaved women had to endure the fear—and the reality—of physical abuse. Rape was common and slave women were at the mercy of masters and their sons, as well as hired overseers. Arbitrary punishment of the most sadistic kind was meted out. "Beat women! Why sure he beat women," Elizabeth Sparks of Virginia reported of her master. "Beat women naked an' wash 'em down in brine." Another ex-slave remembered how his master had treated one "yellow girl": "He tied her across the fence, naked, and whipped her severely with a paddle bored with holes, and with a switch. Then he shaved the hair off of one side of her head, and daubed cow-filth on the shaved part." All this was done "to disgrace her—[to] keep her down."

But enslaved women struggled tirelessly against this unjust system. "Fight, and if you can't fight, kick; if you can't kick, then bite," one slave mother advised her daughter. In the midst of utter degradation, women worked hard to protect their families and to create some joy in their domestic lives. They lived in bleak surroundings. An 18th-century British traveler described one such dwelling as a "miserable shell, a poor apology for a house." The walls were neither "lathed nor plaistered," the one window lacked glass, and as the single room "stood on blocks about a foot above the ground, the hogs lay constantly under the floor, which made it swarm with fleas." Another early observer, Julian Niemcewicz from Poland, wrote of Mount Vernon's "miserable" slave huts, where "husband and wife sleep on a mean pallet, the children on the ground." Yet in the midst of their poverty he noticed a touch of gentility—"some cups and a teapot."

Incredibly resourceful, enslaved women did whatever they could to ease the plight of their families. One enterprising slave made extra money by selling her quilts for as much as ten dollars each to local whites. Mothers scavenged scraps of thread and material to make extra clothing for their families. Using natural dyes, some women made brightly colored dresses which they wore proudly for special occasions. Fannie Berry

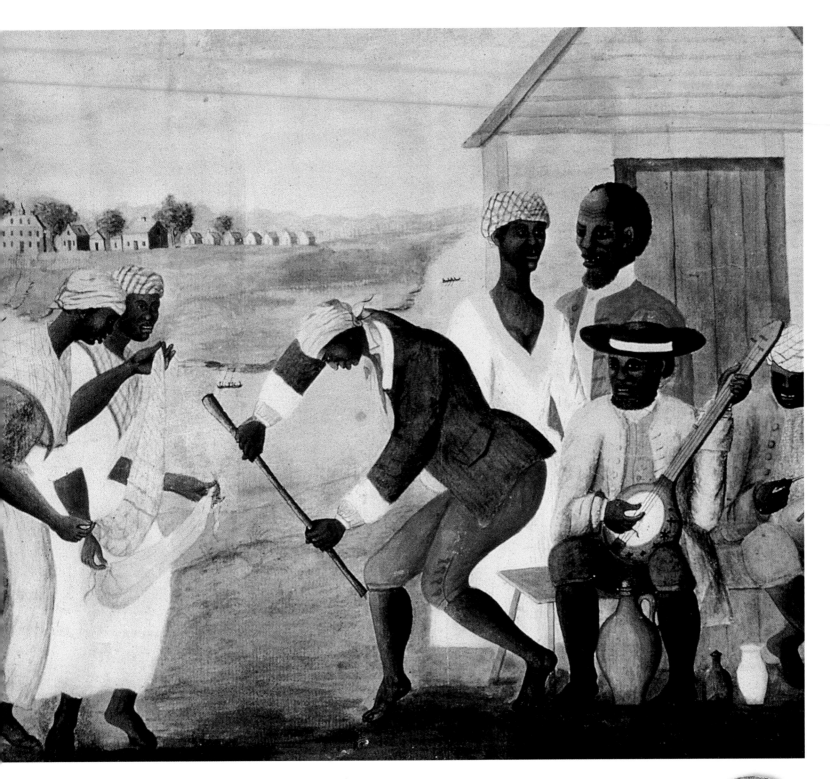

This 1790s watercolor entitled "The Old Plantation" offers a rare glimpse of life in the slave quarters. A man and two women dance joyously to the accompaniment of a banjo and drum (far right). Despite the degradation of their lives, enslaved people created a world apart from their masters. The brass charm at right was one of three hand-wrought amulets, all in the shape of fists, that were unearthed at the slave quarters of The Hermitage, Andrew Jackson's Tennessee plantation. Such a charm may have been thought to bring good luck or fend off evil; whatever its precise meaning, this haunting artifact offers clear evidence of a vibrant slave culture.

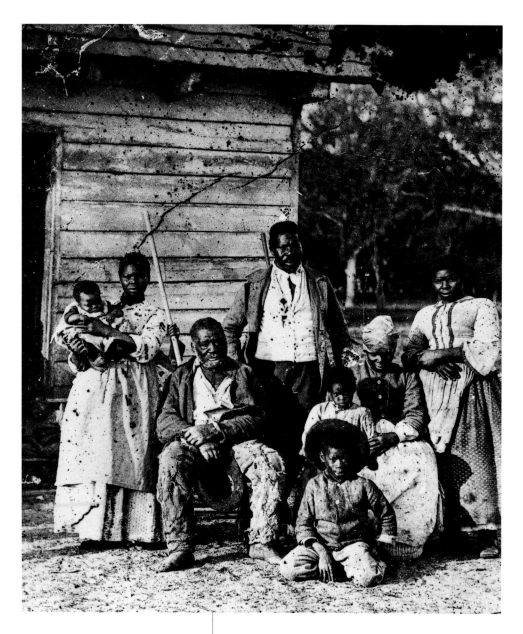

recalled "snitchin' lace an' beads fum de big house" for "fixin' up party clothes." Enslaved Mary Wyatt could not resist one of her mistresses' dresses. Sneaking it out of the Big House beneath her petticoat, she wore it at the slaves' Christmas dance and held her breath the entire time. "Was scared to death dat Missus gonna come in, but she didn't. Marsa come, but I knowed he warn't able to tell one dress from 'nother. Sho' was glad when I slipped dat dress back in place de nex' day."

An 18th-century visitor described the scene at a "Negro Ball" that took place on a tobacco plantation on a Sunday, "the only day these poor creatures have to themselves." They danced exuberantly to a homemade banjo made out of a gourd and horsehair strings. Though the outsider considered the dancing to be "violent exercise...so irregular and grotesque," he had to admit that all of the slaves appeared to be "exceedingly happy at these merrymakings." He added, "they seem as if they had forgot or were not sensible of their miserable condition."

In the face of "their miserable condition," the enslaved people created a society of their own. At night, the slaves crept away from the plantation and met furtively in the forest, away from the prying eyes of the master. There they held dances—joyous affairs where young women danced, each one with a glass of water on her head; the young men placing bets on which woman would be able to dance the longest without knocking the glass over. They danced to the rhythm of carved bones that were slapped against their palms. Religious gatherings were also held in the forest, and both men and women risked punishment to attend them. Groups of white patrollers searched for slaves who were off the plantation without a pass; if caught they would be severely beaten on the spot.

The forest was a place beyond the white world where enslaved men and women could gather strength as a community. It also became a refuge. One slave woman ran off and lived in the woods because she had been treated "like a dog." Runaways like her were taken care of by other slaves who would secretly bring them food and clothing. Fewer women than men tried to escape—not surprisingly, given the fact that women had to hold onto and take care of their children as best they could. In at least one case, however, an entire family—mother, father, and 15 children—lived in a cave in the forest for 15 years.

Enslaved women played a critical role in helping others in their community to escape. Forced to become textile workers under slavery, they used that skill to help subvert the system itself. Slave women gathered together to create complex quilts for themselves. The quilts were made from colorful scraps of calico discarded by their mistress or left behind on the plantation's sewing room floors. Quilting had to be done during a slave woman's free time—a rare commodity, as evening chores might stretch until 10 p.m. After that, especially on winter evenings, women would hunker down to their quilts, working by the dim light of candles or smoky wooden torches. On one occasion, a woman patching a quilt rescued a man being sought by the hated patrollers. When a white posse knocked on her door, she stashed the fugitive beneath her handiwork and calmly kept stitching. They left without their man.

According to oral tradition, the quilt designs themselves became signals used by members of the Underground Railroad who guided fleeing slaves along secret escape routes to the North. Quilts would be placed one at a time on a fence; and since airing out a quilt was a common occurrence, no suspicion would be aroused. But the design embedded in the quilt would dictate the actions of those seeking freedom. A monkey wrench quilt indicated that the fleeing slaves should gather together all their tools and belongings. A

In this page from a plantation ledger book, "blanket" written next to a name indicates that a child was born to a slave and a blanket dispensed. The parsimonious mistress kept track of her blankets, and in the process, inadvertently created a genealogy of her enslaved families. Timothy O'Sullivan's 1862 portrait of one newly freed family (opposite) included five generations.

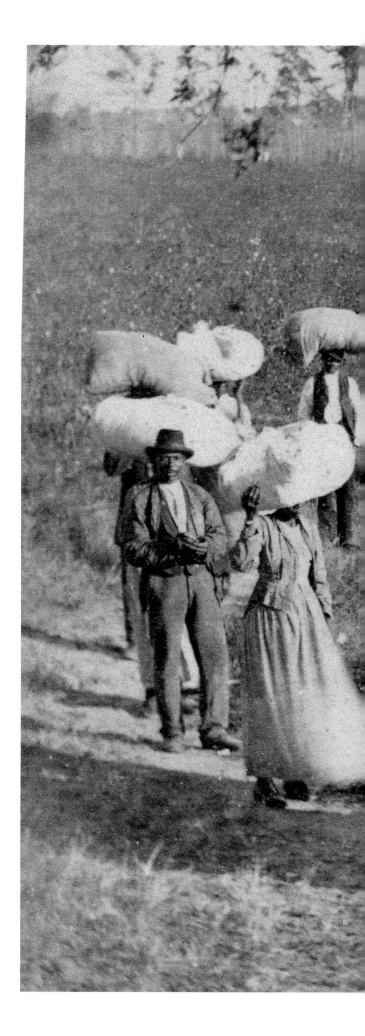

Returning at sunset from plantation fields near Charleston, South Carolina, laborers including men, women, and children walk in single file while balancing loads of picked cotton on their heads. One woman boasted that she could pick 200 pounds of cotton per day, and more than twice that on a good day.

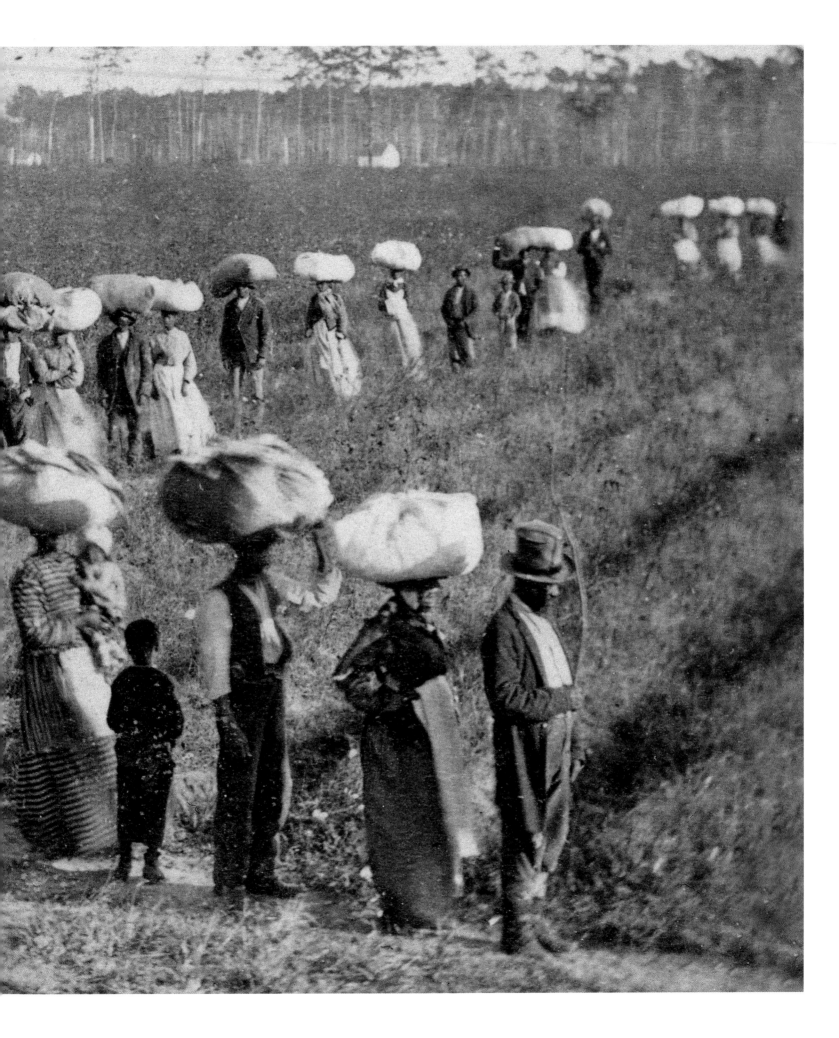

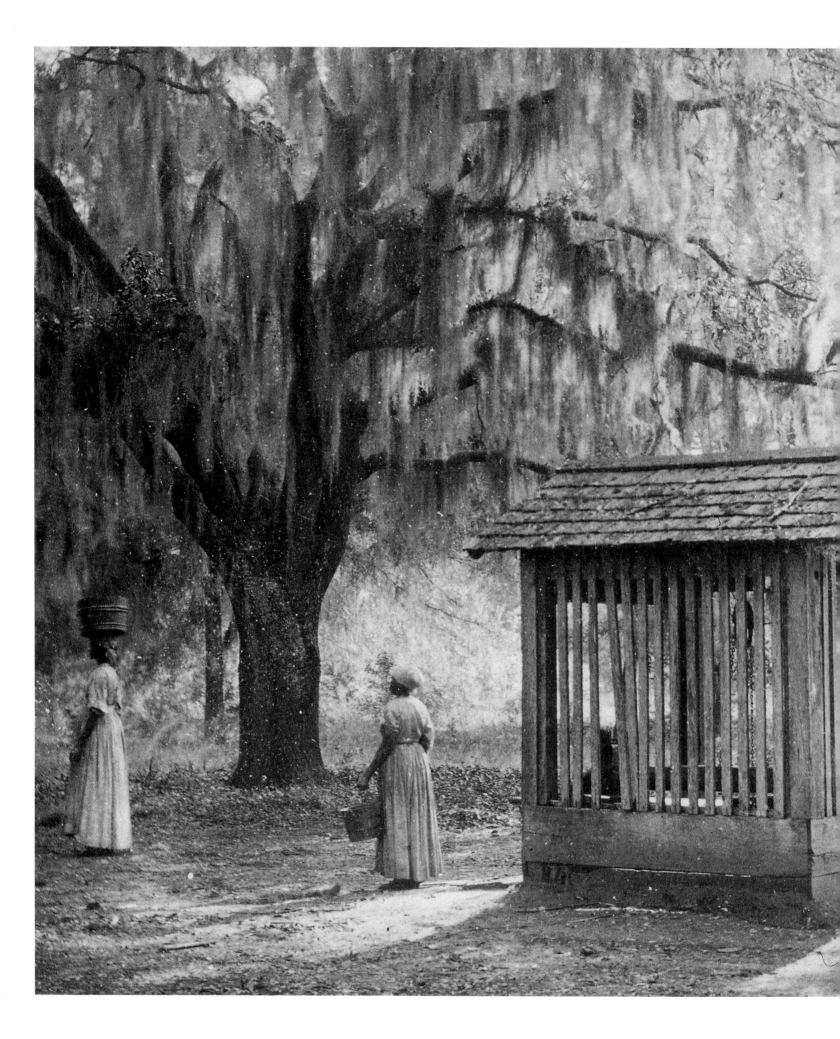

tumbling box pattern meant departure was imminent. Oral history indicates that a log cabin quilt placed outside a house served as a beacon for fugitives—a sign that it was a safe harbor. Knots on the quilts also served as a practical and spiritual guide for the slaves. The placement of the knots was a kind of hidden road map, indicating the distance between one safe house and another. According to African traditions, knots—specifically the kind used on these slave quilts—invoke spiritual protection for those about to set off on a journey. Africans believed that evil traveled in a straight line; reflecting that belief, the drunkard path quilt pattern with its zigzag design urged fleeing slaves to travel in unpredictable ways in order to avoid capture by slave catchers pursuing them. Thus, slave women's handiwork helped guide others to freedom.

One extraordinary woman went even further. Harriet Tubman, an escaped slave turned conductor on the Underground Railroad, personally brought hundreds of enslaved people North to freedom. For her efforts she became known as the Moses of her people. A field hand on a Maryland plantation, Tubman was often whipped as a child and she "prayed to God to make me strong and able to fight." Fight she did. When her master died in 1849 and she learned that she and her brothers would be sold to the Deep South, she decided to flee. Unable to convince her husband or brothers to join her, she courageously set off alone, hiding during daylight hours and walking in the dead of night. When she crossed the state line into free Pennsylvania she could barely comprehend her joy and relief. "I looked at my hands to see if I was the same person," she later recalled. The sun streamed "like gold" over the countryside and a "glory" infused everything. "I felt like I was in heaven," she noted.

Free but alone, she soon resolved to share her freedom with her family. She was determined to make a home for them in the North and then bring them up to join her. Working in Philadelphia and New Jersey as a cook, laundress, and scrubwoman, she saved every penny she could to fund a rescue. In 1850 Tubman slipped into the South and brought back her sister and her sister's two children who were about to be sold. Months later she rescued a brother and two other men. When she returned to Maryland in 1851 to free her husband, she discovered that he had since taken a new wife. Though heartbroken, she grew even more determined: She would free as many slaves as she could. Tubman became a frequent conductor on the Underground Railroad, guiding more than 300 runaways to safety—including her own parents—in a ten-year period. She proved

With Spanish moss dangling from a nearby tree, two African-American women (opposite) carry water from a well on a warm day in Georgia in the 1860s. House servants did the cooking, washing, sewing, and other chores under the intense scrutiny of their mistress. If she were displeased with their work, she could send them back to the fields.

resourceful on the treacherous journey, donning disguises when necessary, sedating wailing infants, and, if need be, strengthening the resolve of weak-kneed fugitives with the help of the gun she carried. Tubman was so effective that enraged southern planters placed a bounty of $40,000 on her head.

When the Civil War broke out, Tubman headed South to get into the action, serving effectively as a Union scout and spy behind Confederate lines. Passing as a freedwoman, she traveled boldly throughout the countryside—disregarding the price on her head—to pinpoint strategic spots such as cotton warehouses and ammunition depots. She also sought out the location of slaves waiting to be freed. Using her information, the guerrilla fighter, Col. James Montgomery, made a series of raids on the coast of South Carolina, Georgia, and Florida. A number of them were led by Tubman herself. During the summer of 1863 Tubman and Montgomery wreaked havoc on plantations along the Combahee River in South Carolina—and in the process, liberated nearly 800 slaves.

After her dramatic on-the-scene rescues, Tubman worked with the freed refugees, who arrived at Union strongholds penniless and frightened about their futures. Tubman recalled her work with ex-slaves at Beaufort, South Carolina: "Among other duties which I have, is that of looking after the hospital here for [refugees]. Most of those coming from the mainland are very destitute, almost naked. I am trying to find places for those able to work, so…[they can earn] their own living."

Slave men and women who fled plantations during the war were designated "contrabands of war," or a form of property. Union Gen. Benjamin Butler saw the value of contraband men: They could be used in building defenses or even in fighting. As for contraband women and children, Butler had little use: "I am in the utmost doubt what to do with this species of property." Obviously, women were hardly welcomed with open arms into Union camps—even after having arrived there at great personal risk.

Thousands of black women with children in tow escaped from plantations during the war and in the process helped bring about the final dismantling of slavery. One white woman witnessed the world being turned upside down as she approached her aunt's plantation: "Down the road [the Yankees]…came, and with them the slaves…journeying, as they thought, to the promised land. I saw them as they trudged the main road, many of the women with babes in their arms…. Some of them fared better than the others. A

$ 50.00 Reward !!

<u>Ran away</u> from the Yard Corner of Jackson & Broad Streets, Augusta Ga. — on the evening of Tuesday 7th April 1863 a Woman "<u>Dolly</u>", whose likeness is here seen. —
  She is thirty years of age, light Complexion — hesitates somewhat when spoken to, and is not a very healthy woman — but rather good looking, with a fine set of teeth. Never Changed her Owner, and has been a house Servant always. ___ It is thought she has been enticed off by some White Man, being herself a Stranger to this City, and belonging to a Charleston Family. ___
  For further particulars apply to Antoine Poullain Esqr Augusta Ga. ___

Augusta Police Station

Louis Manigault Owner of Dolly

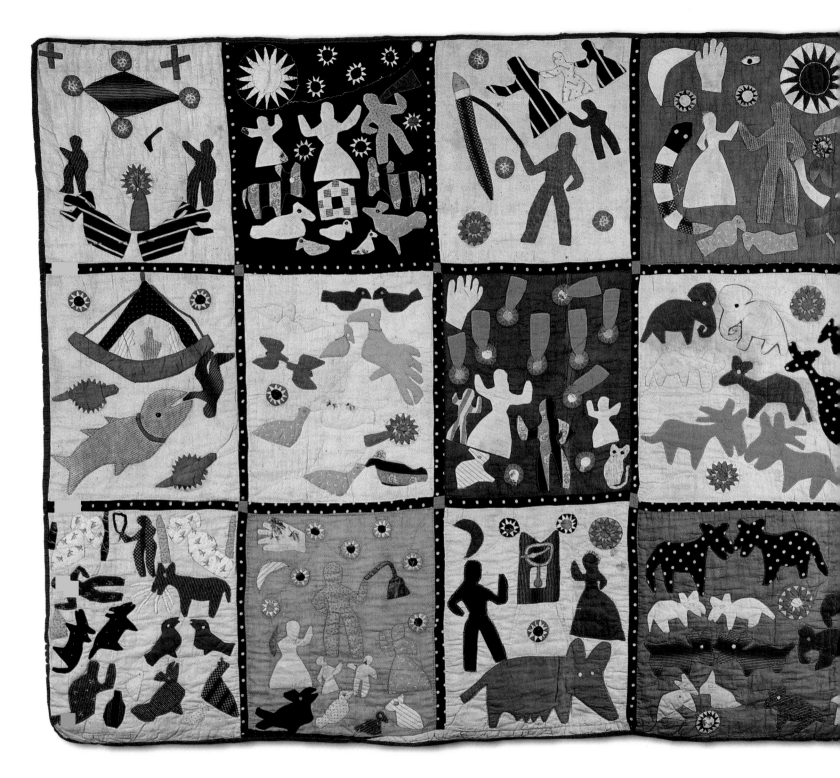

Harriet Powers, a woman born into slavery in Georgia in 1837, made this masterful quilt around the turn of the 20th century. The suffering yet redemptive figure of Old Testament Job is depicted in one of the squares, as is the famous Leonid meteor shower that occurred in 1833, an event so astounding—more than a thousand shooting stars per minute streaked across the sky—and so terrifying that slaves believed it was an omen that war would come and free them. Handed down through oral tradition, the story of how the stars began to fall was turned into a spiritual sung by black troops during the Civil War and eventually incorporated into Harriet Powers's quilt, a folk art masterpiece now in the collection of the Museum of Fine Arts in Boston.

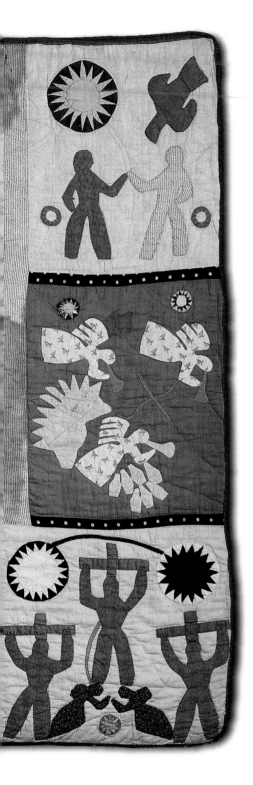

negro woman, Laura, my aunt's fancy seamstress, rode [a] beautiful white pony, sitting [on] the red plush saddle of her mistress."

Many women chose freedom over bondage, despite the risks involved. Capture by Confederates could mean imprisonment or death—or a return to slavery. In some places captured slave women were hanged along with their husbands. One woman disguised herself in men's clothing and proceeded to walk by herself for 200 miles through enemy territory in order to gain her freedom. During the war there were reports in Virginia and Maryland of "women and children...walking, as if for dear life, to reach Washington." Not all arrived safely. One slave mother came into a Union camp clutching her dead child who had been shot by her master as she ran off. She brought the child, she said, "to be buried *free*."

Reaching Union camps, however, did not ensure safety. A northern journalist wrote angrily to the governor of Massachusetts to report that soldiers were abusing refugees: "I am sorry to say that the Massachusetts 24th has been acting outrageously here—robbing, burning houses...ravishing negro women—beating their husbands who attempted protection." In 1862 the military governor of occupied North Carolina permitted slave owners who took an oath of allegiance to the federal government to retrieve their slaves from Union camps. He also closed down a school for black children, arguing that his mandate was to "restore the old order of things." At least in one camp, however, past miseries were repaid in kind. When a cruel slave master turned up at an encampment where a half dozen of his female slaves had taken refuge, the federal officer turned the tables on him. "I laid him bare and [put] the whip into the hands of the Women, three of Whom took turns in settling some old scores on their masters back."

Slave women who did not leave plantations often suffered at the hands of their increasingly desperate masters. When Patsey Leach's husband joined the Union Army, her life changed for the worse. "From that time [the master] treated me more cruelly than ever, whipping me frequently without any cause and insulting me on every occasion." After he threatened to kill her "by piecemeal," Patsey escaped with her youngest child, leaving behind four others to cope on their own.

As the war dragged on and the scent of freedom grew stronger, female slaves became increasingly assertive. One enslaved woman announced to her mistress, Emily Perkins of Tennessee, that she would never be whipped again. Infuriated at what she perceived

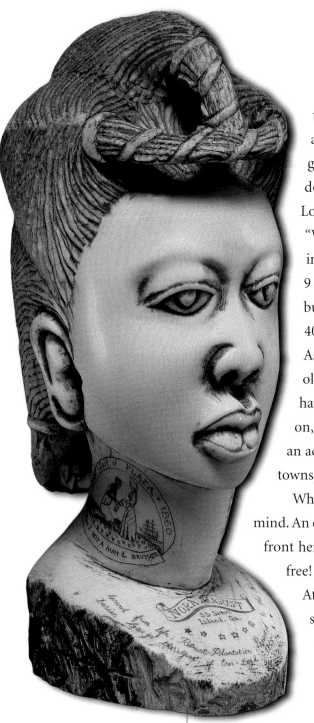

to be the height of insolence, Perkins hit the slave over the head with a broom. When the broom broke and the woman still stood her ground, the mistress called for a male servant to tie the feisty slave down. Perkins then "laid it on." At the Rosedown Plantation in Louisiana, mistress Martha Turnbull was suddenly faced with a strike: "When I ordered Celiame to scrub my kitchen she walked off and sat in her house for 3 days. Stepsy was impudent and would not cook....For 9 days Lucinda refused to come and wait on me." To her horror, Turnbull had to pay her people before they would work: "Julia one week at 40¢....Penny cleaning front yard, gave her 2 lbs. coffee—2 lbs. sugar." As General Sherman's troops marched through Darlington, South Carolina, Amy Spain screamed out in delight, "Bless the Lord the Yankees have come!" Unfortunately for the slave woman, the soldiers continued on, leaving Spain to deal with the consequences of her daring outburst— an act considered so vile that she was hanged for her crime. Most of the townspeople turned out to watch.

When freedom finally did come, once silent female slaves spoke their mind. An elderly slave dropped her hoe in the field and ran seven miles to confront her nemesis. She ran up to her mistress and yelled, "I'se free! Yes, I'se free! Ain't got to work fo' you no mo! You can't put me in yo' pocket now!"

At the Beaver Creek Plantation in Virginia, a slave named Grace had spent decades quietly spinning and weaving, and came to be considered an old "faithful servant." But when Emancipation freed her, Grace went to the Big House, retrieved her granddaughter, and bluntly told her ex-mistress what she thought—Grace said that she had "done a heap" for the white family "but could never do any more." She turned on her heels and left the Big House for good.

Some family members sold off to distant parts of the South were joyously reunited with loved ones, one man reportedly walking 600 miles from Georgia to North Carolina to find his wife and children. A northern observer wrote, "Every mother's son seemed to be in search of his mother; every mother in search of her children." Husbands and wives, their unions not considered legal during slavery time, now rushed to have their marriages officially recognized and their children pronounced legitimate. Ex-slaves put aside their plows and hoes for a day, infuriating the whites who still owned the farmland, to proudly declare their marital status on federal registers. Celebrations full of singing and dancing followed.

The euphoria of freedom soon turned to a grim reality. Many thousands of freed people were unable to locate their family members. In addition, the war had destroyed the southern economy and landscape. Food was scarce and money scarcer. Sharecropping replaced slavery—but many freedpeople suffered as much, if not more, than they did under the old system. Profits were frequently split 50-50 between the white owner and the sharecropper; but first the worker had to pay the owner for his housing and all of his supplies, including seed, fertilizer, farm equipment, and draft animals. By the time all those items were factored in (as well as other creative debits charged to the sharecropper), black workers often found themselves mired in debt to the white planter; or, if owed money, unable to collect it.

A freedwoman named Caroline complained to federal authorities when her employer, Thomas Price of Greensboro, North Carolina, refused to pay her what she was owed. His response was immediate. When she returned to work he "knocked her down and beat her with his fist," calling out to his overseer to fetch "the strap." He then whipped Caroline "on the bare flesh by turning her clothes up." After he had finished, Price commanded his overseer to "ware her out" with more of the same. The overseer complied.

Whites' resentment against African Americans and their new autonomy erupted into acts of violence. Blacks were attacked and murdered for offenses such as refusing to give way to whites on sidewalks, for using what whites perceived as "insolent" language, for having the temerity to send their children to schools, or for trying to buy land.

The Freedmen's Bureau, a federal agency established to protect the rights of the newly freed people, tried—with very limited success—to settle disputes. Unless a bureau's office was located near an Army post and could enlist the aid of soldiers, it often proved useless in enforcing decisions. The official reports of the Freedmen's Bureau's officers attest to the reality of widespread abuse—a kind of guerrilla war being waged against African Americans. Women were not exempt from the mistreatment. An 1867 report from Panola County, Mississippi, stated matter-of-factly: "A woman (colored) has been taken from her house to the woods pulled over fences by the hair of the head; in the woods she is

The regal bust of a 23-year-old woman named Nora August (opposite), was carved in ivory by an unknown Union soldier who wrote of her: "Now a Free Woman." The artist came upon the striking woman at Retreat Plantation on St. Simons Island off the coast of Georgia. Her elaborately braided hair harks back to West African styles.

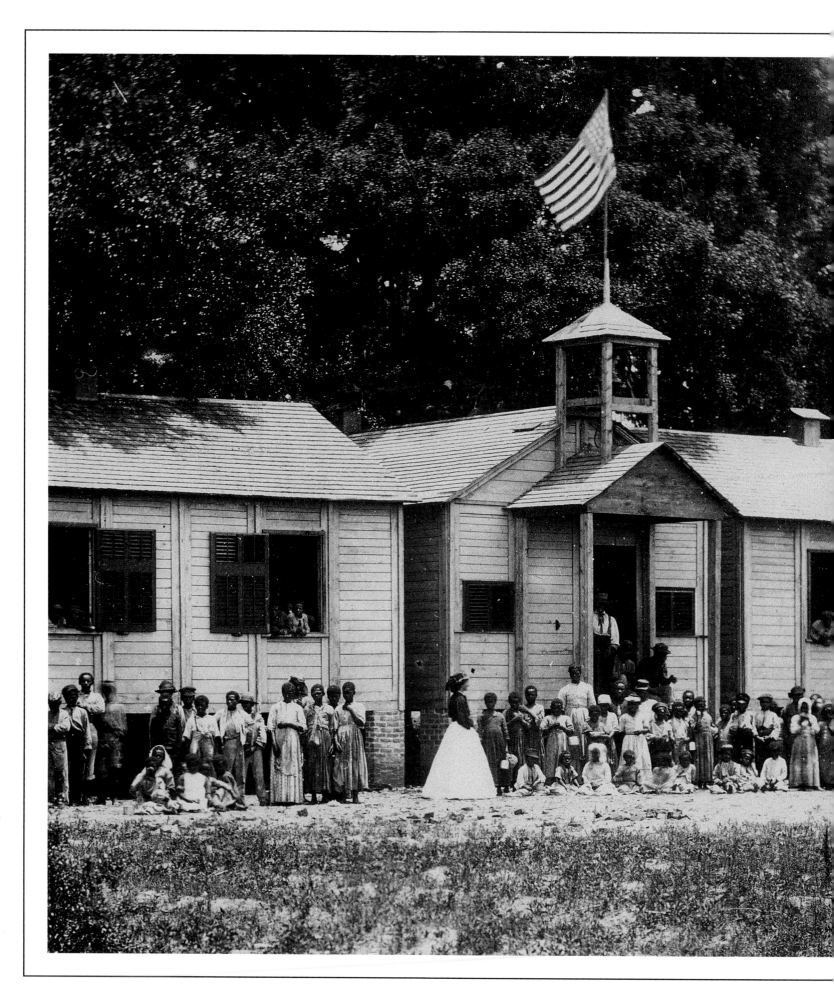

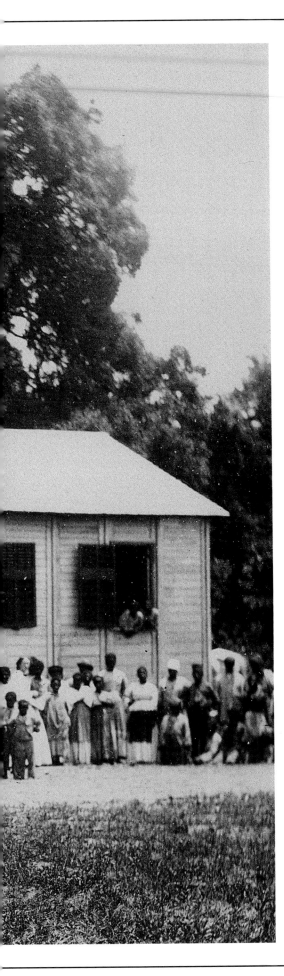

"The people [declare] that no woman could be a lady that would volunteer to come down here to teach 'niggers.'"

FREEDMAN'S BUREAU REPORT, WARRENTON, VIRGINIA

The situation was tense. In 1866 the Freedmen's Bureau, a federal agency created to protect newly freed slaves, announced the opening of a school in Warrenton, Virginia, to teach illiterate freedpeople. Local whites were outraged; to them, such a school would be a symbol of their defeat. Newly established barrooms lining the streets helped fan the town's seething anger. Ex-Confederate soldiers—in uniform and brandishing revolvers—came to town to drink and raise cain.

Into this volatile mix came Serena Wood of Middleboro, Massachusetts, with her hated Yankee accent. She was sent by the New England Freedmen's Aid Society, which helped staff schools for ex-slaves. (The society paid its teachers $15 per month, as indicated in this official Freedmen's

Bureau report.) A highly recommended teacher, she also had nerves of steel. Townspeople vowed not to house her, or even speak to her, but Wood was unfazed. "Fortunately the lady...cares but little for their haughty opinions or 'inuendoes,'" an official wrote. She considers this 'the golden age!' and is glad...[to contribute] her mite."

Bureau of Refugees, Freedmen and Abandoned Lands.
Office Supt. Freedmen's Schools, State of Georgia.

Augusta, Ga., Dec. 1st, 1865.

CIRCULAR }
NO. 3. }

On the 1st day of January, 1866, Teachers of Freedmen's Schools will answer *in the margin,* the questions herein asked; and by mail, or otherwise, return this Circular to this office.

1. Are you white or colored ? *White*
2. How long has your School been organized ? *5 Months*
3. What is your salary per month ? *$15.00 From a Northern Society*
4. By what Northern Society are you employed ? *New England Society Boston*
5. If paid by parents, how much per month, for each pupil ? *$0.50*
6. How many male pupils have you ? *15*
7. How many female pupils ? *7*
8. What is the *average daily* attendance ? *22*
9. How many pupils in Orthography ? *32*
10. How many are Reading ? *9*
11. How many in Arithmetic ? *10*
12. How many in Geography ? *4*
13. How many in Grammar ? *3*
14. How many Writing ? *8*
15. What other branches do you teach ? *no*
16. Is the Bible read daily in your School ? *yes* By whom? teacher or pupils ? *Teacher*
17. What books do you use ? *Mitchell's Geography, Smith's Grammar, Davies Arithmetic, Webster Spelling Book.*
18. Have any books and stationery been furnished gratuitously to your School ? By whom? and what the value? *Pupils furnish books and stationery.*

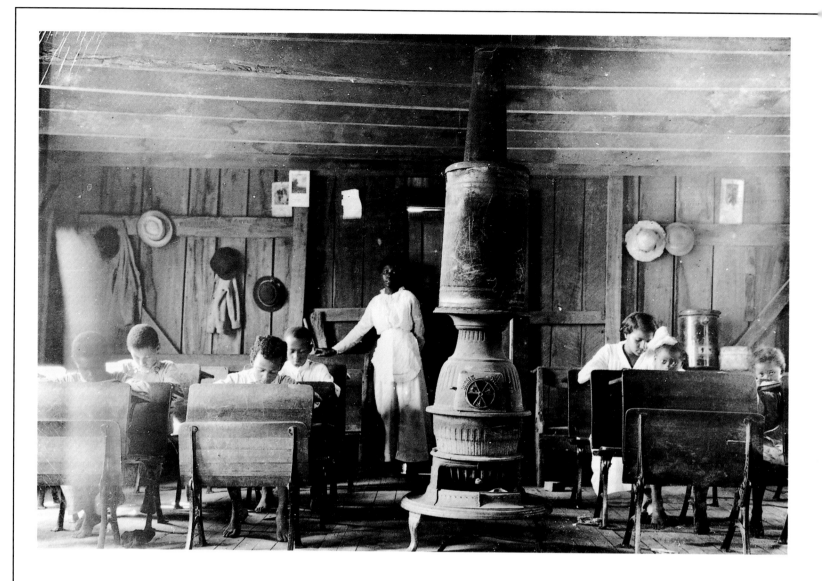

Nearly 4,000 courageous women—dubbed "saintly souls" by WEB Du Bois—joined the crusade. Charlotte Forten, from a well-to-do free black family in Philadelphia, was among the first to arrive. As the Civil War still raged, she came to the island of St. Helena off the coast of South Carolina in 1862. She and other black women educators risked everything: "We thought how easy it would be," Forten wrote, "for a band of guerrillas...to seize and hang us." Left unsaid was another dire possibility—being captured and sent into slavery.

But Forten ignored the danger, writing, "We were in that excited, jubilant state...which makes fear impossible."

Teachers suffered insults and worse—Serena Wood's schoolhouse was moved by "rowdies" in the dead of night; other structures were burned to the ground. The educators persevered, inspired by their eager pupils. Freedpeople sacrificed for the privilege to learn, parents paying from 20 cents to two dollars per month (a substantial sum for them); some children without funds earned their tuition by scrubbing floors,

chopping wood, and carrying water to the schoolhouse.

Though the Freedmen's Bureau schools were in existence less than a decade, they made inroads against illiteracy and helped foster a continuing hunger for education. Many of the teachers who educated later generations of African Americans had been pupils in those early schools. The torch was passed on, though sometimes in reverse—in a poignant scene (opposite), a daughter teaches her own mother to read. ■

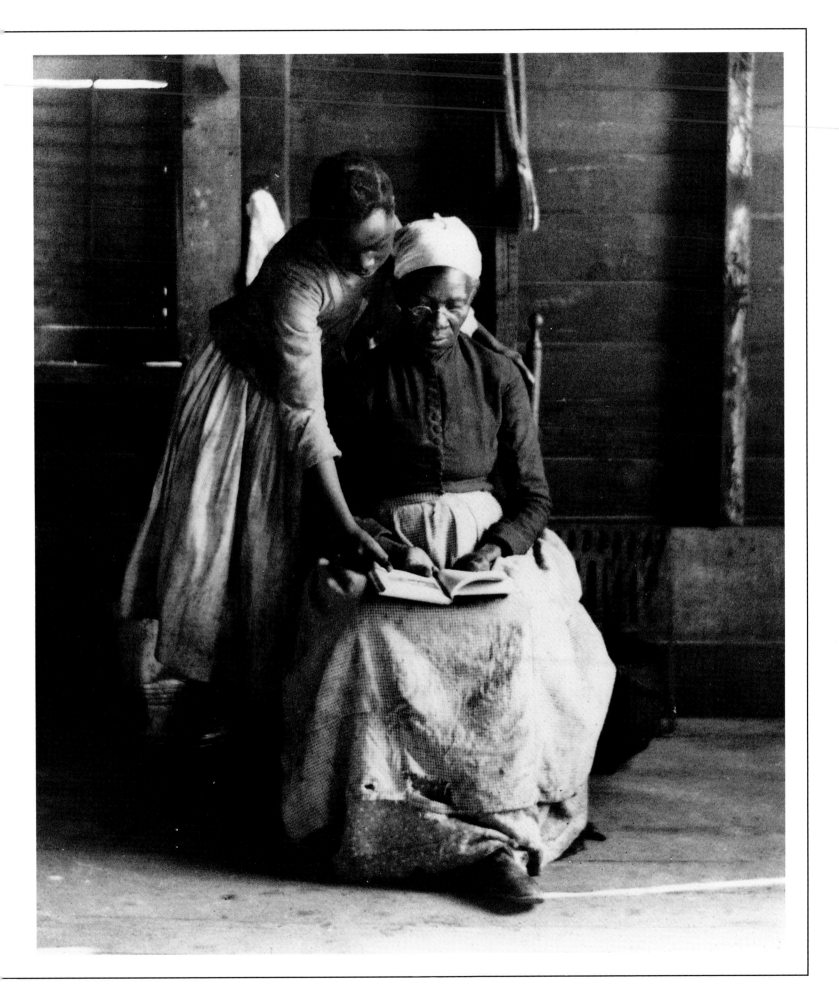

striped naked and tied up by the hands, and whiped untill two men are tired out, then she is laid down on her face, and beaten...."

Bureau agents tried to ensure just treatment for blacks by monitoring the proceedings of local courts, which tended to dismiss complaints against white aggressors. Rhody Ann Hope of Louisiana complained to the Freedmen's Bureau that she had been beaten by her employer, Samuel Davison. Her case was then referred to the Justice of the Peace with the following official result: "After Plaintiff had made her complaint [the Justice of the Peace] said he knew said Davison well and that he did not believe he beat her but that if he did she deserved it. Told her that she had better not have it investigated...[and] if she failed to sustain the charges against Davison she could be sent to the penitentiary." Despite the Justice of the Peace's warning, the woman pursued the charges and a warrant was issued for Davison's arrest. In court Davison admitted that he had beaten her, but claimed that he was justified because she had used impertinent language. The result: Case dismissed, and the woman had to pay court costs.

In 1866 a group of prominent southern white men met at a hotel in Nashville, Tennessee, to create "an institution of Chivalry, Humanity, Mercy, and Patriotism"; its primary goal was to maintain "the supremacy of the white race." Thus was born the Ku Klux Klan, a group that launched a well-organized campaign of terror against southern blacks and their white sympathizers. Women as well as men suffered. One woman refused to tell a Klan mob where her husband was. When one of the hooded intruders warned that he would "blow your God-damned brains out," if she did not tell his whereabouts, she calmly replied, "Then you will have me to shoot tonight." They left empty-handed.

African-American women stood up courageously to abuse during slavery and beyond. Theirs is a miraculous story of hard work and survival. The courage, strength, and ingenuity of African-American women who struggled tirelessly against an unjust system make them American heroes of the first rank. Despite every attempt to dehumanize and degrade them, they managed to hold onto their families and nurture them. One ex-slave who had spent most of her life in bondage said she could die happy knowing that her children would be free. And a number of slave daughters went on to achieve remarkable success, including two women who were unrelated but shared a last name.

"I was not born with a silver spoon in my mouth, but with a laundry basket...on my head," Maggie Lena Walker once said of herself. By the age of ten she was work-

Hooded members of the Ku Klux Klan attack an unsuspecting family in this macabre illustration (opposite). During an 1870s Congressional investigation of the violence that had been unleashed against blacks during Reconstruction, one African-American woman described the execution of her husband: "They made me and my children wrap our heads up in bed quilts and come out of the house, and they then set it on fire, burning it up, and my husband in it, and all we had." His crime was that he had refused to give up his post as an elected constable.

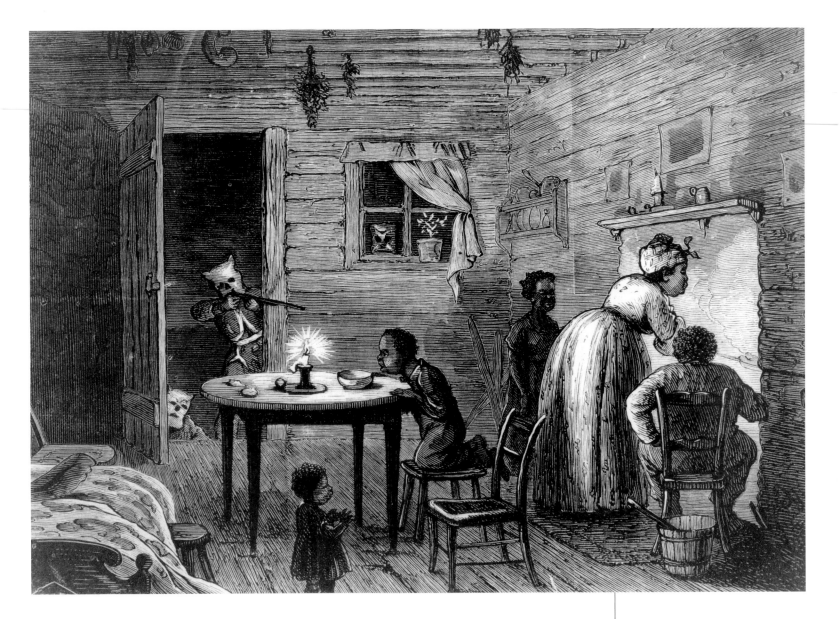

ing alongside her mother as a laundress in Richmond, Virginia, and earning extra pennies by delivering the laundry. Eventually Walker would encourage others to save their pennies and put them in a black-owned and operated bank. In 1903 she founded the St. Luke Penny Savings Bank and became the first woman bank president in the United States.

Sarah Breedlove Walker became a millionaire by developing and selling hair products for black women. An illiterate field hand born on a Louisiana plantation in 1867, Walker recounted her path to success, a path that demanded the perseverance and strength rooted in slavery times: "I am a woman who came from the cotton fields of the South. I was promoted from there to the washtub. Then I was promoted to the cook kitchen, and from there I promoted myself into the business of manufacturing hair goods and preparations." She noted proudly, "I have built my factory on my own ground."

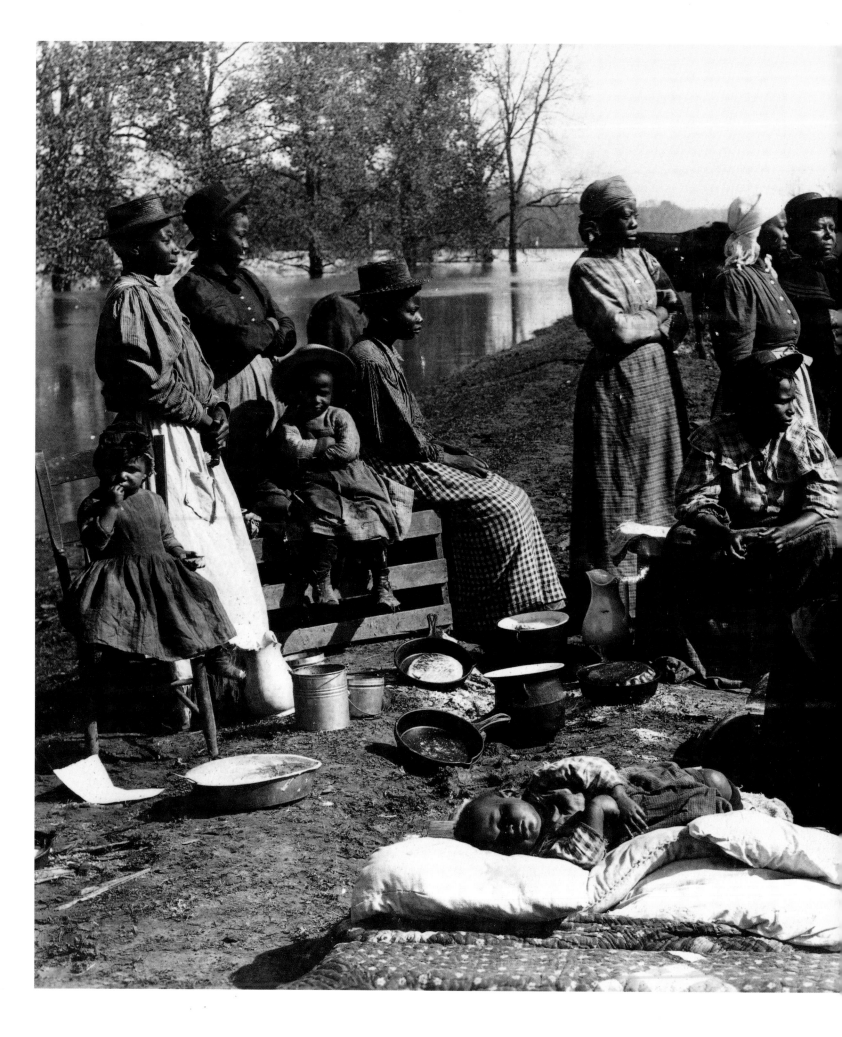

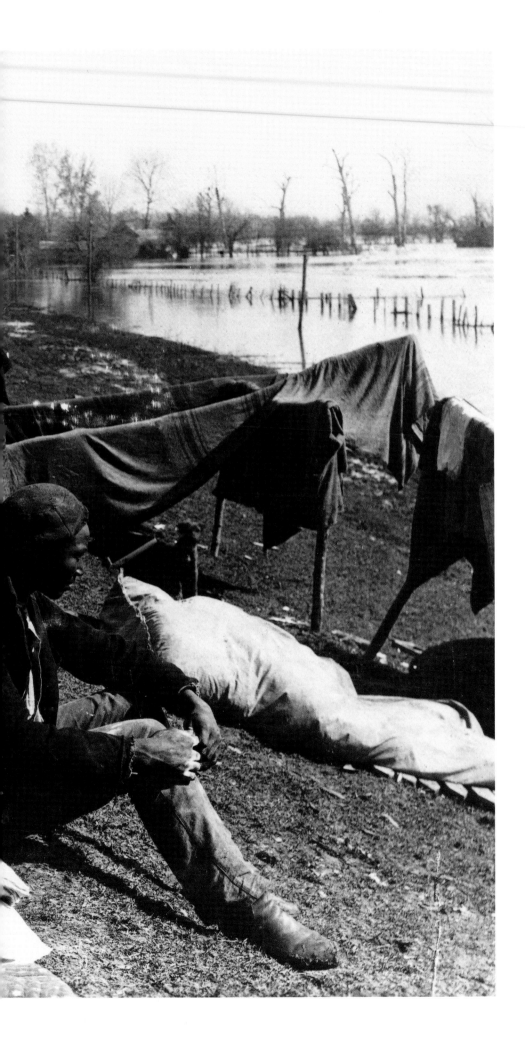

Refugees await a relief boat after flooding on the Mississippi River. As federal intervention in the postwar South ended in 1877 and state laws increasingly limited the rights of ex-slaves, some African Americans looked West for opportunity. Known as Exodusters, over 15,000 of them migrated to Kansas by 1880, many of them drawn by the rumor that the government had set aside that state for freed slaves. One husband recounted his arrival there: "I asked my wife did she know the ground she stands on. She said, 'No.' I said, 'It is free ground,' and she cried for joy."

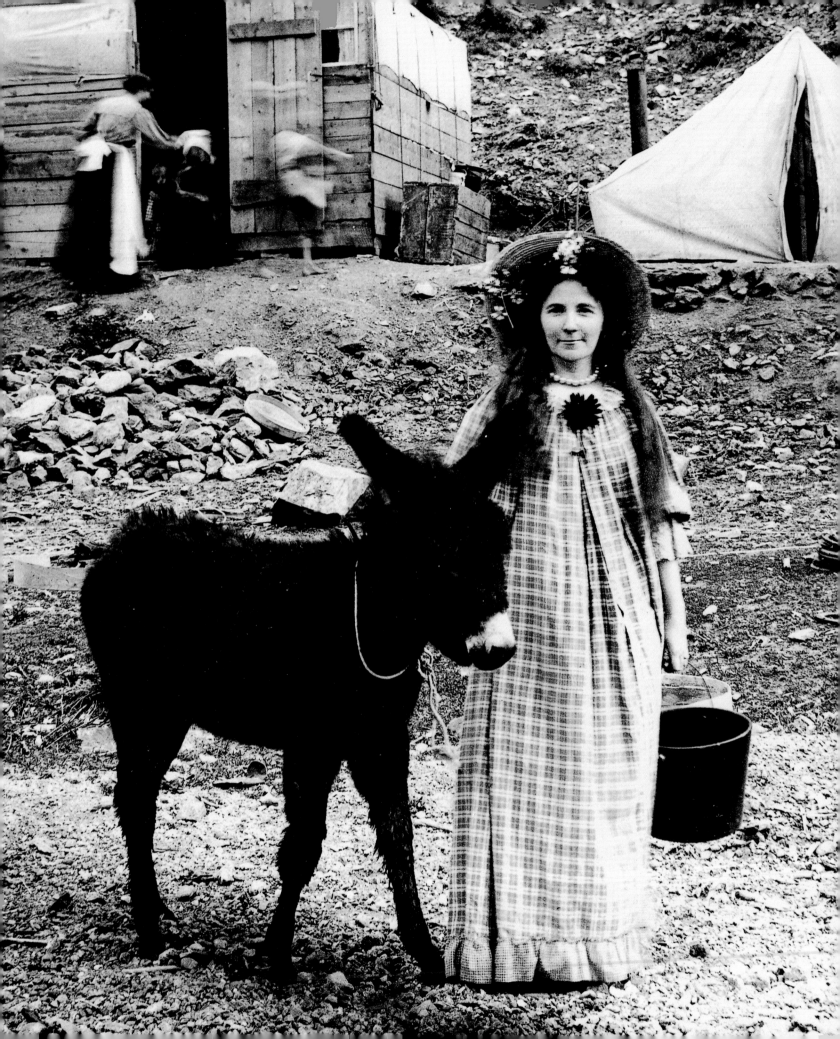

WESTERING WOMEN

*T*HE ROMANCE OF THE 19th-century American West still resonates in the popular imagination. The lone cowboy riding across the high plains represents the archetypal American—the rugged individual fighting for survival in a spectacularly beautiful, yet forbidding, landscape. The mythic West was supposedly a male paradise.

But what of the woman at left in a Colorado mining camp? She looks directly at the camera with a serene half smile. With one hand she holds her burro, with the other

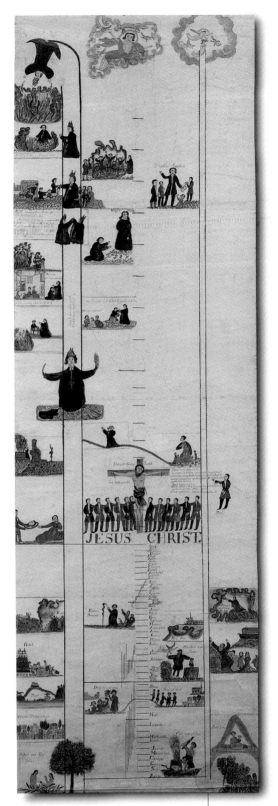

a pail of water. She is prepared to work in this wilderness. Yet she appears to be doing it with an element of joy, and perhaps a sense of humor; flowers adorn her bonnet and dress, and she wears a pearl necklace in the midst of the roughhewn surroundings. Behind her are two other women and the blurred images of children moving too fast for the camera, all of whom probably lived in the makeshift cabin and tent pictured.

According to the enduring myth of the West, men were the primary actors on this immense stage, and women somehow ruined the place; they wanted to civilize and subdue the wildness of the landscape (as well as its rough denizens), taming its very essence. Women were supposedly driven mad by the cruel vagaries of the vast wilderness: blizzards, locust plagues, droughts, attacks by Native American warriors, and sheer loneliness. Teddy Roosevelt famously pronounced that the frontier was "hard on women and cattle." Indeed it was—but it was hard on men as well.

Women were not victimized by the West; in fact, many flourished there. The West offered unique opportunities. In an era when women did not generally own land, single women could claim free acres—160 of them—under the Homestead Act of 1862. Wyoming, while still only a territory, gave women the right to vote—and became the first place in the country to do so. Other western states followed suit. Women went out West—with or without husbands—to take part in the American Dream. Settling into tiny cabins or tents or dirt-floored sod houses, women made do with very little and built on it; in the process they helped create the mining and ranching and homesteading cultures of the West. They contributed immeasurably to the economic and social development of the region, and they forged a pioneer spirit that is at the heart of the American experience.

Ingenuity and hard work were the hallmarks of the western pioneer woman, even en route. Fortunately, many women chronicled their journeys in letters and diaries, including the doughty Algeline Ashley: "I write on my lap with the wind rocking the wagon." She was one of 350,000 people who headed west by wagon across the continental United States—some 2,400 rugged miles from the Missouri River to Oregon and California in the period from 1841 to 1866. The vast majority of the emigrants were young (most between ages 16 and 35) and healthy—they had to be to endure the trek. Many women, of course, were not eager to be separated from their homes and loved ones, knowing well that they would probably never see either again. Others, however, embraced the new challenge: "I was possessed with a spirit of adventure and a desire to see what was new and strange," Miriam Thompson, a teenage bride, wrote.

Halfway across the country, Thompson and her traveling mates received a dire prediction: a man "gave us the consoling information that the Indians would kill us before we got to Oregon." But the emigrants were "indifferent to fear," according to Thompson, and, for her part, she found the Native Americans "better than represented." In fact, women frequently bartered with the native people they met on the trail, exchanging calico and cash for foods such as salmon, mountain trout, and buffalo (the men in the emigrant trains not being nearly the hunters that the Native Americans were). Similarly, Indians helped ferry emigrants across dangerous rivers, one woman noting that her family's trip across the Deschutes River "cost a good many shirts." A newlywed couple in 1845 met with disaster at one of the first river crossings they encountered. Their raft was swept out of sight, with all of their possessions on it. Disconsolate and alone they huddled on the bank trying to keep warm. Two Native American women found and rescued them, sending word of their plight to a nearby white settlement.

Yet as more and more whites poured into Native American lands, the relationship between the groups soured. The herds of buffalo upon which the Indians depended were being thinned and their patterns disrupted; diseases like cholera, smallpox, and measles, illnesses unknown to the native people—and for which they had no resistance—decimated the tribes. Indians began to burn the grass needed to feed the emigrants' livestock; they also attacked the arriving wagon trains. A new fear gripped the emigrants. One woman traveler slept every night with an ax by her side to protect her family in the event of an attack.

In September 1857 an overland emigrant reported that traders had found a woman who had been scalped and assumed dead. She survived, only to die a year or two later of "melancholy." The same woman chronicler noted that a party ahead of them had made a chilling discovery on the trail: "the body of a nude woman on the bank of the slough....A piece of hair rope was around her neck....From appearances it was thought she had been tortured by being drawn back and forth through the slough by this rope around her

Protestant missionary Eliza Spalding painted this six-foot-long "learning ladder" (opposite) around 1845 as a teaching aide in proselytizing Native Americans in the Far West. Though she and her husband set up a mission in the wilderness, they undoubtedly felt a keen competition for souls. In addition to depicting scenes from the Bible, Eliza clearly illustrated how the Presbyterian faith, represented by the straight and narrow path at right, led directly to heaven, while the broader road at left, dominated by a sword-wielding Roman Catholic pope, led only to the flames of damnation.

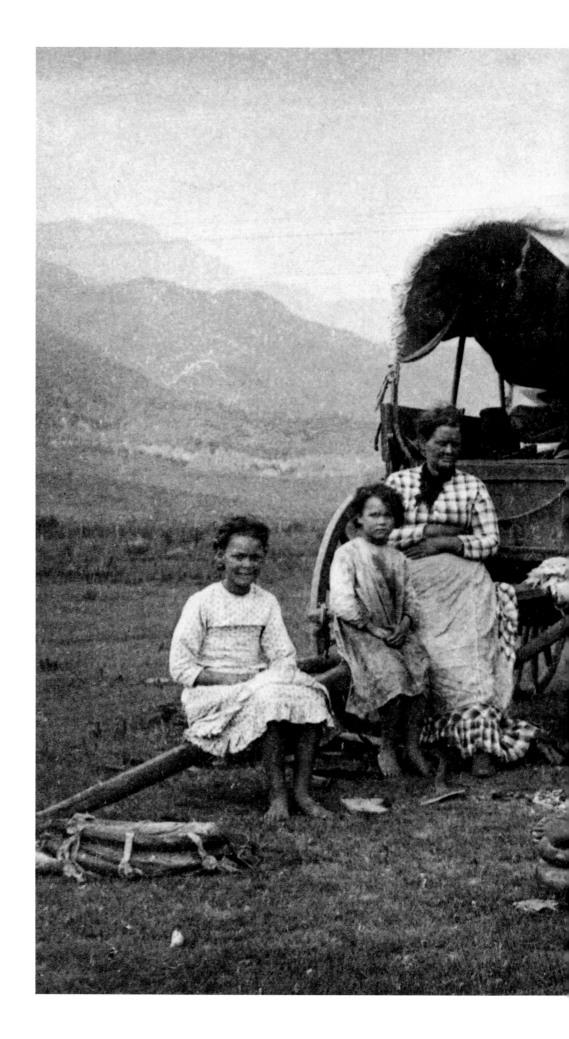

Bearing the haunted look of exhausted travelers, a westering family pauses on the trail with mountains looming in the distance. One California-bound wagon train had no guide and so little information on how to get there that, according to a member of the party, they had to "smell" their way west.

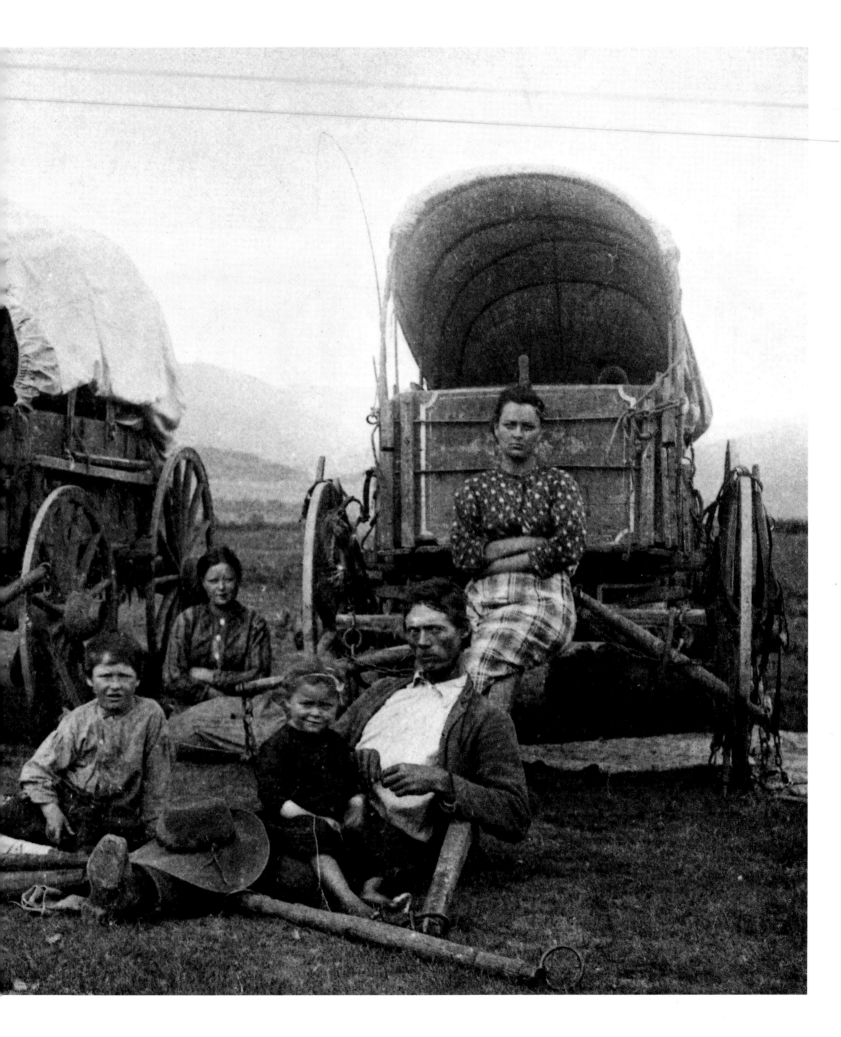

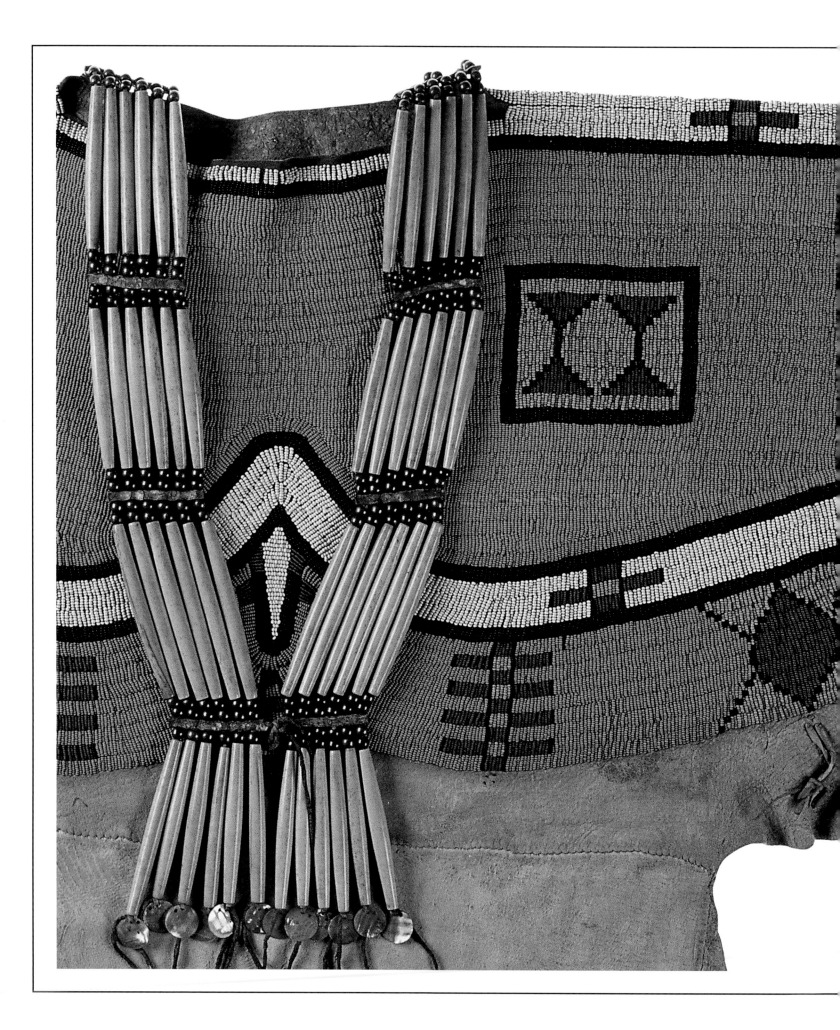

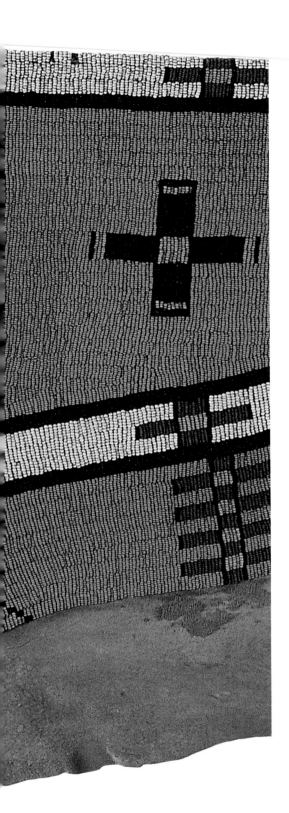

"A basket is a song made visible."

Native women from tribes throughout the West have left behind an astonishing array of traditional artwork: elaborately beaded clothing and cradleboards, vividly designed Pueblo pots and Navajo weavings, and intricately woven baskets of varying sizes and shapes. Yet there is not even a word for "art" in Native American languages; the concept does not exist. Women have fashioned utilitarian objects of great beauty, but the creative process has been almost more important than the finished products themselves.

In the 19th century, northern plains tribal women made handsome beaded buckskin dresses like the one at left to be worn on special occasions. The creation of such a garment was viewed as a kind of prayer. Women prepared the animal hides and took pride in their tanning skill: Just as men kept track of their conquests in war, women kept a running tally of the hides they prepared by marking the handles of their elk-horn scrapers. Using colorful glass beads acquired from white traders, women incorporated meaningful symbols into their designs. On this dress, for instance, the cross on the blue background represents the morning star; the blue beads symbolize water, or life; and the design within the white band of beads represents a turtle, another symbol of fertility, rising from the water.

Pueblo women of the Southwest made masterful *ollas* (storage jars) and bowls for daily and ceremonial uses. In the Zuni pueblo it is still said that water tastes better when drunk from a pottery jar. Living in the parched desert, the potters frequently used geometric patterns that represented rain-filled clouds or stylized rain birds.

According to Pueblo tradition, the origin of pottery stretches back to creation itself, and in fact, their ceramics exhibit a timeless quality. The black-on-white jar, below, dates to around 1050 A.D., but such bold graphic design, still used centuries later, right, could be mistaken for Cubist art by Picasso.

Pueblo potters considered the clay a living entity. Traditionally, they prayed as they collected it, and they sang while shaping it into bowls, jars, plates, and figures. The craftswomen were working the spirit of the Earth itself into useful vessels.

An anthropologist studying the Zuni pueblo in the late 19th century reported on the creative process: "When a woman has made a vessel, dried, polished, and painted it, she will tell you with an air of relief that it is a 'Made Being.'" ■

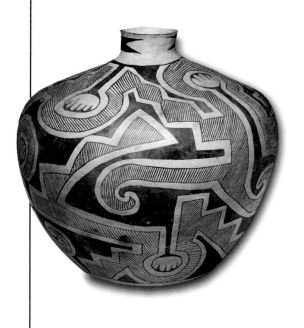

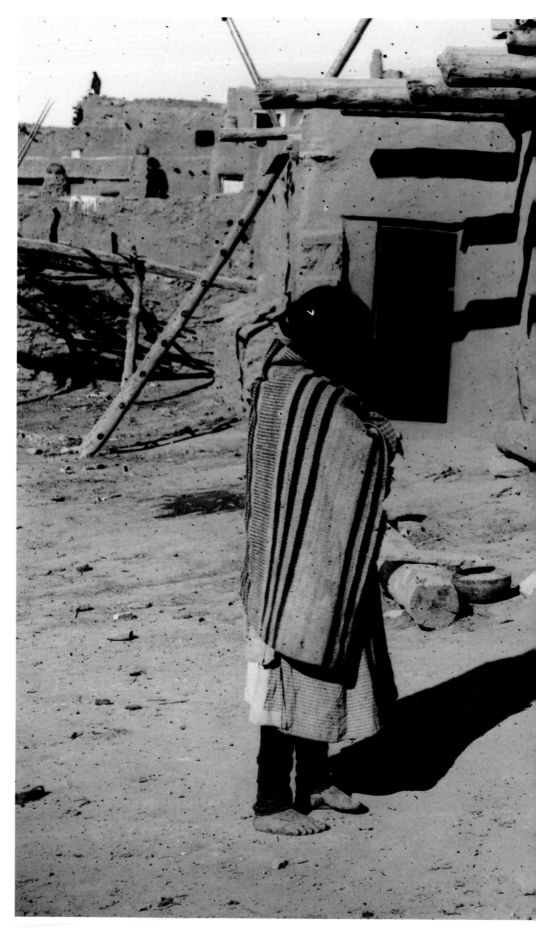

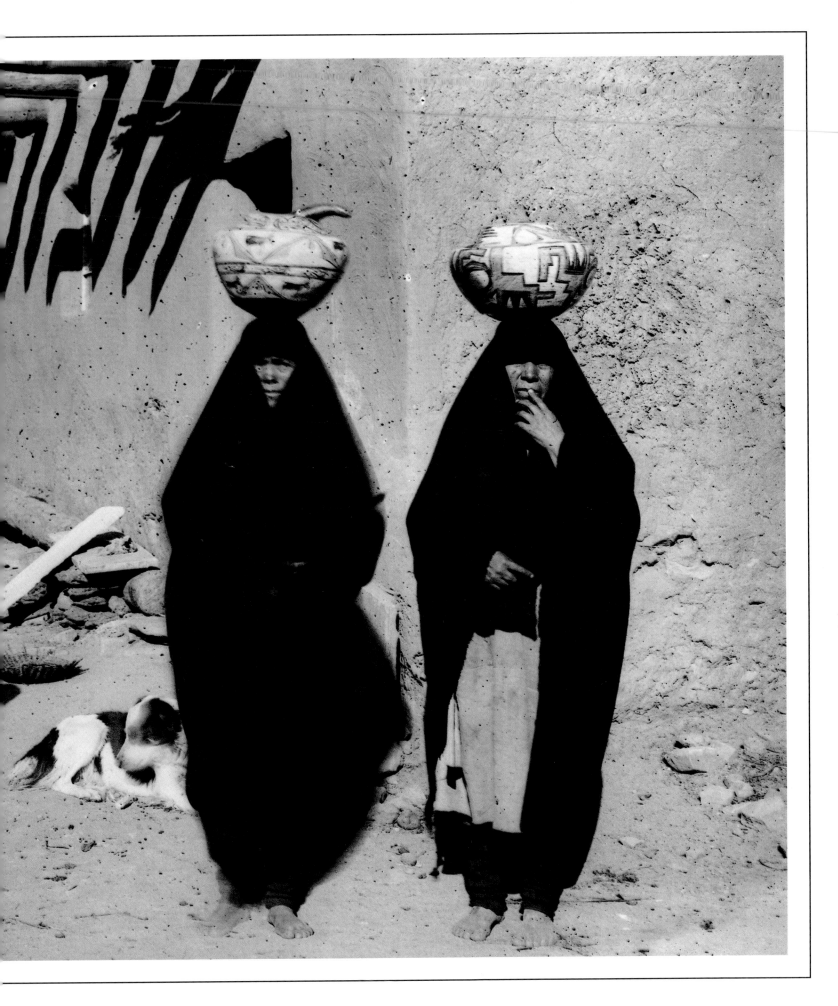

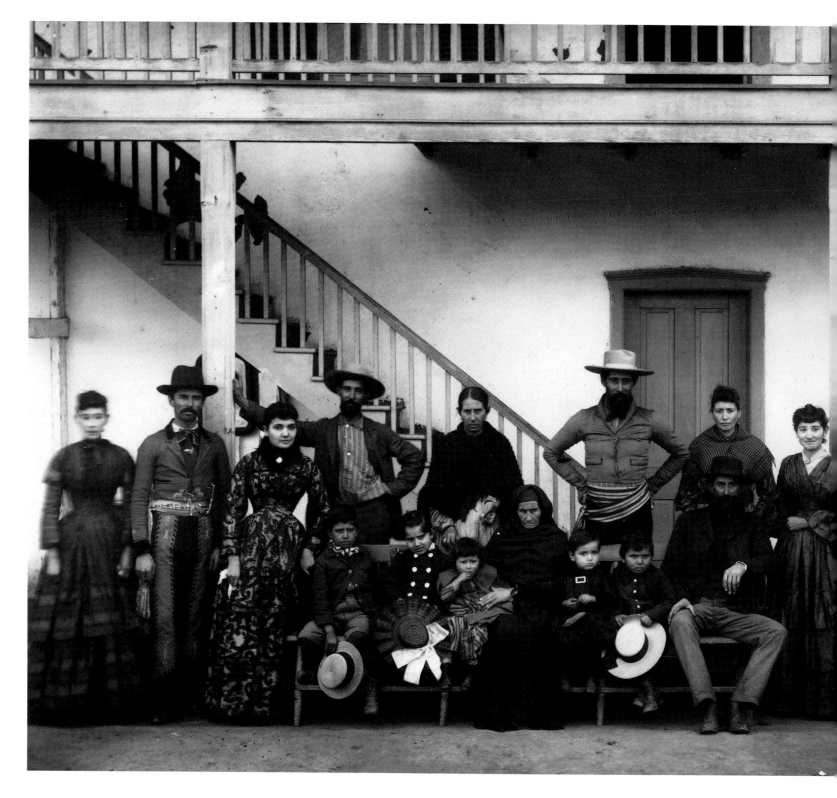

In 1870 the widow of Don Vicente Lugo is surrounded by her family at their Los Angeles ranch, a once sprawling 30,000-acre estate reduced to 400 acres. The dominant Hispanic society of early California was overwhelmed by hordes of gold and land seekers who flooded the West in the mid-19th century. Many Hispanic landowners were victimized by unscrupulous lawyers, government officials, and rustlers. "Our cattle were stolen by thousands," one Hispanic woman later recounted. "Men who are now prosperous farmers and merchants were guilty of shooting and selling Spanish beef 'without looking at the brand,' as the phrase went."

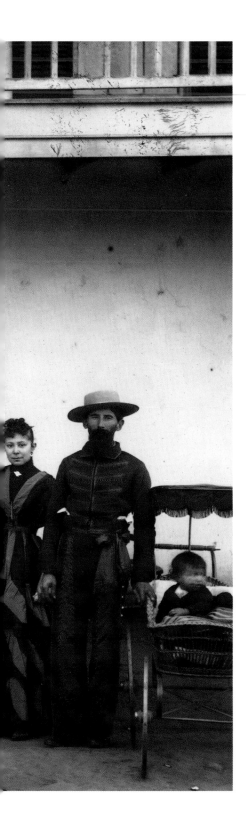

neck. The body was given the best burial that was possible, under the circumstances."

Death was a constant presence on the trail, but many more died from diseases and accidents than from attacks by Native Americans. In the mid-19th century, at the height of gold rush fever then luring adventure seekers to California, cholera swept through the emigrant ranks with an astonishing fury. Two-thirds of some large wagon trains—and entire families—died. In June 1852 Jane Kellogg vividly described the devastation in her diary: "All along the road up the Platte River was a grave yard; most any time of day you could see people burying their dead; some places five or six graves in a row, with board head signs with their names carved on them. It was a sad sight; no one can realize it unless they had seen it."

In an attempt to ward off cholera, one family followed the advice of a grizzled mountain man by putting pepper sauce in every bit of water they drank along the way. Tainted water was a common problem on the trek, and many emigrants believed in the purifying power of whiskey, mixing it liberally with any suspicious water. The same remedy was used on livestock sickened by alkali-fouled water. Whiskey, or sometimes melted lard, was poured down the animals' throats.

Women generally took charge of the family's health, and they counted on a simple bag or chest full of medicines, which included such necessities as castor oil and essence of peppermint, which reportedly "would cure anything that ailed you—from colic in newborn babes—to aches and pains accompanying old age." Porter was so young and healthy that she had not bothered to bring even the basics—despite being pregnant. Suffering from a severe bout of dysentery on the trail, Lavinia went nearly mad with the constant roiling and jolting of the wagon. She begged her husband "to take me out, make my bed on the sand and let me die in peace." An old prospector advised a big dose of castor oil. They had none, so Porter improvised: She drank her hair tonic and "it acted like a charm."

When the time came to give birth on the trail, the wagon trains would sometimes, but not always, have the luxury to stop for a day or two. Fellow women travellers assisted as midwives during childbirth. One woman gave birth during a terrific storm. The wagon flooded so badly that the midwives had to hastily move the mother's bed on top of several chairs, and they literally waded through water as they tended to the mother and her newborn. Another woman gave birth amidst the cliffs of the Sierra Nevadas—and then had to trek over the precarious mountains with her infant.

Traveling in the outdoors for five or six months with babies and young children was fraught with peril: blistering sunburns, mosquito bites, drenching rains, childhood illnesses. The families marched on regardless. Children fell out of wagons and broke bones, became lost among hundreds of other families, and got into endless mischief. One little girl broke into the family medicine bag and drank an entire bottle of laudanum. She was buried in the desert; her mother gave birth to another girl three days later.

Members of one ill-fated wagon train were stricken with both typhoid and bad luck. They got lost in the wilderness and ran out of supplies. While trying to take charge, one man suffered a heart attack. His widow, Ellen Smith, was left on the trail with nine children—one of them a crippled six-year-old, another a 16-year-old daughter who was mortally ill. Before she died, the teenager begged her mother to dig a hole deep enough so that wolves would not be able to eat her. The party stopped just long enough to bury the young girl. The mother selected a "prity little hill," and the men on the wagon train set to work digging the grave. They had such poor tools that after about four feet they gave up. The mother was distraught. It was not deep enough to keep out marauding wolves. Frantic, the mother began digging her daughter's grave herself; the sight was so piteous that the men took up their shovels again. And then she had to set off—by foot, with the younger of her offspring strapped to the oxen. There was no time to grieve; she had to save her remaining eight children. They scavenged mice from the woods and finally straggled into Salem, Oregon, just two days before Christmas in 1846. Ellen Smith claimed 640 acres of land in Oregon Country (it was still not officially part of the United States), and with the help of her children cleared the land, built a house, and created a new life.

A decade earlier, the first white women to take the overland route across the Rocky Mountains had a different objective. Narcissa Whitman and Eliza Spalding were missionaries eager to christianize Native Americans. Narcissa Whitman made the arduous journey through the wilderness to the Pacific Northwest while on her honeymoon (her trousseau included an inflatable life preserver). On the trail she shared her tent not only with her groom, but with the other missionaries in their party—including Eliza Spalding and her grim husband, Henry. (It was an ill-advised grouping. Henry had once courted and proposed marriage to Narcissa. Rebuffed by her, he remained embittered and took it out on the bridegroom during the trip.)

Arriving at Fort Walla Walla (in present-day Washington) in September 1836, the Whitmans set up a mission nearby among the Cayuse Indians. The Spaldings—mercifully parted from their traveling mates—began work among the Nez Percé in what is now Idaho. Both missions would last only 11 years.

"This is a cause worth living for!" Narcissa had written enthusiastically after an early encounter on the trail with western Indians and fur traders. But life in their mission proved different. Narcissa had no understanding of—nor sympathy for—the native culture. The Cayuse resisted all of the Whitmans' efforts to convert them and to change their way of life. Narcissa noted that the Indians seemed to "blame us for telling [them] about eternal realities"; one of them admitted to her that "it was good when they knew nothing but to hunt, eat, drink and sleep; now it was bad."

The Whitmans' only child, a two-year-old girl, drowned in 1839. Narcissa sank into a depression. She largely gave up her work among the native peoples, branding them "insolent, proud, domineering, arrogant." She took in 11 children—7 of them orphaned during their trek westward on the Oregon Trail—and turned her attention to them. As more and more emigrants poured into the area, the Cayuse grew restive. An epidemic of measles came with the wagon trains in 1847. More than half of the Cayuse died, including many children. Narcissa's husband, a doctor, tended to the sick with little success and was blamed for their deaths. On November 29th three Cayuse Indians—one a father who had lost three children to the disease—arrived to see the doctor. They shot and hacked him to death. Narcissa came next—warriors shot and killed her and then lashed her lifeless face with a riding crop. Others at the mission—including Narcissa's adopted children—either died or were carried off as captives. When word of the massacre reached the Spaldings, they abandoned their mission. The clash of cultures proved deadly, yet failed to dissuade other whites from joining the exodus West.

To Anglo eyes the vast landscape appeared free for the taking. But native tribes had lived throughout the West for a thousand generations. And a thriving Hispanic culture had taken root in the Southwest since the early 17th century. (Santa Fe was founded a full decade before the Mayflower arrived on New England shores.) As a young bride, Susan Magoffin accompanied her trader-husband to Santa Fe in 1846, and in her diary she recorded her startling impressions of Hispanic women. They smoked cigarettes, gambled, and wore shocking attire: low-cut blouses and short skirts, or even petticoats

"The death of one out of a community of four women might well alarm the remainder."

DAME SHIRLEY,
CALIFORNIA MINING CAMP

and chemises—what white women used as undergarments. "I am constrained to keep my veil drawn closely over my face all the time to protect my blushes," the prim Anglo observer wrote.

Yet the Hispanic women's lack of formality and warmth won Susan over; they were, she wrote in her diary, "decidedly polite, easy in their manners, perfectly free." In fact, Hispanic women did enjoy a measure of personal and legal freedom unknown by their Anglo peers. Upon marriage a white woman lost most of her legal rights, and her husband took over ownership of her property and wages. In marked contrast, an Hispanic woman retained her own property, wages, and even her maiden name after she married. She used the courts to settle disputes over her property, or, in the case of the renowned gambler, Doña La Tules, to collect debts built up in her gambling den. (A foreigner would write of La Tules's expertise: "The cards fell from her fingers as steadily as though she were handling only a knitting needle.")

A number of Hispanic women received substantial grants of land from the governor of the Mexican province of California. The formal possession ceremony consisted of "entering on the land, walking over it, breaking off branches of trees, picking up handfuls of earth and throwing stones to the four winds." The women established enormous ranches stocked with cattle and horses.

But in the mid-19th century, an unprecedented wave of Anglos flooded into California. They had little interest in grazing land; they were following the siren of gold. The newcomers quickly overwhelmed the Native American and Hispanic populations, stripping them of land and power. Mining camps sprang up overnight—and they were decidedly male places. In 1850, women composed not quite 8 percent of California's entire population. Louise Amelia Knapp Smith Clappe, whose pen name was the mercifully shorter "Dame Shirley," wrote about the California mining camp that she and her husband came to in 1851. When they arrived in Rich Bar, a grand total of four women were living there; a little over a week later, one of them died. "The death of one out of a community of four women," Dame Shirley wrote darkly, "might well alarm the remainder."

If they did not pan for gold themselves, women found surer—and sometimes even more lucrative—ways of making money. As soon as Luzena Stanley Wilson arrived in the tent town of Nevada City, California, she surveyed the scene. Her husband went off to look for wood to put a roof over their wagon home, and she immediately set up for business:

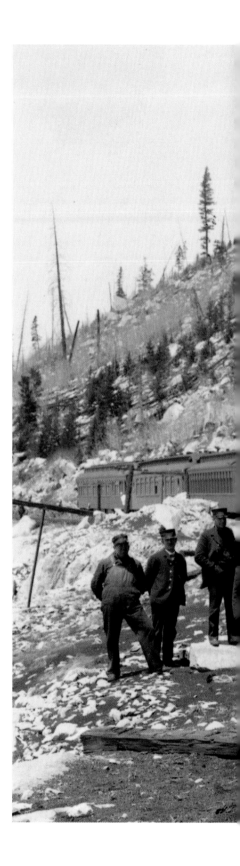

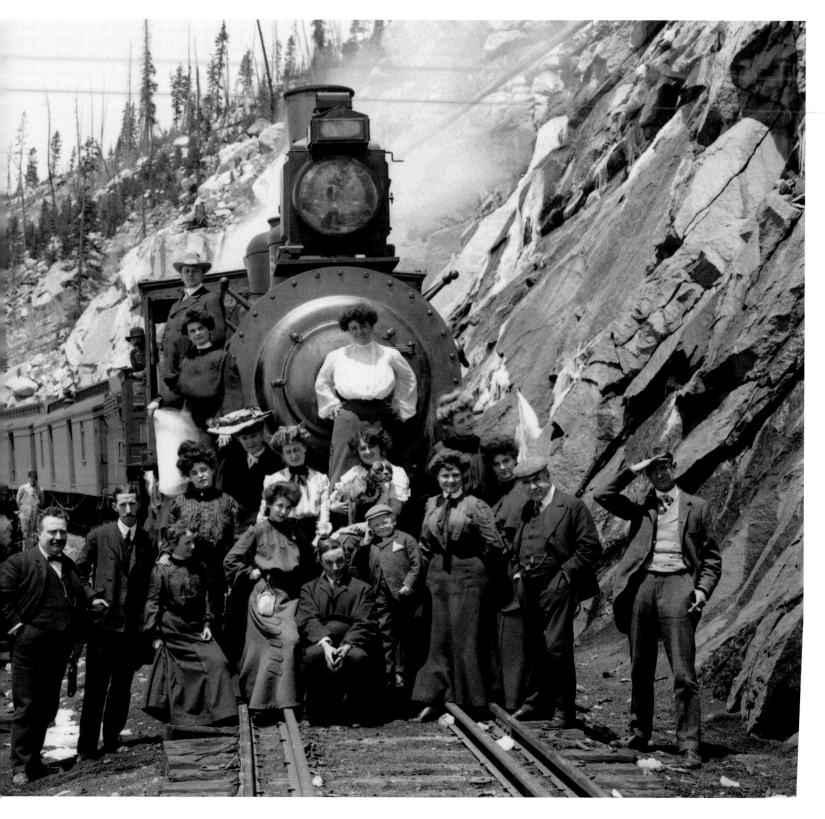

Singer and actress Anna Held, in the white blouse, presides over a jolly theatrical troupe touring the West in 1904. Enjoying the view from the highest railroad in the United States, they have paused at Hell Gate, a scenic gap in the Colorado mountains. Entertainers took advantage of the rail lines to reach amusement-starved western towns and mining camps. The company here includes a midget, a dog, and master showman, Florenz Ziegfeld (seated, center), who was married to the star.

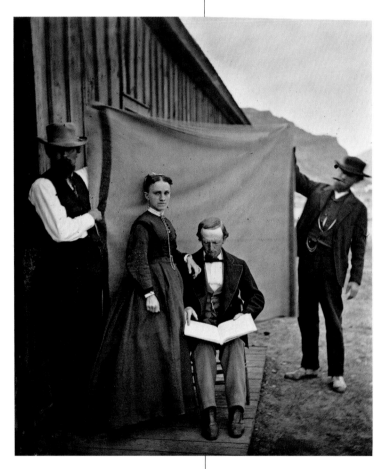

I thought of taking boarders....With my own hands I chopped stakes, drove them into the ground, and set up my table. I bought provisions at a neighboring store and when my husband came back at night he found...twenty miners eating at my table. Each man as he rose put a dollar in my hand and said I might count on him as a permanent customer. I called my hotel "El Dorado."

Luzena eventually served up to 200 boarders a week and was able to hire a cook and waiters. The miners also entrusted her with their loot: "Many a night have I shut my oven door on two milk-pans filled high with bags of gold dust and I have often slept with my mattress lined," she wrote. "I must have had more than two hundred thousand dollars lying unprotected in my bedroom." A shrewd businesswoman, she soon turned to lending money at an "extravagant rate of interest"—10 percent per month. A year and a half of prosperity went up in a puff of smoke—literally. Fire swept through town and Luzena and her family lost everything except what was in their pockets (fortunately Luzena's husband had $500 stuffed in his). They had to start all over again.

Such was the fate of many mining fortunes. Eilley Orrum, born in poverty in Scotland, eventually wended her way west to the Sierra Nevada silver mines. Having already discarded two husbands, she rolled up her sleeves and began to cook and wash clothes for miners. To settle an unpaid bill, one miner gave her a ten-foot claim. It turned out to be part of the fabled Comstock Lode. Eilley joined forces with another boarder who owned the adjoining ten-foot claim and married him. Soon the mines belonging to Eilley and Sandy Bowers were coining money—to the tune of $50,000 a month.

In 1861 Eilley set out to build a grand mansion where she could reign as "Queen of the Comstock." She hired a San Francisco architect and imported stonecutters from her native Scotland. Her husband did not object, boasting "I've got money to throw at the birds." The couple went on a European shopping spree to fill the house. Rebuffed in her attempt to meet with Queen Victoria, Eilley returned home with some ivy cuttings that she swiped from Westminster Abbey, claiming that they were a personal gift from the monarch. She planted the ivy next to her mansion and tended it lovingly.

But then the wheel began to turn. In 1867 the mine played out. A year later her 35-year-old husband died of lung disease. In less than a decade she would lose everything. Her 12-year-old daughter, the Bowers' only child, died suddenly in 1874, and two years later, Eilley's mansion and furnishings were sold at auction. Before leaving the house forever, she poured lye on her royal ivy to kill it. Eilley became a fortune-teller in Reno and San Francisco, peering into a crystal ball that she called a peepstone. Her own future was not very bright; she died penniless in California in 1903.

Other women reaped more enduring benefits from the mining boom. African-American Clara Brown, enslaved since her birth in 1800, went west when given her freedom in 1857. Her husband and three children had been brutally taken from her years earlier—auctioned off and sold to distant masters— but Clara would never forget them. Hired as a cook for a wagon train headed to Pikes Peak, she walked more than 600 miles to the goldfields (the wagons were bursting with provisions). She settled in Central City, Colorado, in 1860, when it was nothing more than a tent city. She opened a laundry, scrubbed miners' shirts for 50 cents each, invested in property, and soon had saved $10,000. Her generosity was renowned—she nursed sick miners, took in weary travelers, and opened her own house for church services. When the Civil War ended, she headed back to Kentucky to search for her lost family, but she could not find a trace of them. Clara Brown returned to Colorado with 16 African Americans, most of them former slaves, in the hope that they, too, could share in the opportunities available on the western frontier. Brown spent most of her remaining money helping to establish the newcomers in Colorado.

At age 82, in declining health and fortune, she received amazing news: Her daughter, Eliza Jane, was in Iowa. Clara set out east and had a joyous reunion with her long-lost daughter. She returned to Colorado with her granddaughter, where they lived together for the last three years of Clara's life—an unexpected and treasured gift in her old age.

Around 1868 famed railroad photographer Andrew J. Russell composed this enigmatic portrait of a well-turned-out couple in a remote corner of the West. The woman's dress barely clears the plank sidewalk, which ends abruptly and turns to dirt.

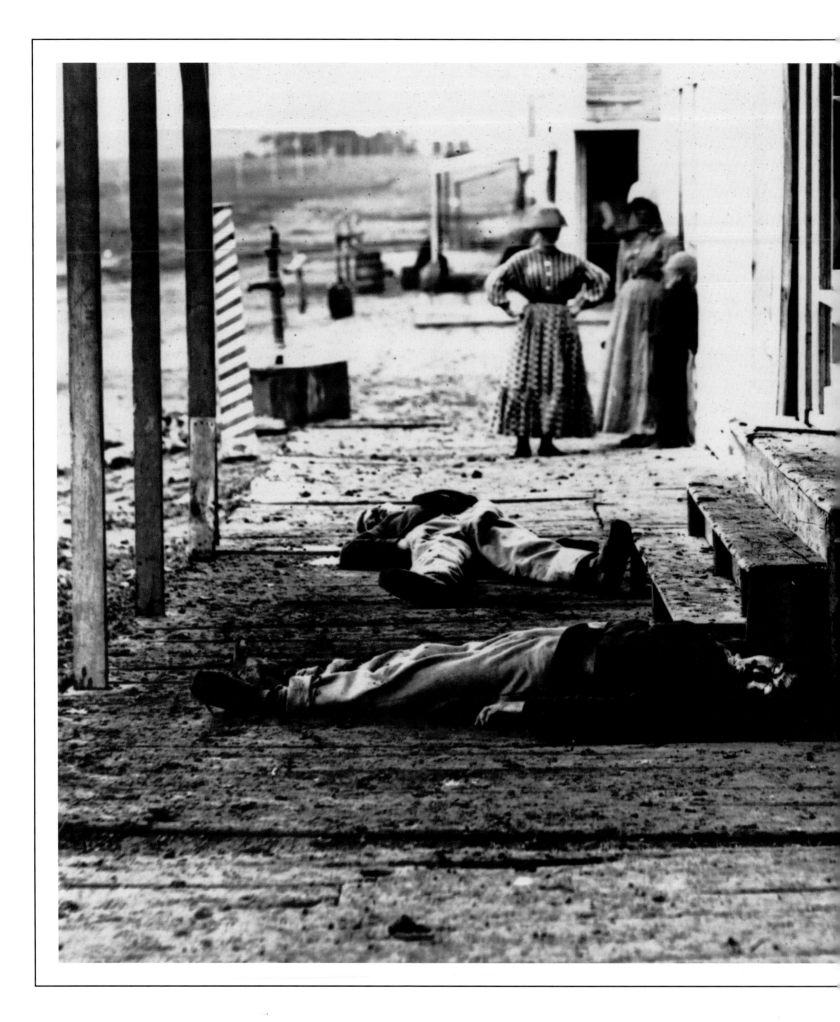

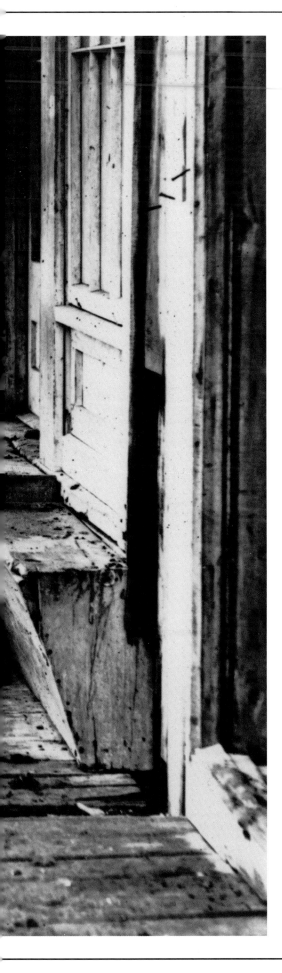

> *"I went into the sporting life for business reasons and for no other. It was a way for a woman in those days to make money and I made it."*

MATTIE SILKS, TURN-OF-THE-CENTURY MADAME

With the freedom offered in the West came all manner of lawlessness and episodes of hideous violence. The women at left view the bloody carnage outside a dance hall in Hays, Kansas, where soldiers capped a night on the town with a shoot-out in 1873. Saloons, dance halls, and brothels flourished on the frontier, where men vastly outnumbered women. Enterprising madams made the most of it. Mattie Silks started a traveling bordello using a tent (equipped with portable canvas tub) that she moved from one mining camp to another. Flush with her earnings, she moved to grander quarters in Denver and—sporting a lace parasol and a gold-encrusted cross around her neck—became a famous character in town. She even advertised using this imaginative folding card shaped like an oyster, a food thought to boost virility. The wording might fool the wife of an out-of-town visitor who had pocketed the card, but everyone in Denver knew what was being sold. Mattie and other madams got rich, but young prostitutes often suffered the hazards of the trade: diseases, assaults, too much alcohol, laudanum, and botched abortions.

PHONE MAIN 1173

M. SILKS

GENTS' FURNISHING GOODS

1916-22 MARKET STREET
DENVER. COLO.

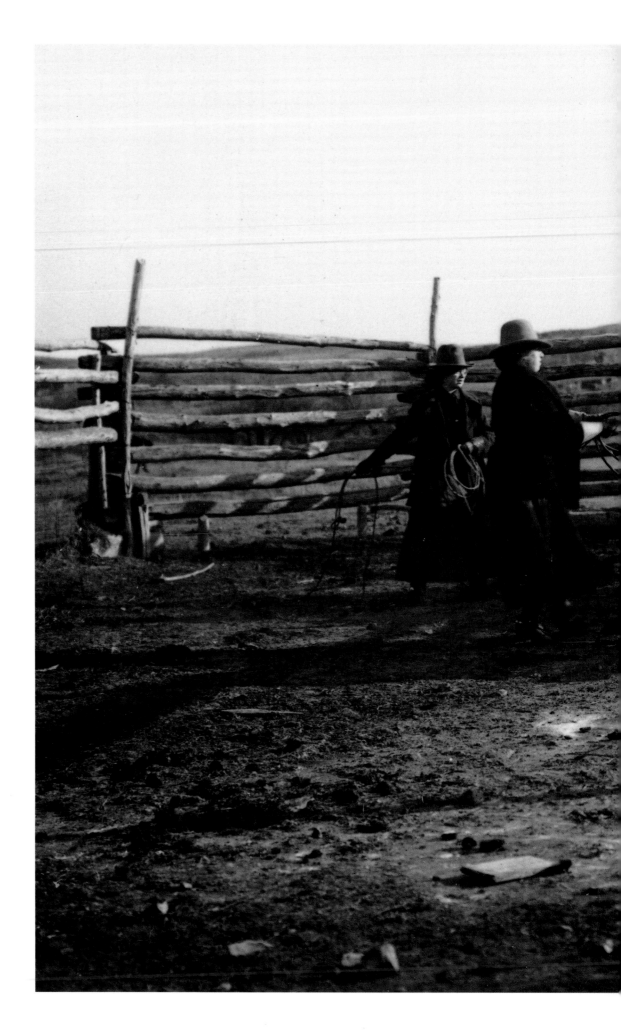

Pioneer photographer Evelyn
Cameron caught an action shot
of the Buckley sisters at work
on their eastern Montana ranch.
Known as the "Red Yearlings"
because of their reddish hair and
their skills as horsewomen, the
trio was asked to perform for
Teddy Roosevelt. The shy young
women declined.

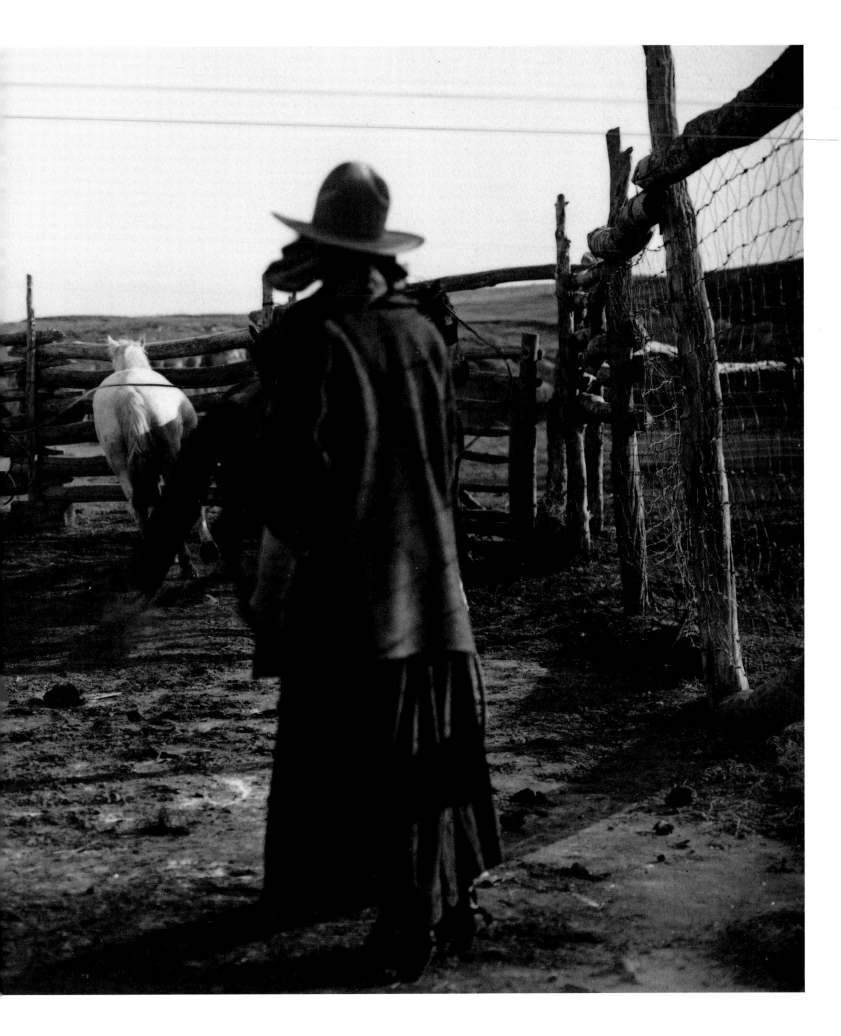

Gold and silver were not the only draws to the West. After the Civil War, a new boom took hold—a rush for the land itself. The Great Plains that stretched from the Dakotas south to Texas and westward to the Rockies—semiarid land once considered so barren that mapmakers referred to it as The Great American Desert—were now being touted as a great verdant paradise, a veritable Garden of Eden, where wheat and other crops would flourish. Of course, the purveyors of that optimism had more than a little self-interest at heart. Railroad tracks were being laid all across the West, and some 180 million acres of land along the routes had been given to the railroad corporations by Congress. The head of the Northern Pacific put it bluntly: "You can lay track to the garden of Eden, but what good is it if the only inhabitants are Adam and Eve?"

They needed people—lots of them—to settle the land; the larger the population, the busier the railroad lines would be. Thus began the selling of the West not only in this country but around the world. Agents fanned out throughout Europe all the way into Russia to entice farmers to this new paradise. As if on cue, the 1870s and 1880s turned out to be rainier than usual, which was a boon to crops and seemingly confirmed the promoters mostly baseless claims.

U. S. citizens—many of them midwestern farmers eager to cash in on opportunity—flooded the rail lines to stake their claims on western land. The Homestead Act of 1862 had made it simple. For a nominal filing fee of ten dollars (plus a small commission), both married and unmarried men and women could claim 160 acres of free land, the only requirement being that they had to work and live on the land for five years. Overnight, jerry-built shacks appeared on the prairies and plains. Some were covered in tar paper; others were mere caves dug out of the side of a hill. And a new architectural phenomenon appeared on the treeless horizon—houses literally made of the landscape itself. Strips of sod were laid as if they were bricks; most houses boasted two layers, so the walls were about 30 inches thick. (The price could not be beaten: One pioneer claimed to have built a sod house for a grand total of $2.78.) Cool in summer and easily heated in winter, sod houses were immovable objects—the heavily weighted sod withstood brutal prairie winds and blizzards. But it did have a tendency to leak—and then it was literally a muddy mess. One Nebraska woman recalled a leaky one-room soddy after a four-day rainstorm: "Father said, 'Let's get under the table.' So we did. The long ridgepole of the roof began to crack from the heavy weight of the wet sod and finally the roof caved in, with the pole resting on the table. We were buried beneath the sod and muck. Finally Father saw a patch of light and dug his way out." If the sod did not give way, other creatures might emerge from it, as an anonymous poet made clear:

How happy am I when I crawl into bed;
A rattlesnake hisses a tune at my head!
A gay little centipede, all without fear,
Crawls over my pillow and into my ear.

Despite the primitive homesteading conditions, women took up claims eagerly. In 1886 one eyewitness estimated that women held fully one-third of the land in the Dakotas. Wives, sisters, or daughters would claim land that adjoined their relatives' property to make for a larger farm (after all, one could barely scratch a living out of 160 acres of semiarid land). Friends took up claims side by side and helped each other out. Some women looked upon the land as purely an investment; after "proving up" on the property and earning outright title to it, they would sell it. In this way, North Dakota homesteaders Anna and Ethel Erickson planned to earn money for college.

Others, however, yearned to own a home of their own. Elinore Rupert, a young widow with a two-year-old daughter, fell into this latter category. Scraping by as a laundress and house cleaner in Denver in 1909, Elinore dreamed of exchanging "the rattle and bang, the glare and the soot, the smells and the hurry" of city life in Denver for "the sweet, free open" of the country. She advertised for a job as a housekeeper on a ranch, so that she could learn the ins and outs of the business before settling on her own claim. She secured a position in Burnt Fork, a tiny outpost in southwestern Wyoming, 60 miles from the railroad. Her employer was one Clyde Stewart, a Scottish rancher about whom Elinore wrote: "Mr. Stewart is absolutely no trouble, for as soon as he has his meals he retires to his room and plays on his bagpipe, only he calls it his 'bugpeep.' It is 'The Campbells are Coming,' without variations, at intervals all day long and from seven till eleven at night. Sometimes I wish they would make haste and get here."

She must have gotten used to the song, for within six weeks of her arrival Elinore married Stewart. Though she fully intended to get her own homestead, by mid-April she had not yet filed on her preferred location—mountain land that was still covered by 15

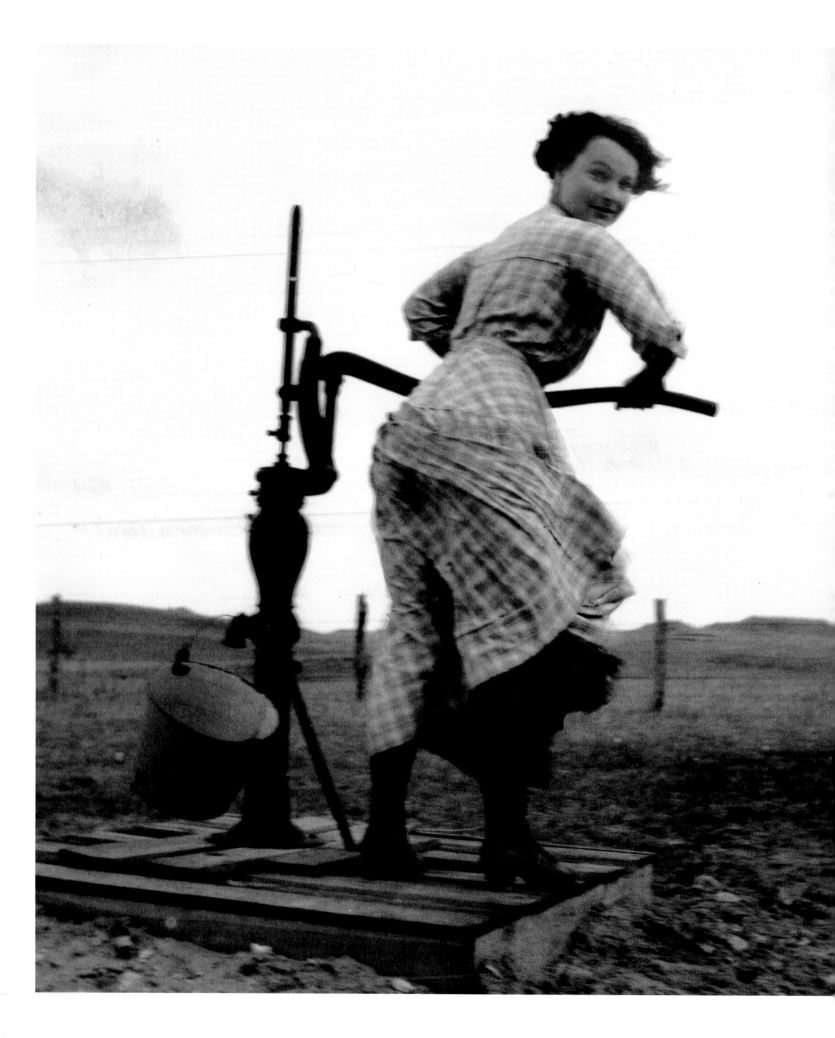

feet of snow. She decided to delay claiming the land, as "I think I would rather see what I am getting." By the end of the next month, the land still covered with snow, she opted instead to claim a homestead in the valley. In fact, it was a tract next to her husband's land. "I have filed on my land and am now a bloated landowner," she wrote proudly to a woman friend in Denver. Her house, as well as her land, literally adjoined her husband's; yet she insisted that "I should not have married if Clyde had not promised I should meet all my land difficulties unaided; I wanted the fun and the experience." Elinore milked the cows, tended chickens and turkeys, mowed the hay, raised large crops of potatoes and other vegetables, and gave birth to three sons—one of whom died as a baby. Elinore believed that the life of homesteading was a bracing tonic and an antidote to urban ills. "When I read of the hard times among the Denver poor, I feel like urging them every one to get out and file on land," she wrote. "I am very enthusiastic about women homesteading....but I realize that temperament has much to do with success in any undertaking, and persons afraid of coyotes and work and loneliness had better let ranching alone. At the same time, any woman who can stand her own company, can see the beauty of the sunset, loves growing things, and is willing to put in as much time at careful labor as she does over the washtub, will certainly succeed; will have independence, plenty to eat all the time, and a home of her own in the end."

Similarly, another ranch woman—a gently bred Briton named Evelyn Cameron who had gladly turned her back on the drawing rooms of London to embrace a primitive cabin in Montana—found even the air on the western frontier to her liking. "What lovely pure exhilarating air this is in Montana, it would cure many nervous & other ills if it was only given the chance," she wrote to a friend. As a newlywed, Evelyn had arrived in Montana Territory in 1889; she and her Scottish husband, Ewen, had come on their honeymoon to hunt. With an English cook and one of Custer's old scouts to guide them through the wilderness, they set off into the badlands of eastern Montana to track down mule deer, mountain sheep, pronghorn antelope, and grizzly bear. They fell in love with the region—its esoteric beauty, the plentiful game, and the untamed wildness of the place;

Resourceful women concocted ingenious remedies such as the multipurpose solution (above), which removed grease and paint, worked well as a shampoo, and even killed bed bugs. An energetic young homesteader in North Dakota (opposite) pumps water, one of her daily chores. Some women, including rancher Evelyn Cameron (following pages), reveled in the outdoor life and hard work the West demanded. In a pair of self-portraits, Evelyn stands atop her horse and feeds a grasshopper to a falcon.

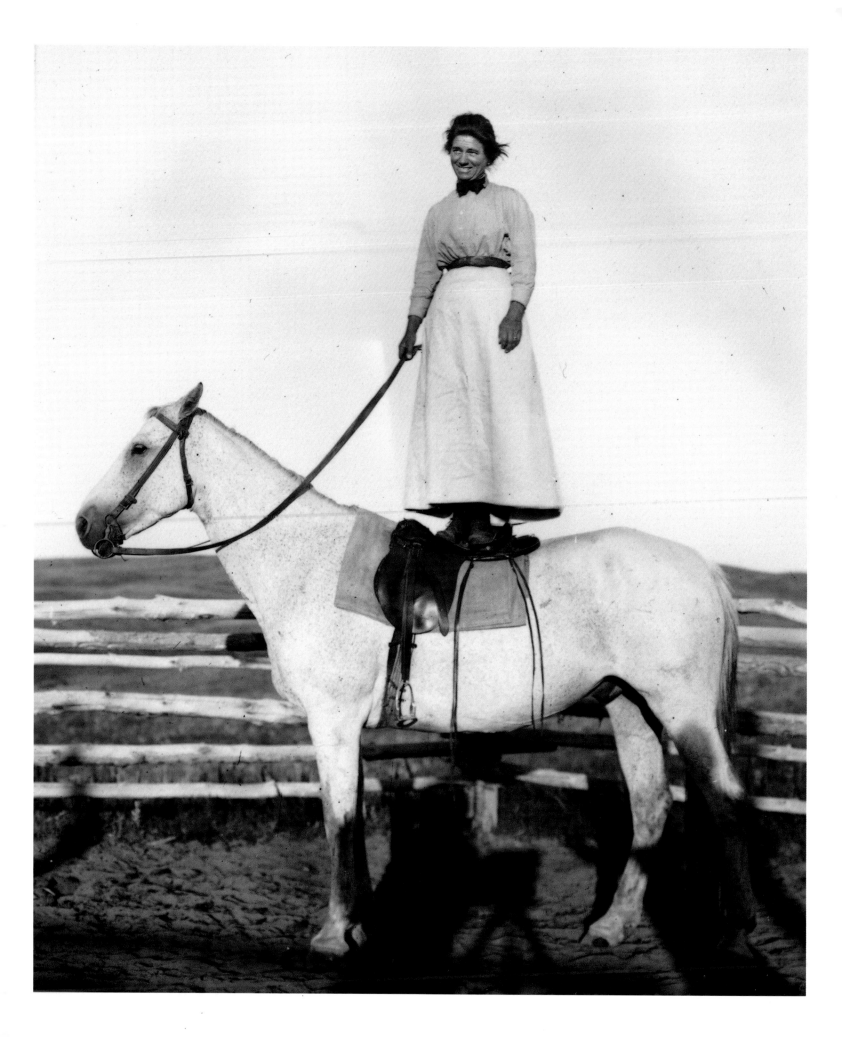

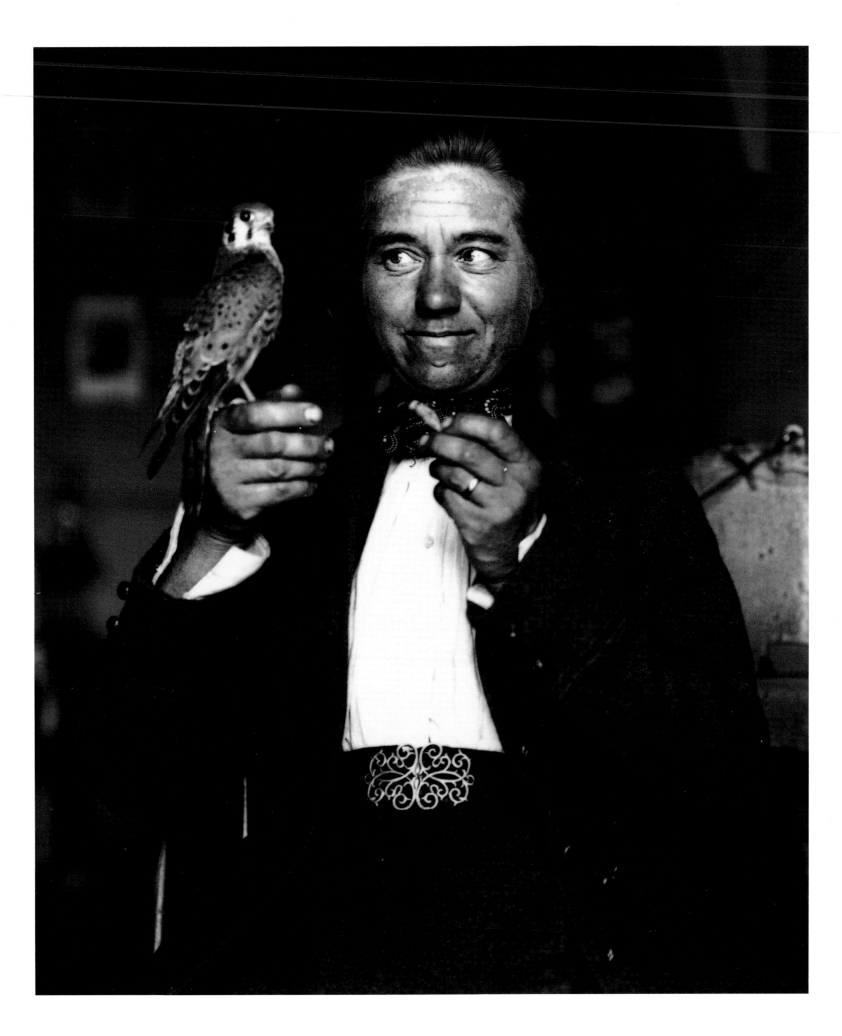

and they came up with an unusual plan to stay there: They would raise polo ponies for export to the playing fields of England and the Continent. It was a disaster. After years of breeding and raising ponies, and spending almost all of Evelyn's money in the process, many of the horses died en route to England. The Camerons were ruined financially.

Even before the final fiasco, Ewen was ready to give up, return to Britain, and live off his wife's family money. Evelyn would have none of it. She was determined to stay in Montana, and she took up several ingenious moneymaking schemes (all of which added substantially to her ranch work): she raised and sold vegetables to cowboys, once even venturing into a saloon to make a sale; and she took in well-to-do Britons, two at a time, as boarders in the hope that they would invest in the ranch. They never did. Despite the aggravation they caused, the boarders did leave a lasting legacy—two of them were amateur photographers and they helped introduce Evelyn to the nuts and bolts of that art. She took it up with enthusiasm and made money by selling her prints, thus helping to keep the ranch afloat.

Through trial and error, Evelyn painstakingly taught herself the intricacies of glass-plate photography. She began to document everything around her in her photographs—the badlands and plains of eastern Montana, the wildlife, and the colorful frontier characters that populated that remote world. In addition, Evelyn was an obsessive diarist who kept a detailed account of everything that happened in the course of a day—and she dutifully wrote an entry every day for over 35 years. With her diaries and photographs she created a kind of home movie of pioneer life, a unique record of that time and place.

Evelyn documented her world with unflagging energy and enthusiasm. She would set off on horseback with her large-format camera, traveling for hours or even days in search of remote subjects. "My hip is bruised from the camera's pressure," she admitted in her diary once, after having spent the entire day on horseback with a camera dangling from her waist. That, however, did not deter her. She was fascinated by the how-tos of pioneer life—how to shear a sheep, how to herd cattle across the Yellowstone River, how to harvest a wheat crop—and she photographed all of it. She sought out solitary frontier characters (the "New World type," in her words) who followed herds of sheep and cattle across the lonely landscape. Cowboys, herders, "wolfers" who tracked coyotes and wolves for bounties—all of these grizzled pioneers were captured by her camera.

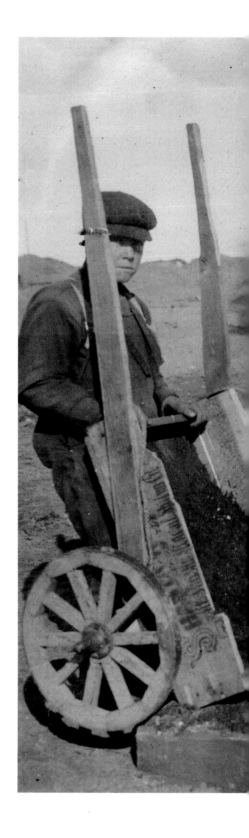

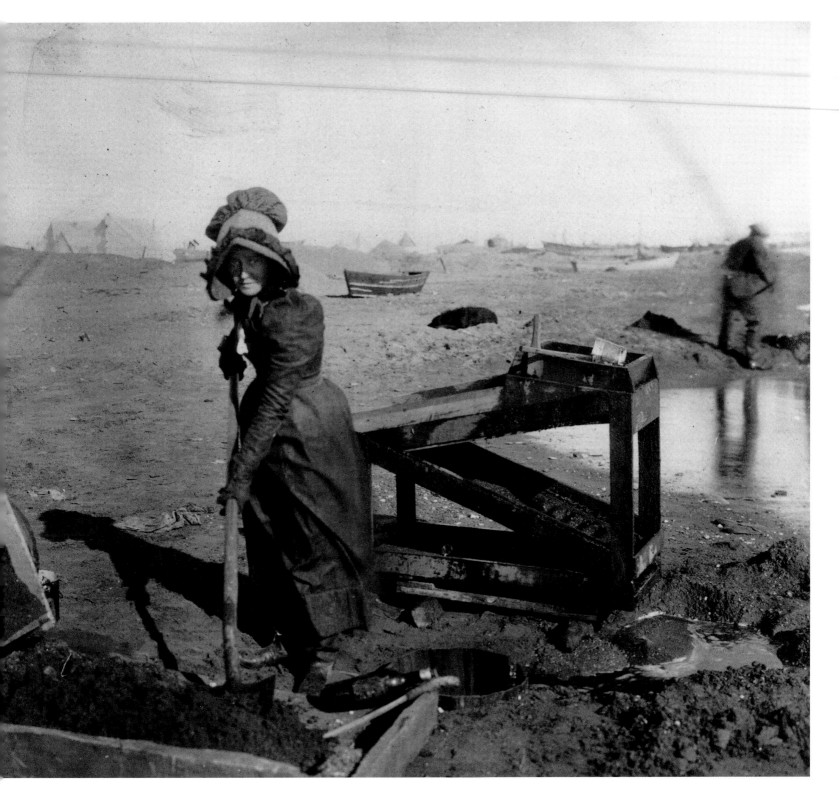

A woman prospector, eager to strike it rich, digs into the beach at Nome, Alaska. Thousands of women joined the rush for gold in Canada's Klondike, but when word got out in 1898 that the sand in Nome was laced with the precious metal, many headed there. If digging proved futile, women could earn good money by opening roadhouses, restaurants, and laundries.

The elegantly clad Margaret Tobin Brown, better known as Molly Brown, stands amidst western trappings in her hotel room in Newport, Rhode Island, in 1915. After her husband made a fortune in Colorado gold mines, Brown set herself up as a Denver socialite and activist. But her real fame came after she survived the sinking of the *Titanic* in 1912 and earned herself the nickname "Unsinkable." She embodied the feisty and independent western spirit; not long before her death, *Fortune* magazine proclaimed her "as legendary as Paul Bunyan but as real as Pike's Peak." Later Broadway and Hollywood versions of her life would further embellish her myth.

But she was equally fascinated by the women drawn to this rugged world. These women were not the beaten-down martyrs of western stereotype. They were industrious, rugged women who took the same pride as men in the work that they accomplished. Evelyn so admired a trio of cowgirls—the sisters Myrtle, May, and Mabel Buckley—that she wrote and illustrated an article about them for the British publication *Country Life*. "All three sisters," Evelyn wrote, "may be said to have been born in the saddle, and are accomplished in the incidental work of branding cattle, breaking horses and throwing the lasso....A book might be filled with their exploits and hair-breadth escapes when riding 'broncs.'" In the same 1914 article, Evelyn went on to extol the virtues of the hard-working women then taking up homesteads:

> *Dry-farming...is developing a new phase of the woman on the ranch. The female members of the Russo-Germans who have swarmed over the prairie like ants take outdoor work even more seriously than the cowgirls whom they replace. Russo-German girls in their teens successfully perform every kind of farm labour, and may be seen ploughing from daylight to dark, sacking and hauling grain, haymaking, or driving up the cows on their great draught colts, ridden bareback.*

As if to prove the point, Evelyn took a photograph of "the Reisler girl ploughing with four horses which I think will be of interest as showing how hard these Russian and German girls work."

Evelyn was no slouch in the work department herself, writing proudly to a niece in England, "Manual labour...is about all I care about, and, after all, is what will really make a strong woman. I like to break colts, brand calves, cut down trees, ride & work in a garden." She worked from dawn to dusk doing rough ranch work. The Camerons had no regular hired hands—and husband Ewen was often less than helpful. He conducted himself as if he were a man of science with few other responsibilities. A trained naturalist, Ewen became obsessed with studying the birdlife of eastern Montana. He wrote a number of articles for ornithological journals, which Evelyn illustrated with amazing close-up photographs of wild birds (all without benefit of a telephoto lens).

Evelyn somehow managed to do all of her ranch chores—milking the cows, churning the butter, tending the chickens, gathering the eggs, digging coal for fuel, chopping wood, harvesting vegetables, in addition to all of the daily cooking and cleaning—and still find time for her photography. After a full day of back-breaking work, she would sometimes develop her negatives in the middle of the night. She printed these by day, often using nothing more than the sunlight and a homemade printing frame.

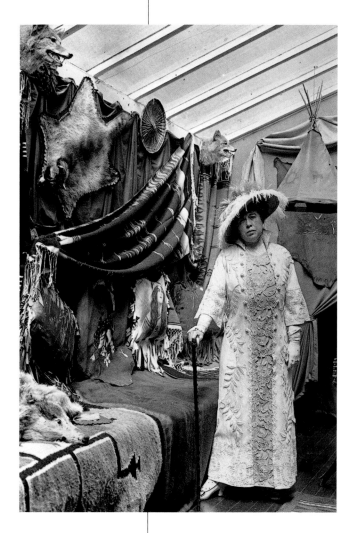

As the years went by Evelyn seemed to gain ever more energy and love for her adopted land; Ewen, on the other hand, grew ever more sickly. In February 1915 Evelyn took him by train to California, hoping that the ocean air would revive him. It did not. Ewen died in Pasadena that spring. Evelyn's family in England assumed she would return to Britain, but she refused. She went back to her Montana ranch and ran it by herself without benefit of ranch hands, electricity, or running water.

"I am living quite alone on the ranch," she wrote to a concerned relative in 1917, "but I have plenty of occupation—cattle, photography, reading etc., that I do not feel lonely." Evelyn had a profound attachment to the landscape itself, to the very air of Montana. In fact, her story turns the myth of the West on its head: It was Evelyn who found strength and purpose on the frontier, while her husband withered and died. And Evelyn was not alone; other women also found a new freedom and meaning in the western life. After the death of her husband, one army wife wrote of her feelings about the Nevada wilderness that had become home to her:

> *To mount a horse...and gallop over prairies, completely losing*
> *one's self in vast and illimitable space...is [to] leave every*
> *petty care, and feel the contented frame of mind which*
> *can only be produced by such surroundings. In those*
> *grand wastes one is truly alone with God. Oh, I love the West...*

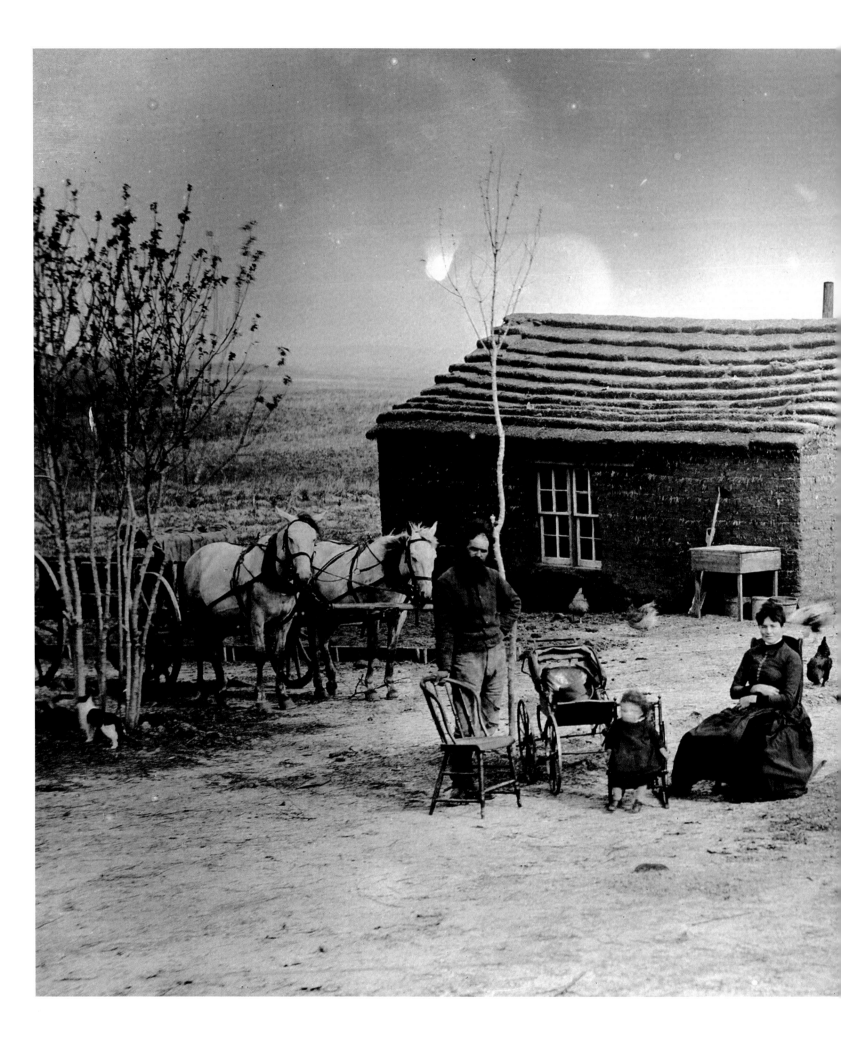

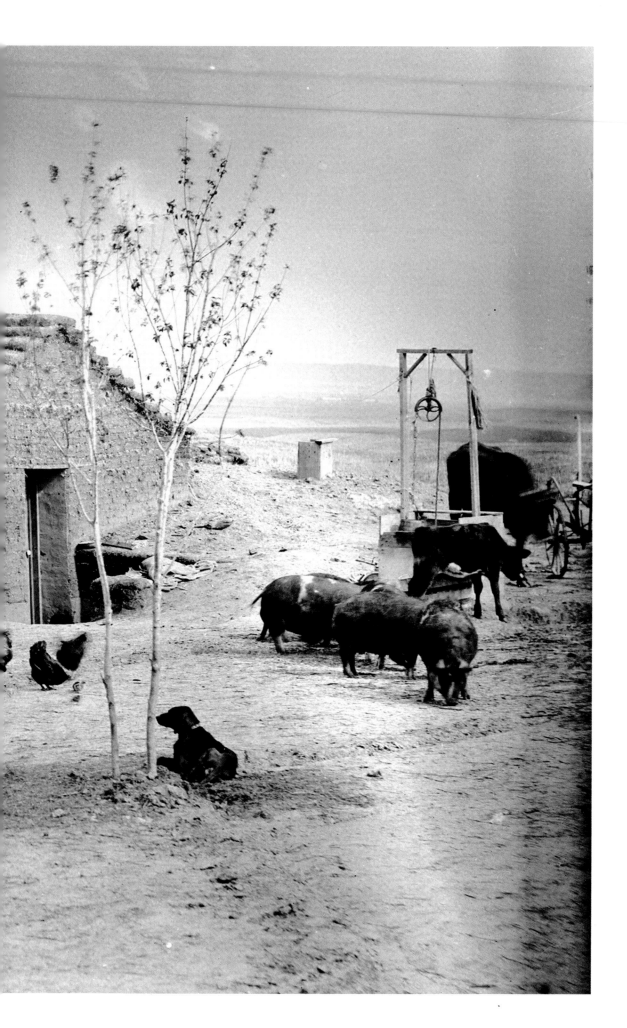

With arms folded, a young woman in 1887 sits resolutely in front of her domain—a house on the prairie made from thick slabs of sod, a building material the locals playfully referred to as "Nebraska marble." She is surrounded by the key elements in her pioneer world—husband and young child, livestock, pets, wagon, well, and the land itself. The couple has planted trees in front of the house in the hope that one day they will create an effective shield against the winds that roar across the open landscape.

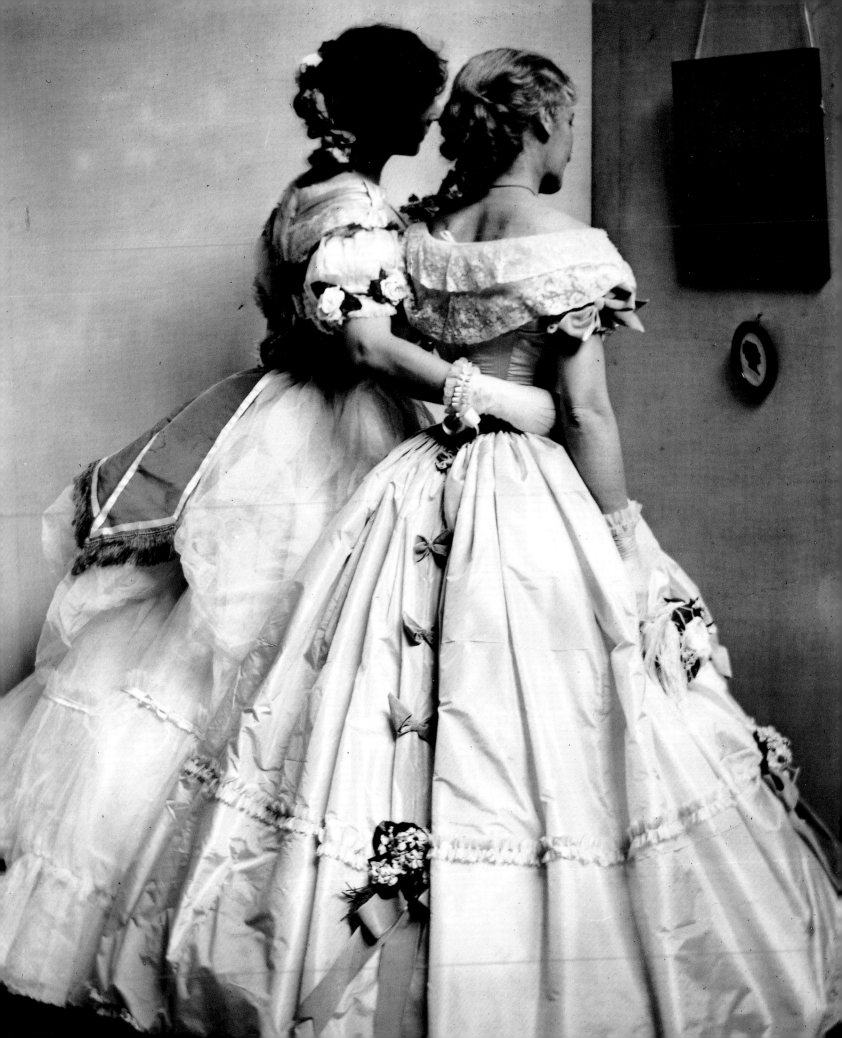

THE GILDED AGE

STANDING BENEATH a life-size portrait of herself and glistening with so many diamonds that one observer compared her to a chandelier, Caroline Astor— *the* Mrs. Astor—imperiously welcomed her guests, beautifully gowned socialites like this pair, to her Fifth Avenue mansion. Her annual winter ball was the most important social event in New York in the late 19th century. Four hundred guests had been carefully selected, as that was the number her ballroom could comfortably accommodate.

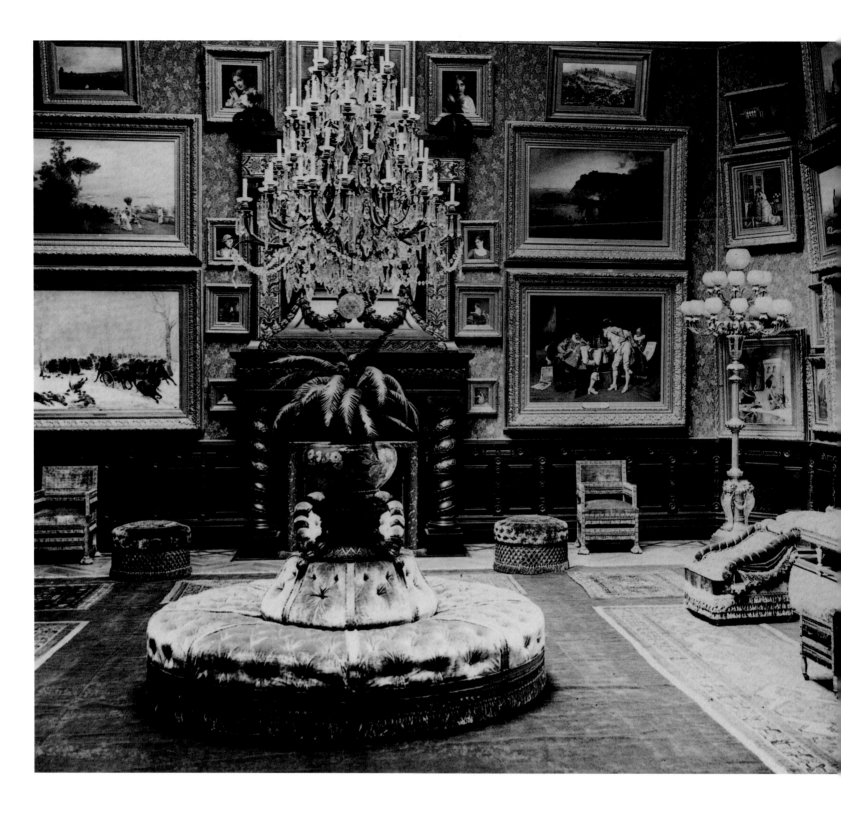

Added to the family's Fifth Avenue mansion in 1875, Mrs. Astor's art-encrusted ballroom (above) became the absolute epicenter of New York society. Four hundred people could comfortably fit in this room; thus "The Four Hundred" invited by Mrs. Astor to her balls were deemed the ne plus ultra of the Gilded Age. A contemporary book noted that the grande dame held equal sway in Newport, Rhode Island, where it was "as imperative for a social aspirant's claims to be passed upon by Mrs. Astor as it was for a potentate of the era of Charlemagne to go to St. Peter's, Rome, for coronation."

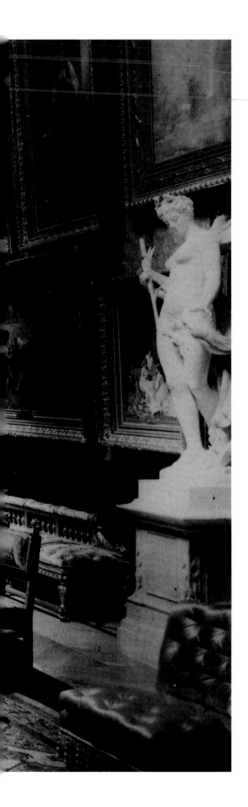

(A snobbish confidante of Mrs. Astor's also admitted that "when you get above that number you get into people who do not feel at ease in a ballroom.") Her invitation was the most coveted in New York, as it conferred instant membership to the inner sanctum of high society. "The Four Hundred," as decreed by Mrs. Astor, were henceforth the crème de la crème—and they included blue bloods from old-line New York families as well as newly minted millionaires who had made their fortunes in the post-Civil War industrial boom.

The glittering, turn-of-the-20th-century society of the very rich and the very well-born came to be known as the Gilded Age. A culture based on ostentatious display, it spawned the mansions of Fifth Avenue and the vast seaside "cottages" of Newport. Here the rich entertained and created a world of almost unimaginable wealth and a society dictated by the most intricate rules of etiquette. Ruling over all this were women—"beautiful, gracious and glittering with gems," as Henry James described them. Mrs. John King van Rensselaer, a member of top-drawer New York society pointed out: "Women brought Society across the Atlantic, nurtured it, and made it their sphere." The cultural life of the nation was enriched and reshaped forever by Gilded Age women, and New York society quivered under the dictatorship of Mrs. Astor.

As undisputed queen, Caroline Astor combined both lineage—her family, the Schermerhorns, dated back to 17th-century New York—and fabulous wealth from her husband, William Backhouse Astor, Jr. (shortly after they married she made him drop his middle name, which she considered vulgar). William had no use for high society—nor much use for his wife. He preferred the company of his racehorses, his club cronies, and other women. He was usually conspicuously absent at his wife's social galas, opting instead to cruise on his steam-powered yacht.

His absence did not deter Caroline Astor at all. After greeting her guests, the elegantly clad hostess would take her accustomed spot on a large divan set on a raised dais at one end of the ballroom. There, as the orchestra played, she held royal court. "She ruled with a distaff of gold," according to one awed observer. Her ballroom throne could accommodate six other women—and to be chosen to ascend to her level was the ultimate honor and social coup in New York. One woman who failed to receive the royal summons rushed out of the ballroom in tears. "She doesn't love me!" the woman sobbed. "I won't stay one minute longer in a house where I am not loved." Mrs. Astor, for her part, could be brutally frank in sizing up those deemed worthy. "How can I have her up

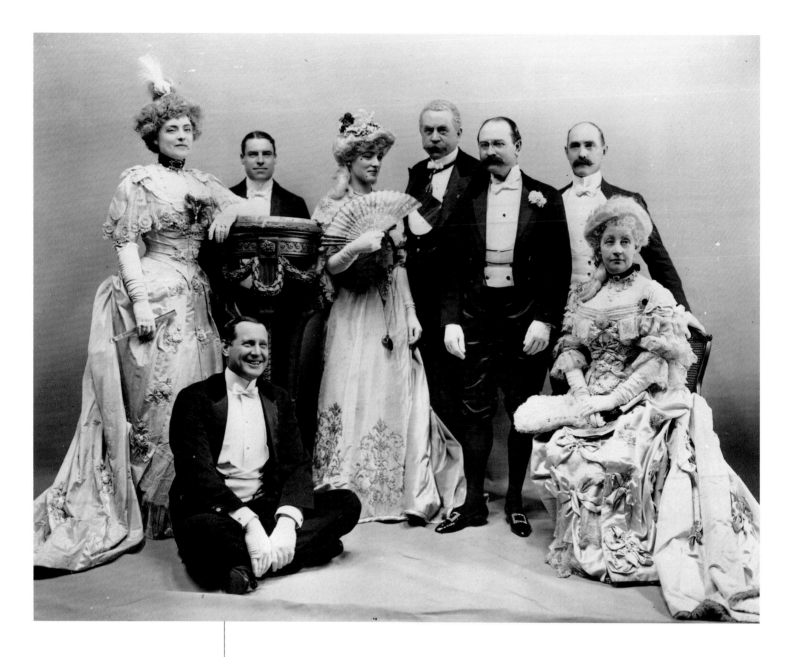

here," she said of one amply proportioned dowager, "when she takes two seats?"

Mrs. Astor herself cut an imposing figure. Not that she was a beauty. In fact, one of her nieces recalled that "she was really homely, no looks at all." But her regal bearing, magnificent wardrobe, and the sheer quantity of precious jewels that she wore overrode any deficiency in the looks department. The *New York Times* opined that she wore her diamonds "with the most effective prodigality"—an understatement by any stretch of the imagination. On special occasions she sparkled with jewels from head to toe. A diamond tiara crowned her jet black hair, and layers upon layers of diamonds were often looped around her neck, including a choker and two longer necklaces, one in a sunburst pattern that boasted nearly 500 stones. Wearing diamonds on her back was one of Mrs. Astor's trademarks. She hung a diamond-studded necklace over her neck in reverse; she also had her dressmaker sew diamonds into the back of her gowns. (In fact, Mrs. Astor's regal posture could be credited in part to her jewelry: She had to sit up perfectly straight without leaning back on her chair in order to avoid being pinched by her diamonds.) Cinching her waist was perhaps her most celebrated accessory—a diamond-encrusted "stomacher" that had once belonged to Marie Antoinette. The sheer excess led one magazine to quip, "Perhaps she should wheel her jewels to the next ball in a barrow."

Mrs. Astor defined high style, and her choice of dressmaker helped create a vogue for all things European. Her gowns were made in Paris by Charles Worth, who became the most sought-after designer of the day and the founder of haute couture. Between the social seasons in New York and Newport, Mrs. Astor would go to Paris to replenish her wardrobe. With women like Mrs. Astor in the lead, other wealthy Americans followed suit and rushed to Worth's atelier on rue de la Paix to be fitted for gowns. One gossip columnist reported on the scene at his studio: "There was not one word of French to be heard among the ladies who were grouped in the various rooms holding conclave together...they were all American." Another wag reported that there were two sets of prices at Worth's, "one for Americans and one for Christians of every other denomination." A single Worth gown might fetch as much as $10,000 (at the time, the average American earned roughly $500 per year), but cost was no object for these Gilded Age women. An etiquette book published in 1884 quoted the designer himself: "Worth says that American women are the best customers he has—far better than queens. They ask the price; American women never do. They simply say, 'Give me the best, the most beautiful, the most fashionable gown.'" Another contemporary book, entitled *Women of New York,* mused on the sheer number of gowns necessary for a well-dressed woman, as well as the time it took to amass such a wardrobe:

> *The elite do not wear the same dress twice. If you can tell us how many receptions she has in a year, how many weddings she attends, how many balls she participates in, how many dinners she gives, how many parties she goes to, how many operas and theatres she patronizes, we can approximate somewhat to the cost and size of her wardrobe. It is not unreasonable to suppose that she has two new dresses of some sort for every day in the year, or seven hundred and twenty. Now to purchase all these, to order them made and to put them on afterward consumes a vast amount of time. Indeed, the woman of society does little but doff and don dry goods.*

Revelers in New York (opposite) pose for a society photographer at the French period ball given by insurance magnate James Hazen Hyde on the night of January 31, 1905. Despite the winter season, Sherry's Ballroom was festooned that evening with $28,500 worth of flowers; the floor was strewn with rose petals. Among the guests shown are the haughty Mrs. Stuyvesant Fish (seated at right) who commissioned architect Stanford White (standing third from right) to build her a 35-room Venetian palace on East 78th Street. Mrs. Fish was noted for her own eccentric brand of parties. She once gave a dinner for the pet dogs belonging to a hundred of her dearest friends. One dog sported a $15,000 diamond collar.

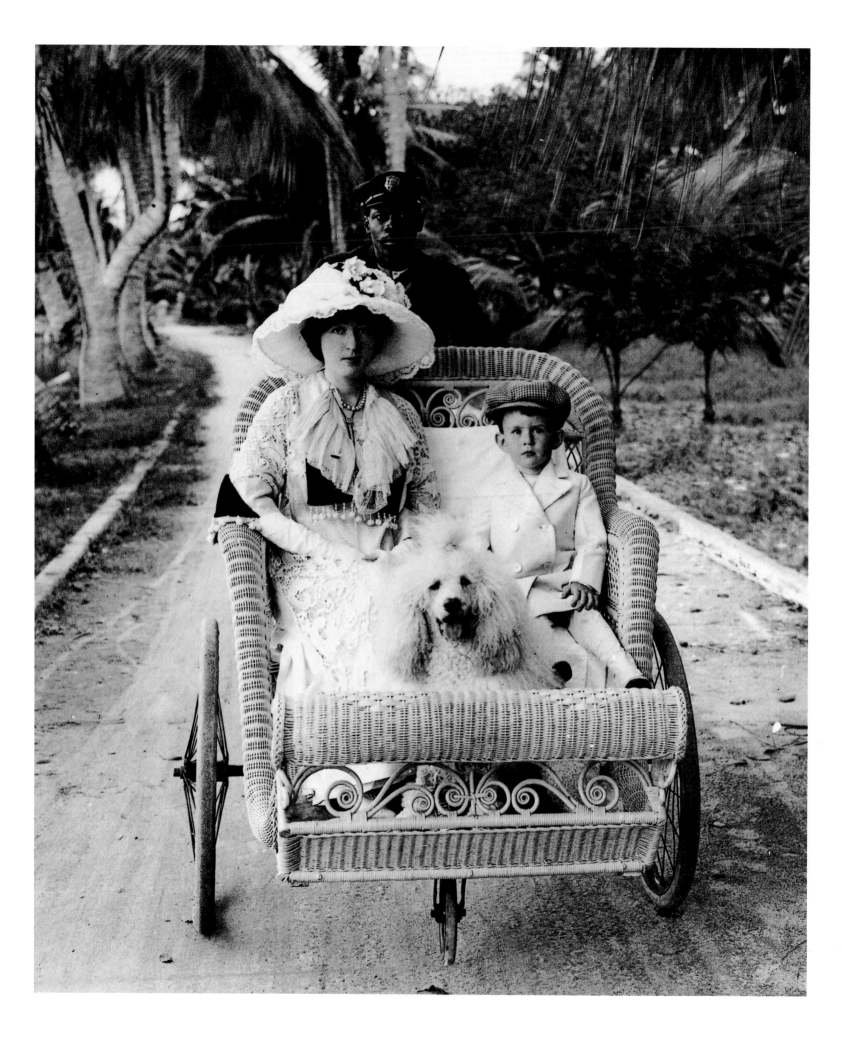

Indeed, a socially ambitious mother understood how important it was for her daughter to be dressed properly; it might make all the difference in snagging a good husband—preferably a well-born magnate or a European aristocrat. The nouveau riche Wilsons, a southern family who had made their fortune by profiteering during the Civil War, became renowned for their skill in marrying up the social ladder, and thus earned the nickname the "marrying Wilsons." There was no luck involved; rather it came about due to skillful plotting by Mrs. Wilson. As her daughter May was no great beauty, Mrs. Wilson devised an ingenious plan. She arranged to have May presented to two of the most powerful people in Europe, Queen Victoria and the designer Charles Worth. From the former, May acquired a social luster, and from the latter, a wardrobe that "transformed [her] from a quite ordinary looking girl into one that was notably distinguished in appearance." The plan worked to perfection. May married Ogden Goelet, possessor of impeccable social credentials and heir to a vast Manhattan real estate fortune.

Mrs. Wilson's scheming worked just as well with her other children. Her son married Caroline Astor—*the* Mrs. Astor's daughter, much to the social monarch's consternation; another daughter married Cornelius "Neily" Vanderbilt III, also over strenuous parental objections. Cornelius Vanderbilt II disapproved of the arriviste Wilsons; so much so that when the engagement was announced in 1896 he went to the press and declared that it was "against his expressed wish." A month later he suffered a stroke, which family members blamed on the stress caused by his son's impending marriage.

The Vanderbilts' objections, however, were rich with irony. After all, despite their great wealth, they had long been considered beyond the pale socially. The original "Commodore" Cornelius Vanderbilt had amassed a fortune in steamboats and railroads and left behind over a hundred million dollars in 1877, an unheard of sum at the time. The elite sneered that Vanderbilt money was so new that you could hear freshly printed bills crackling in their pockets as they passed by. Barely literate, coarse, and cheap to a fault, the Commodore outraged New York high society—pinching servant girls, spitting tobacco juice on rugs, and swearing a blue streak in front of well-bred hostesses. In short order the Vanderbilts were blackballed socially; even the Commodore's grandchildren still felt the sting of rejection—particularly by Mrs. Caroline Astor, arbiter of the social order.

It was not until 1883 that Mrs. Astor relented and permitted the Vanderbilts to join the golden elect. And it took years of strategic planning by Alva Vanderbilt, wife of William

Evalyn Walsh, heir to a mining fortune and married to a newspaper scion, is pedaled around Palm Beach in a wicker carriage with her young son Vinson and their pet dog. Owner of the Hope Diamond, a reputedly unlucky stone, Evalyn's pampered life did not bring her happiness. Not long after this photograph was made, her adored son would be run over and killed by a car.

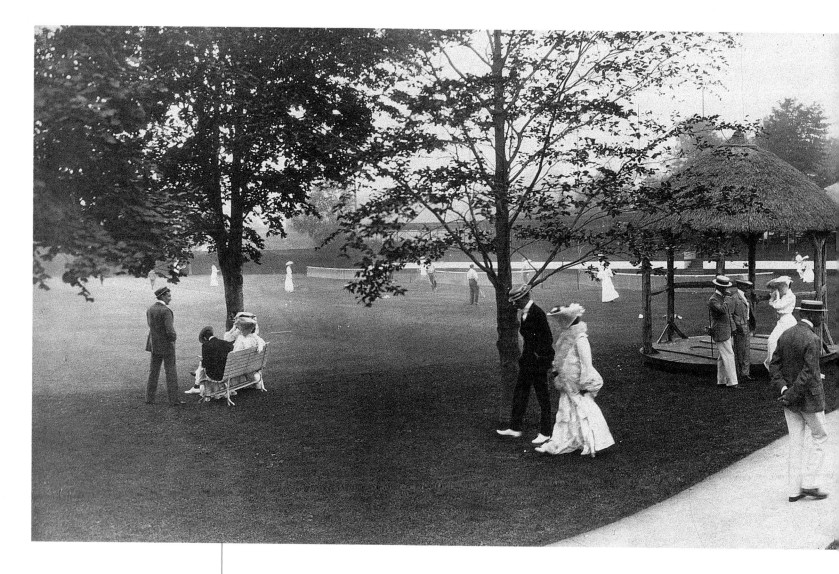

Kissam Vanderbilt, to achieve the feat. Alva, from a gently bred but financially strapped southern family, was rather plump and was described by one acquaintance as resembling a frog. She seemed hardly suited to launch a social juggernaut; yet she had the drive and steely disposition to challenge the haughty Mrs. Astor. Alva's own daughter succinctly summed up her mother as a "born dictator."

Alva determined that architecture would be the key to her success, and she used it as a battering ram to force her way into elite society. She commissioned the architect Richard Morris Hunt, darling of the upper crust, to design a French Renaissance château-style mansion on Fifth Avenue. It took three million dollars and three years to construct. A distinctive round tower rose above the main entrance, and a playroom on the top floor was so large that the three Vanderbilt children biked and roller-skated in it. The mansion also included vast and sumptuous rooms perfect for entertaining. Alva decided that the only thing the Vanderbilts and their new palace lacked was a coat of arms, so she promptly drew one that featured three acorns and pronounced that "great oaks from little acorns grow."

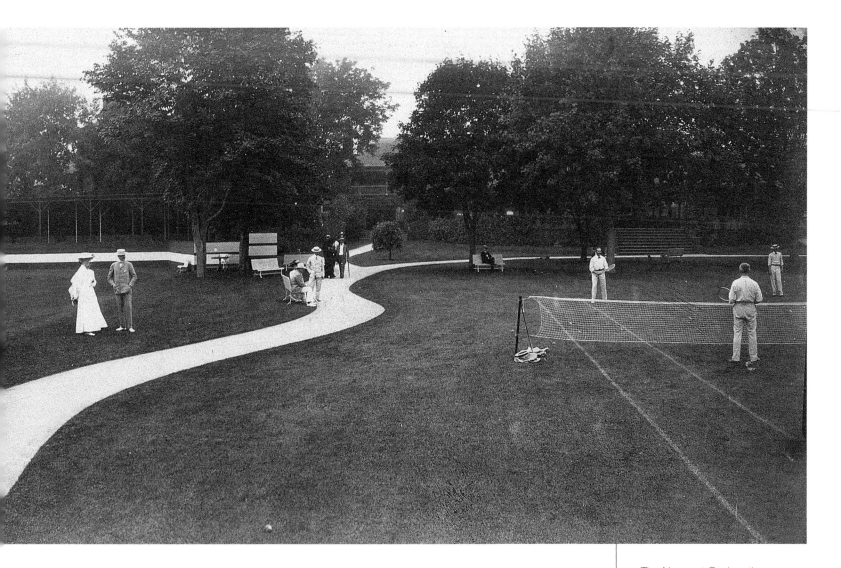

The château completed, the next phase of Alva's social assault began. To showcase her grand new quarters, she decided to host a costume ball. It would take place on March 26, 1883, immediately following Easter, and the anticipation leading up to it was so great that the *New York Times* observed: "The ball has disturbed the...waking hours of social butterflies both male and female for over six weeks and has even interfered to some extent with the rigid obedience of Lenten devotions which the church makes."

Mrs. Astor studiously ignored the buzz about the upcoming event—that is until her own daughter was slighted. Twenty-two-year-old Caroline and her friends had been practicing a special dance for the ball, but Alva Vanderbilt made it known that she would be unable to invite the young woman because her mother, Mrs. Astor, had never paid her a call. Seeing how deeply disappointed her daughter was, Mrs. Astor conceded defeat. "I think" the social maven announced, "that the time has come for the Vanderbilts." Summoning her carriage, Mrs. Astor made her way up Fifth Avenue and left her card at the Vanderbilts' new château. Within hours, an invitation to the ball arrived at the Astors'. Henceforth the Vanderbilts were part of the charmed inner circle.

The Newport Casino, the exclusive club for Gilded Age socialites, boasted lawn tennis that players of both sexes enjoyed at the turn of the 20th century. The game's popularity among women members soared after Mrs. John Jacob Astor took up the sport. The club offered other amenities: a theater (where Oscar Wilde once appeared), a restaurant, and the Horse-Shoe Piazza, where a string orchestra played every morning.

The ball itself—with Mrs. Astor in attendance—was the greatest social event of the era. Footmen in knee breeches and powdered wigs directed the 1,200 guests. Roses lined the halls and drawing rooms; palms, orchids, and bougainvillea turned the two-story gymnasium into a tropical garden, where supper was served after midnight. Alva Vanderbilt, inspired by a painting from the family's art gallery, appeared as a Venetian princess—in a Worth gown, naturally. Her sister-in-law Alice Vanderbilt came as "The Electric Light," her costume flashing at intervals, powered by batteries in her pocket. The dancing went on all night; at 6 a.m. Alva led a Virginia reel, signaling that the ball was over, though some refused to take the hint and continued dancing.

The event was a huge triumph for the Vanderbilts, and for Alva in particular. She had breached the social fortress, and now, at age 30, had made her way to the center of New York society. It had required hard work. She would later complain that she knew of "no profession, art or trade that women are working in today as taxing on mental resources as being a leader in society." At least one gossip columnist of the time dismissed Alva as a mere social climber and castigated the society that she aspired to. The March 5, 1895 edition of the *New York World* described Alva's world as consisting of "Society, Fifth Avenue, terrapin, Newport, dry champagne, servants in livery, men who don't work, women with no serious thoughts, and all the other charms of fashionable existence."

But Alva did indeed have "serious thoughts" to go along with her serious social aspirations. The critic failed to credit Alva's significant contribution to American architecture. It was Alva, not her husband, who commissioned the architect Richard Morris Hunt and then worked closely with him on her Fifth Avenue château, a building which injected a dazzling European splendor and sophistication to New York. She then moved on to her greatest architectural triumph—what she referred to as her "fourth child"—the grand Marble House in Newport. This would be hers entirely, and she insisted that the property be put in her name, a wise decision in light of her troubled marriage with William. (Her husband was notoriously unfaithful, a pervasive trait among the Gilded Age set. One Newport socialite sarcastically noted that she was a wife, but that she had "an assistant down the street.")

An 1894 paper doll set featured Newport socialites in costumes, but the women of Newport left behind a social and architectural legacy much more substantial. Imposing Marble House (opposite) was completed there in 1892 under the watchful eye and design dictates of Alva Vanderbilt.

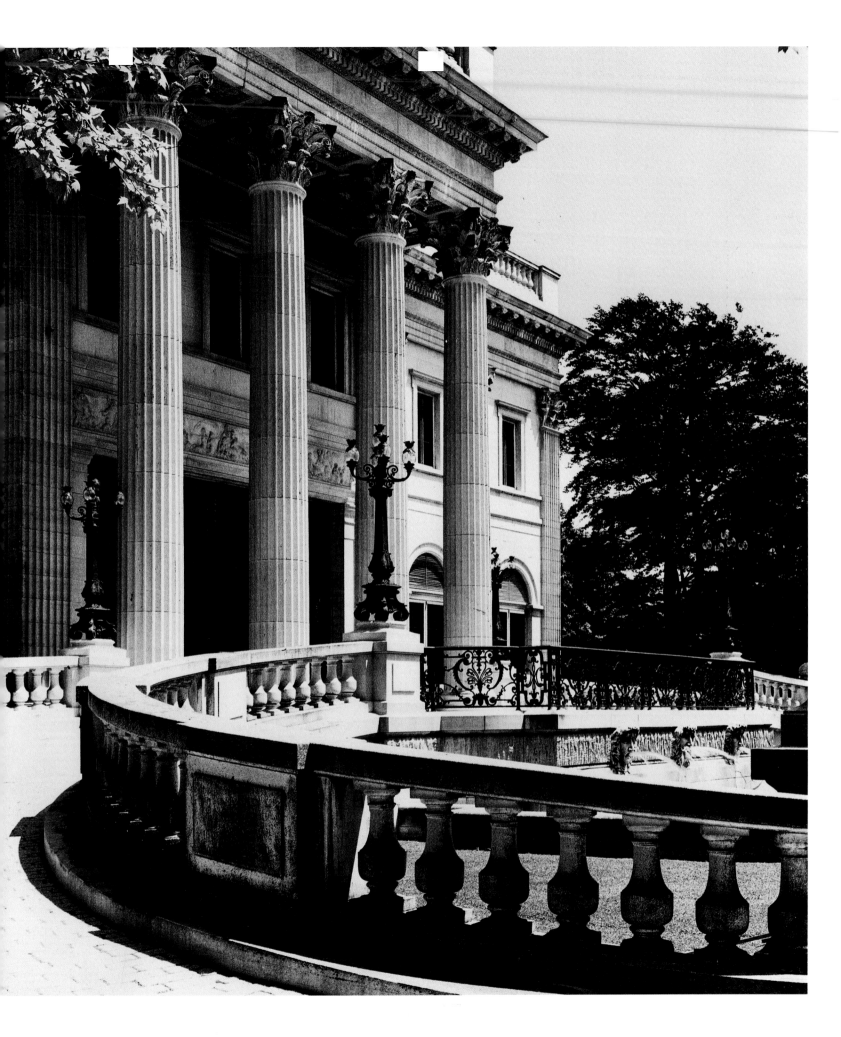

Julia Morgan, a talented Gilded Age architect, painted this water-color while a student at the prestigious École des Beaux-Arts in Paris. Though initially turned away because of her sex, in 1898 she became the first woman admitted to its architectural program and while there won medals (including the one below) in a number of competitions. Morgan went on to design over 700 buildings, her most famous being San Simeon, William Randolph Hearst's spectacular hilltop castle in California.

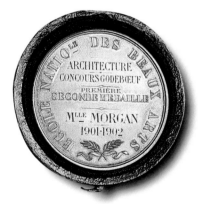

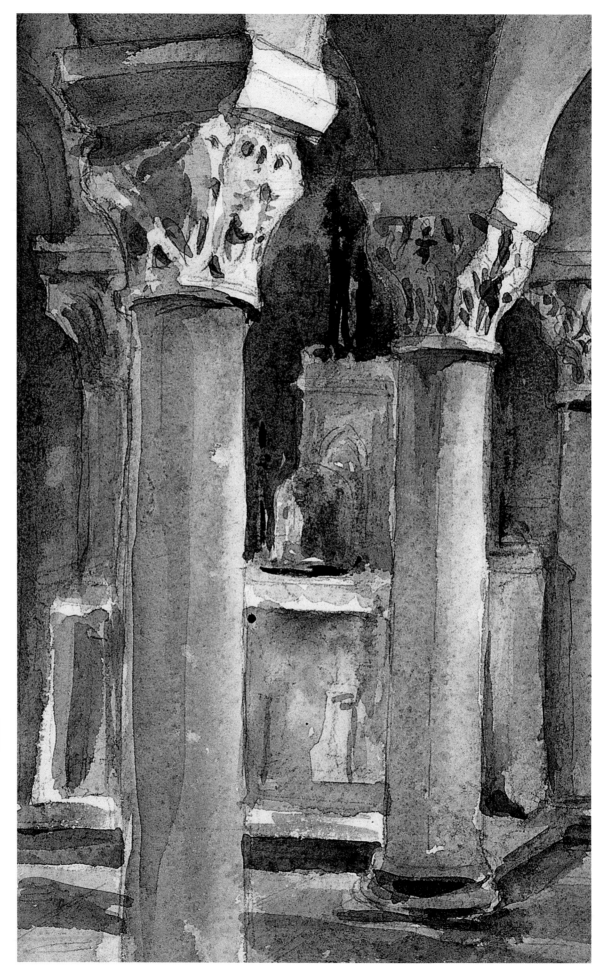

Alva threw herself totally into the planning and construction of her Newport "cottage." The official architect, Richard Morris Hunt, acknowledged his debt to her, admitting that she was "immersed [in] every aspect of the design." She worked hand in hand with him, offering suggestions, researching architectural details, and rendering final approval or disapproval. She scrutinized the smallest detail, down to every single molding and cornice.

The striking exterior of Marble House—constructed of half a million cubic feet of marble and fronted by four massive Corinthian columns—was largely Alva's concept. She fondly recalled gazing at the Parthenon by moonlight from her yacht and being struck by the realization that "the effect of art upon the soul is to make it long for beauty, which is the highest morality." At Alva's insistence, the exterior was fashioned out of Tuckahoe marble, a substance so hard that it could not be carved, but so white that it would practically glow in the moonlight. The Marble House was to be her work of art.

The interior and its furnishings were just as sumptuous, if not more so. The dining room had walls of rose-colored Numidian marble imported from Algiers; the solid bronze dining chairs weighed 70 pounds each, and footmen had to push guests to and from the table. The Gothic Room, created to house the medieval and Renaissance art that Alva had collected in France, included a polychrome ceiling and stained-glass windows which kept the room dimly lit—and never hinted at the fact that it faced out onto the sea. Alva's daughter, Consuelo, would describe the room as "melancholy" and "propitious to sacrifice," as it was here that she became betrothed—against her wishes, but at her mother's command—to the Duke of Marlborough.

Perhaps the most astonishing of the 50-odd rooms in Marble House was the ballroom, aptly named the Gold Room. A sculptor hand-carved the oak-panelled walls, which were covered entirely with gilt. It was literally the gilded room for the Gilded Age. It exuded excess in a town not noted for simplicity.

Alva oversaw the construction of it all; a friend once described her as only happy when "knee-deep in mortar." Adding an element of suspense to the entire project, Alva demanded complete secrecy. High fences shielded the grounds from onlookers, watchmen patrolled with St. Bernards, and the workers were searched at the end of each day to make sure they were not carrying off building plans. Alva's security measures, however, did not prevent one journalist from disguising himself as an electrician and surreptitiously photographing the site. Neighbors, naturally miffed at the stalag-like conditions, referred to the place as "a marble house for a woman with a marble heart."

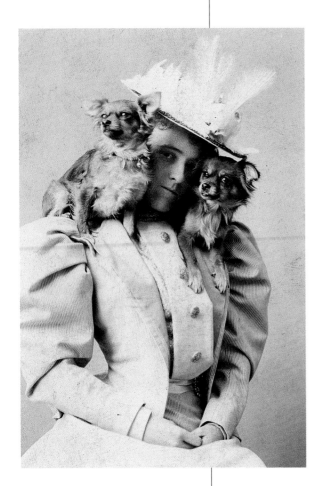

After three years of secret construction, the upper crust was nearly bursting with curiosity. On August 18, 1892, guests invited for the opening of the house were kept waiting at the gates to the mansion. The house was in darkness. Suddenly all the lights were turned on at once, dramatically illuminating the imposing facade and grounds. The *New York Times* gushed, "The grand portico was a blaze of light and liveried attendants were on hand from carriage to cloakroom." Dinner was served on gold plates.

The total cost of Marble House was staggering—11 million dollars for its construction, decoration, and furnishings. Willie Vanderbilt presented it to his wife as a birthday gift. Within three years she would divorce him—and get to keep the house.

Alva never did things half way. Divorce among polite society was unheard of at the time; even her lawyer had a simple piece of advice for her: "Don't do it." Willie Vanderbilt begged her, for her own sake, to consider separation rather than divorce. But she would have none of it. She detested the double standard of the day—the "J. P. Morgans and Jack Astors" could do as they pleased, she complained, while the poor abandoned wives had to look the other way to save their own reputations.

She relished her role as a pioneer, boasting: "I always do everything first," and, with some exaggeration, "I was the first society woman to ask for a divorce." She certainly felt the cold shoulder of Newport society. They were, in Alva's words, "by turns stunned, horrified, and then savage." Upper-crust women greeted her with stony silence and glares—even at church. Alva took it in stride, and would later quip that it was the women most in need of a divorce who were the most vociferous in their denunciations.

A trio of Newport's most powerful matrons came to her rescue, including her old rival, Mrs. Astor, whose word was final law in Newport. Thus, the divorcée was still ensured invitations to the finest homes—though the hostess might be the only woman to speak to her. According to the arcane social rules of that set, men could speak to the scandalous Alva, though they certainly did not want their wives to do so. Before long, however, the elite closed ranks behind Mrs. Astor's lead, and Alva regained her position. But Alva's headstrong personality and remarkable architectural panache had helped transform high society and its rules forever.

The nuances—and cruelties—of this rarefied world were captured brilliantly by another woman, the Pulitzer Prize-winning fiction writer Edith Wharton, who vividly described one of her upper crust characters as having a mind "like a kind of moral fly-paper, to which the buzzing items of gossip were drawn." Wharton was able to evoke the very texture and manners of Gilded Age society because she was herself a member of that exclusive tribe. Part of the old-guard elite—her mother was a Rhinelander, an aristocratic New York family dating back to the colonial era—Wharton was raised in proper fashion, shuttling between Paris, New York, and Newport.

As a child, Edith was bookish by nature and interested in writing—traits frowned upon by her mother, who was more concerned that she make an advantageous marriage. To that end, her mother decreed that writing supplies should be limited, and the date of her formal debut into society pushed forward, so that Edith would have less time to read. Edith did make an "appropriate" marriage—to the handsome, socially prominent, but intellectually lightweight Teddy Wharton; they had little in common save an interest in dogs, horses, and the outdoors. The marriage was a disaster. Edith took to writing. She published her first book, *The Decoration of Houses,* in 1897. Written in collaboration with the Boston-Brahmin architect Ogden Codman, Jr., the work was an influential design book for the Gilded Age rich: a guide to the graceful decoration of every room in an upper-class house, from the library to the ballroom. Edith drew upon her deep knowledge of European architecture and interior decoration, scorning the cluttered Victorian interiors of her youth.

A few years later, Edith took her own advice to heart and directed the creation of a magnificent European-style mansion. Bored with the lack of intellectual stimulation in Newport, she decided to build her new summer home in Lenox, Massachusetts, another Gilded Age playground. Set in the picturesque Berkshire Hills, Lenox was less flamboyant than Newport, though just as grand, with residences like Shadow Brook, a sprawling hundred-room mansion. (The owner's son, Anson Phelps Stokes, Jr., member of the

Twenty-eight-year-old Edith Wharton poses with her two small dogs in 1890. Years later, in enumerating the "ruling passions" in her life, dogs ranked second on the list, just behind "Justice and Order." The esteemed author who brilliantly dissected the social mores of her era once wrote in her diary: "I am secretly afraid of animals...I think it is because of the *us*ness in their eyes."

Using her opera glasses, a well-to-do woman in black (opposite) is absorbed in the spectacle unfolding on a Parisian stage, and is totally unaware of the patron in a nearby box who has fixed his gaze on her. This intriguing oil painting by American-born Mary Cassatt captures the offstage drama in the world of private theater boxes (a preoccupation in the glamorous Gilded Age), as well as the atmospheric lighting cast by the era's gas chandeliers. In 1874 Cassatt settled permanently in France; five years later her work would be featured in an avant-garde Impressionist exhibition. One critic hailed the expatriate's work as "bold, mysterious, and fresh....There is nothing more graciously honest and aristocratic than her portraits of young women."

Yale class of '96, once telegrammed his mother: "Arriving this evening with a crowd of '96 men." Her response: "Many guests already here. Have only room for fifty.")

Edith carefully situated her new house on a high point overlooking a lake and named it The Mount. In addition to a grand residence, she set about creating an entire landscape that would be a "prolongation of the house," in the manner of an Italian villa. She designed the gardens herself, with only minimal help from her niece, the landscape architect Beatrix Jones Farrand (the only woman among the founders of the American Society of Landscape Architects at the turn of the 20th century).

Edith had an innate understanding of the nuances of architecture and landscape design and their effect on the human psyche. In one of her stories, "The Fullness of Life," she used architecture as an image of the sad seclusion of a woman's soul:

> I have sometimes thought that a woman's nature is like a great house full of rooms: there is the hall, through which everyone passes in going in and out; the drawing room, where one receives formal visits; the sitting room, where the members of the family come and go...but beyond that, far beyond, are other rooms, the handles of whose doors are never turned; no one knows the way to them, no one knows whither they lead; and in the innermost rooms, the holy of holies, the soul sits alone and waits for a footstep that never comes.

Wharton held a chilling mirror up to her own world. Her 1905 novel, *The House of Mirth,* chronicles the destruction of Lily Bart, a patrician by birth with neither parents nor money. Attempting to keep up with the ultra-rich, she falls hopelessly into debt and tumbles from her social perch. She dies alone and destitute, a victim of that glittering but harsh society. Looking at poor, struggling Lily, one of the male characters notices "her hand, polished as a bit of old ivory, with its slender pink nails, and the sapphire bracelet slipping over her wrist." He suddenly realizes that she was "so evidently the victim of the civilization which had produced her, that the links of her bracelet seemed like manacles chaining her to her fate." *The House of Mirth* sparked admiration and a stream of praise from members of the upper tier. Her friend Henry James, a novelist who shared her knowledge of the nuances of gilded society, declared the book to be "altogether a superior thing."

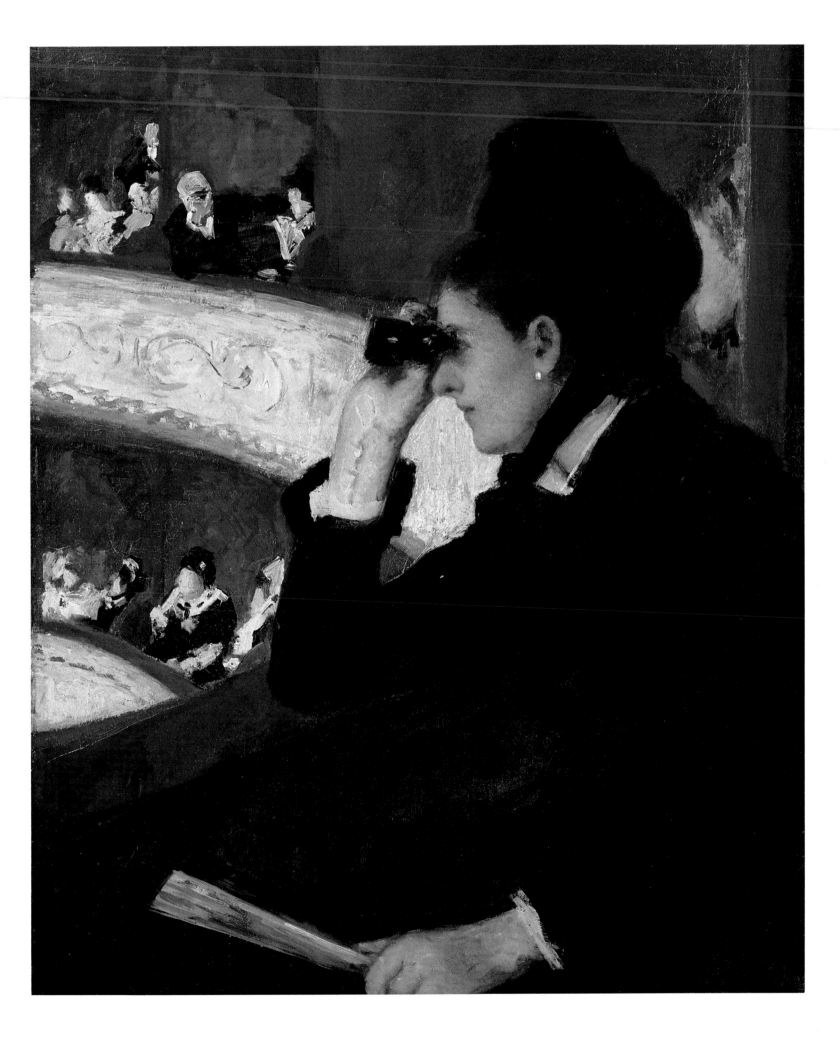

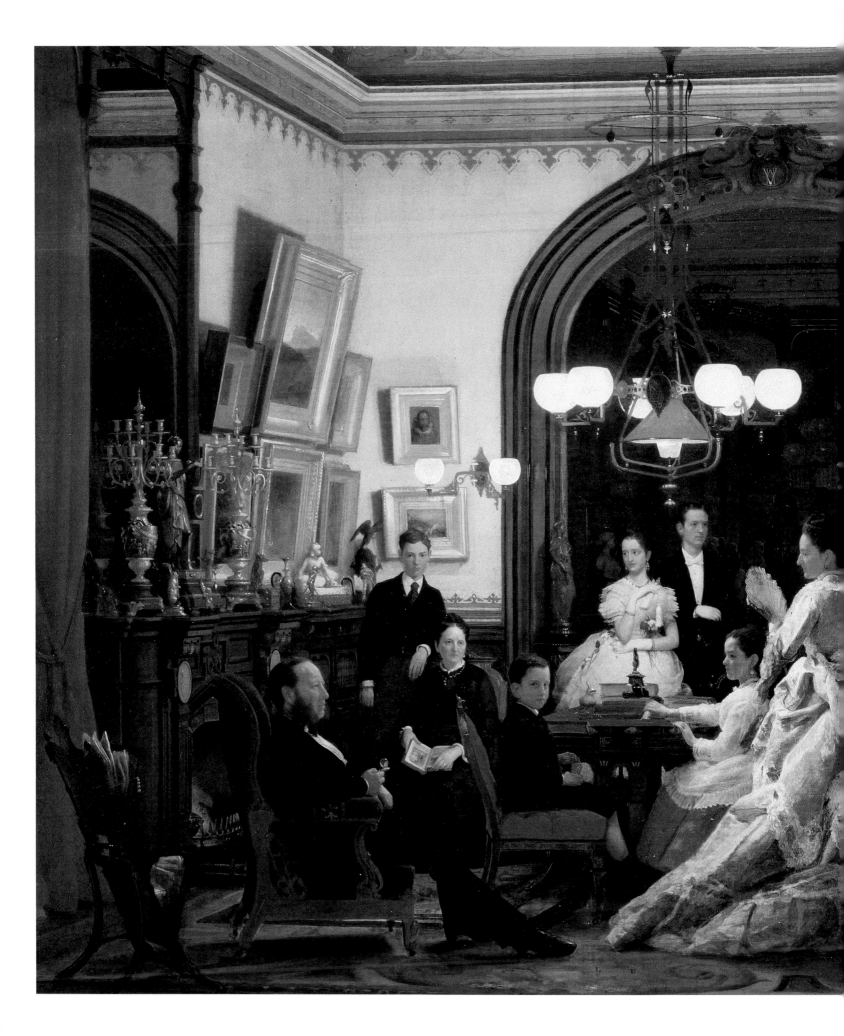

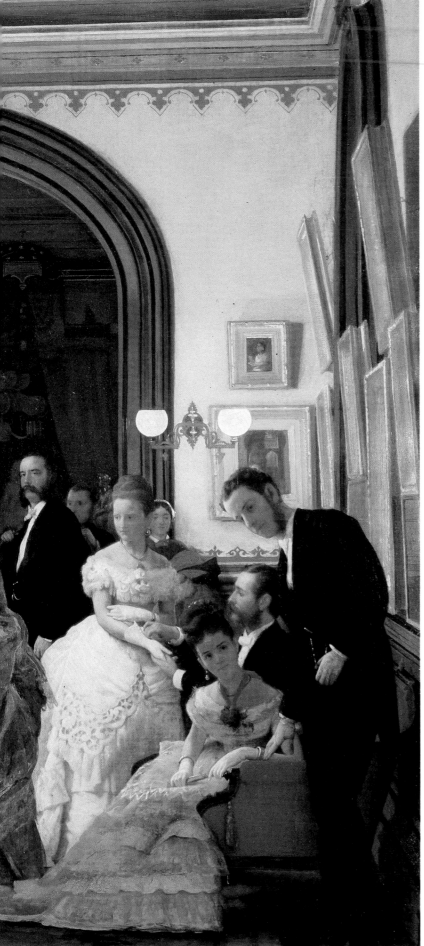

Elegantly attired, three generations of the William H. Vanderbilt family assemble before leaving for the opera in 1873. The Vanderbilts, with their vast railroad fortune, were regarded as arrivistes and sneered at by old New York society. Turned down in an effort to buy a box at the venerable Academy of Music opera house, William H. (seated, far left) would decide to build his own. He joined forces with other scorned millionaires, as well as his formidable daughter-in-law Alva, to create the Metropolitan Opera House in 1883.

Isabella Stewart Gardner drapes pearls around her waist in this regal 1888 portrait by John Singer Sargent. Set against a backdrop that one viewer described as looking like "the heart of a lotus," the seemingly sedate portrait created quite a stir when it was briefly exhibited at the elite St. Botolph Club in Boston. The low-cut dress—as well as rumors of an extramarital affair by the socialite—caused her husband to lock up the painting for the rest of his life. Isabella resurrected the portrait after his death and placed it prominently in the museum she created in Boston.

Despite her criticism of the haut monde, Wharton remained firmly entrenched in that glittering world—and shared in its snobbery. As did many in her set, she preferred the refinements of Europe. On one occasion, when her car broke down in Massachusetts and she had to make an unexpected stop at a resort hotel, Wharton was stunned at what she found:

I have been spending my first night in an American 'summer hotel,' and I despair of the Republic! Such dreariness, such whining callow women, such utter absence of the amenities, such crass food, crass manners, crass landscape!! And, mind you, it is a new and fashionable hotel. What a horror it is for a whole nation to be developing without a sense of beauty, and eating bananas for breakfast.

In a similar vein, she once wrote to a friend: "I think I have found a way of summing up what ails 'our country'…. The American landscape has no foreground and the American mind no background."

And yet, for all of her European proclivities, Wharton's roots remained in America. After two weeks in Paris she once exclaimed, "I would give up all this fine civilization for a sight of my spring blossoms at Lenox." She spent a good part of her life in France, but was the quintessential American—especially when holding a critical microscope to the fabric of Gilded Age society. Bernard Berenson, the era's unrivaled connoisseur and tastemaker, found Wharton's evocation of the privileged world in which they both moved so perfectly on target that he wrote to her: "To a hazardous degree you are bone of our bones & flesh of our flesh." He would declare to a French associate that the four most genuine Americans of his time were Edith Wharton, Henry James, Henry Adams, and, of course, himself.

Americans of the gilded set looked to Europe for style, refinement, art, and culture. Opera became a preoccupation in New York—whether one liked it or not. Since 1854 old-line New York aristocrats had gone to the opera at the Academy of Music on 14th Street, but it was a highly exclusive club—by the late 1860s there were only 18 boxes that were handed down from one generation to the next. Of course, it was just that exclusivity that the old Knickerbocker aristocracy cherished. Wharton's *The Age of Innocence* opens at the 14th Street opera house where "the world of fashion was still content to reassemble every winter in the shabby red and gold boxes of the sociable old Academy. Conservatives cherished it for being small and inconvenient, and thus keeping out the 'new people.'" This did not sit well with ambitious robber barons who were growing richer by the minute—and eager to showcase their bejewelled wives. William Henry Vanderbilt offered $30,000 for a box at the Academy of Music and was unceremoniously turned down.

Blocked by the old guard, Vanderbilt and other like-minded millionaires, including J.P. Morgan, Jay Gould, and William Rockefeller (brother of John D.), banded together to start their own rival opera house. (And, being hard-headed businessmen, the plutocrats could not resist including rent-producing apartments in the building to ensure year-round revenue.) Alva Vanderbilt, among others, worked diligently behind the scenes to make the opera house a reality.

On October 22, 1883, the Metropolitan Opera had its grand opening. The jewel-bedecked members of the audience probably outshone the performance of Faust that evening—if indeed anyone was even paying attention to it. The performance began at precisely 8:23, and the final curtain calls did not end until after 12:30 the next morning. "All the nouveau riche were on hand," a reporter from the *Dramatic Mirror* noted disdainfully. "The Goulds and Vanderbilts and people of that ilk perfumed the air with the odor of crisp greenbacks.... The tiers of boxes looked like the cages in a menagerie of monopolists." The occupants in the "Golden Horseshoe" of boxes boasted an accumulated wealth of some 540 million dollars.

The article in the *Dramatic Mirror* went on to contrast the flashy, new-money crowd at the Metropolitan with the audience assembled downtown at the staid old opera house on 14th Street—the Knickerbocker set "distinguished by their brilliant social altitude and by the identification of their names with Manhattan's history"; an old guard willing "to support an opera season backed by

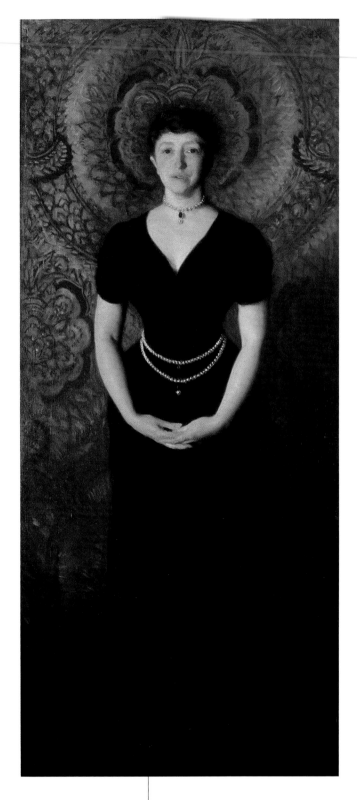

In broad-brimmed hats and white gloves, a pair of women pause with their children to gaze at Emanuel Leutze's monumental "Washington Crossing the Delaware." The painting was presented to the Metropolitan Museum with great fanfare in 1896, though humorist Mark Twain was less than impressed: "A work of art," he called it, "which would have made Washington hesitate about crossing, if he could have foreseen what advantage was going to be taken of it." The satiric Twain coined the term "Gilded Age" to characterize—perfectly—that flamboyant era.

something more than the money bags of indiscreet speculation." Despite the reporter's vitriol, at least one socialite decided to hedge her bets. She had boxes in both opera houses, and on opening night she attended the first act at the Metropolitan Opera House on 40th Street and then raced by carriage to 14th Street to be seen at the old Academy during the second intermission.

The critic's snide remarks proved moot: When Mrs. Astor decreed that Monday would be her night at the Metropolitan Opera, all of high society rushed to join her. The old Academy of Music slowly fell from grace, and the Metropolitan assumed social ascendancy. An 1892 fire forced a reconfiguration of the Metropolitan, and the number of boxes was substantially reduced—making them all the more coveted. The 35 most luxurious boxes, known as the "Diamond Horseshoe," fetched $60,000 each; and, according to a contemporary magazine, "millionaires would willingly crawl on hands and knees up the red velvet stairs to the Diamond Horseshoe and feel that the dust accumulated on their knees in the painful Odyssey was a hallmark of social progress."

A brass plaque with the owner's name hung on the entrance to each box, and the owner could invite guests for the performance—and for wine and other refreshments served during the lengthy intermissions. An anteroom to the box was used for entertaining, and owners tried to outdo one another in its decoration. Blue silk and silver stars covered one woman's compartment; another had the walls "concealed by festoons of orchids." Women controlled the etiquette as well as the decor at the opera. Indeed all eyes were on Mrs. Astor's box, because protocol demanded that society not leave before she did. In Edith Wharton's *The Age of Innocence,* the main character wonders whether even death would change the entrenched rituals of opera society: "[if] Mrs. Selfridge Merry would be there with the same towering ostrich feathers in her bonnet, and Mrs. Beaufort with the same diamond earrings and the same smile—and whether suitable proscenium seats were already prepared for them in another world."

Collecting art became another Gilded Age obsession. Reporting on American society in the 1890s, the French writer, Paul Bourget, noted that "one must hear the Americans utter the word *art,* all by itself, without the article, to understand the intense ardor of their desire for refinement." American millionaires combed Europe to amass Old World treasures in a bid for refinement and prestige—as well as the envy of their social peers. One turn-of-the-20th-century artist complained that collections such as that stockpiled

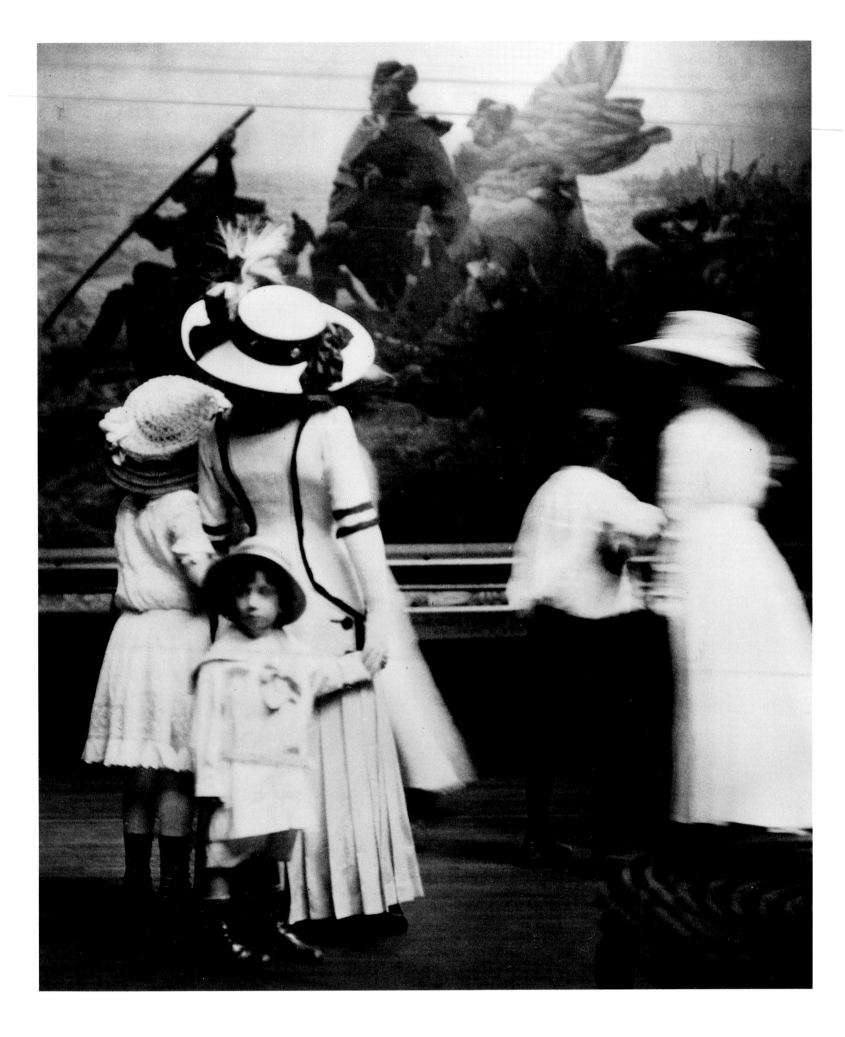

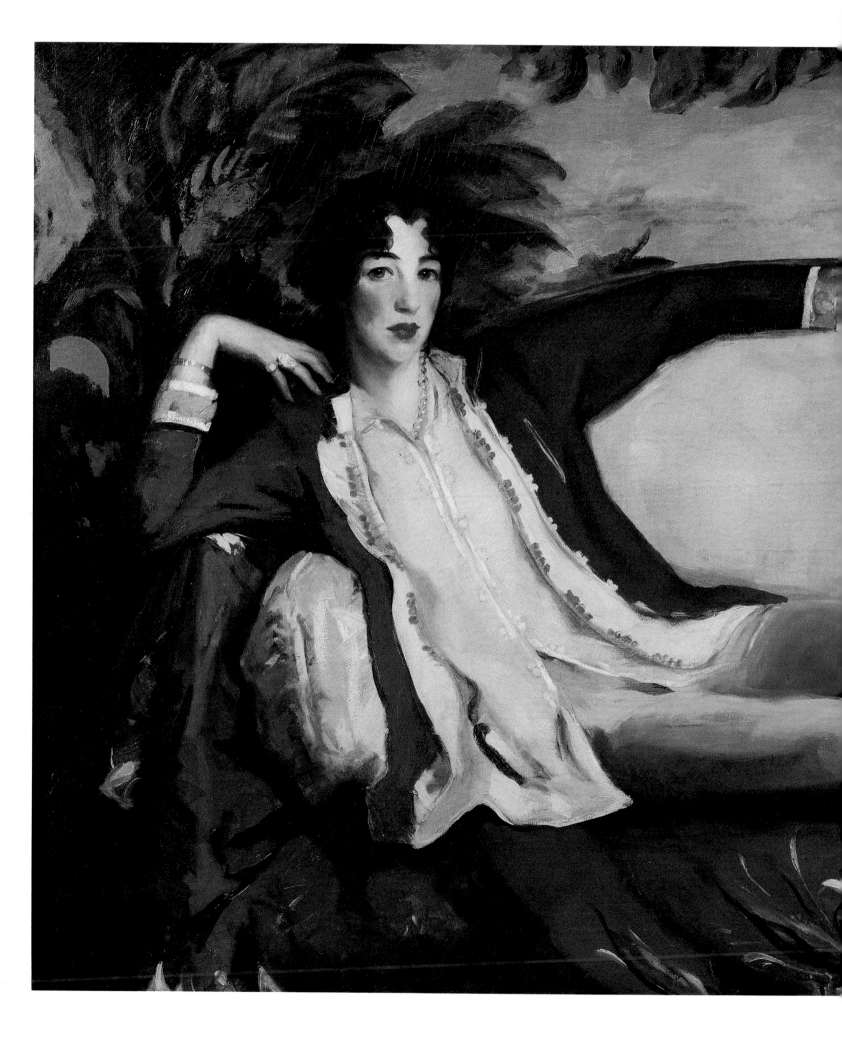

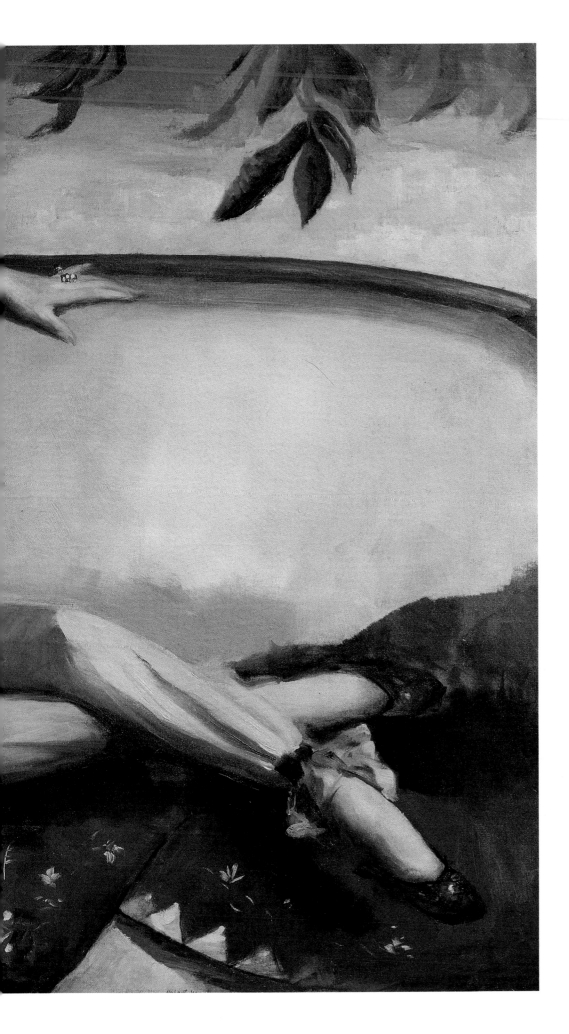

Renowned socialite, sculptor, art collector, and museum founder, Gertrude Vanderbilt Whitney lounges on a couch in a life-size 1916 portrait by American realist painter Robert Henri. Dressed in colorful aqua silk pants, royal blue jacket lined in yellow, and embroidered slippers, she appears more bohemian artist than upper-crust heiress. An avid supporter and collector of contemporary American art, she paid Henri $2,500 to paint her portrait, a substantial sum at the time. She would later establish the Whitney Museum of American Art.

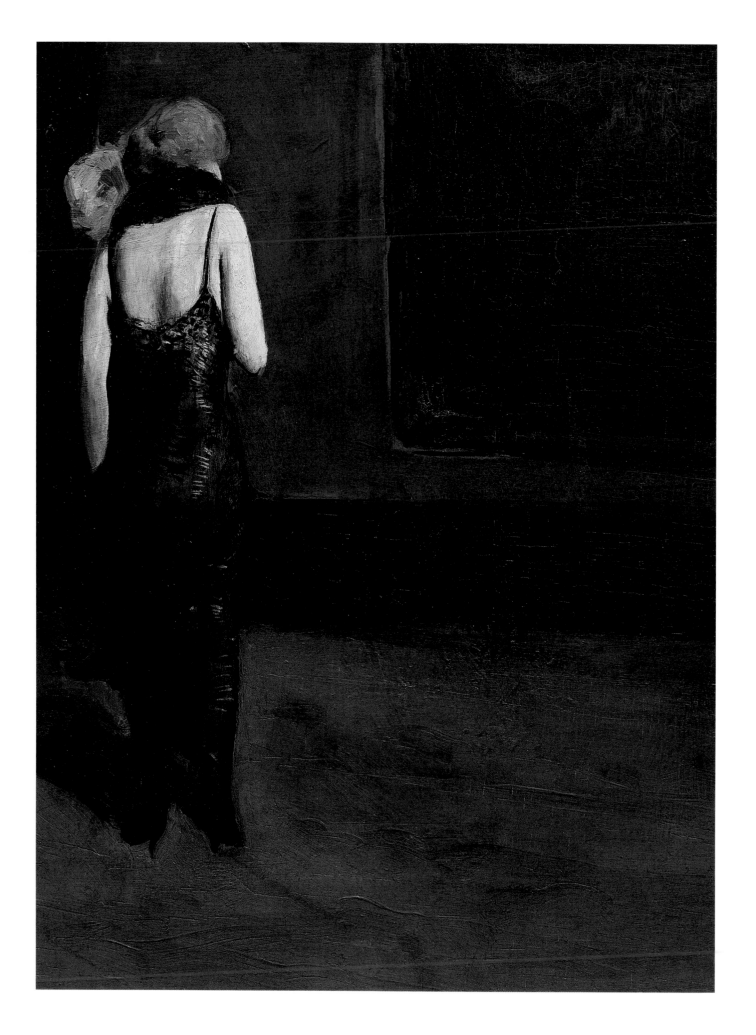

by the financier J.P. Morgan—who spent millions on masterpieces from the distant past but ignored anything contemporary—expressed little real love or understanding of art; it represented merely "the booty of conquerors." Collectors at that time rarely gambled on the work of unknown artists, and few became patrons of living artists; such risk-taking required an unwavering belief in one's own taste. Yet during the Gilded Age, several women emerged as discerning collectors and trendsetters.

By the end of the Civil War, Elizabeth Hart Jarvis Colt had money to burn. Her husband, Samuel Colt, renowned inventor and manufacturer of the Colt pistol, had died in 1862 and had left her some 15 million dollars as well as a controlling interest in his business, which was the largest private armory in the world. The arms company in Hartford, Connecticut, boomed during and after the war, with Elizabeth closely overseeing the operation of the factory. Having profited handsomely from war, Elizabeth turned to a gentler occupation in the late 1860s. She began collecting and commissioning art, particularly naturalistic landscapes then being painted by American artists such as Frederic Church, Albert Bierstadt, and John Kensett, all members of the Hudson River school of painters.

Elizabeth assembled one of the most important private collections of paintings in the country and then created her own art gallery, hiring the eminent architect, Richard Morris Hunt, to design a formal viewing space on the second floor of her Italianate mansion. She was the first woman on her own to attempt such an undertaking, and many considered it unseemly. Elizabeth shrewdly blunted any criticism by claiming that it was a fitting memorial to her husband. She commissioned a portrait of him and had it mounted in an enormous gilt frame that featured a rearing colt and invited over a thousand people to view it. Among those who toured her Hartford gallery were Mark Twain and Civil War hero Gen. Philip Sheridan.

At her death in 1905, Elizabeth Colt left her impressive collection to the Wadsworth Atheneum in Hartford, the oldest public gallery in the country. Her gift, boldly made in her own name, included a $50,000 endowment to build a separate wing to house and maintain her art collection, ensuring that her contribution—and her name—would not be forgotten.

Other adventurous women helped revolutionize the art world in the late 19th century. Louisine Havemeyer of New York and Bertha Honoré Palmer of Chicago both began enthusiastically collecting the work of then-obscure contemporary French artists such

Surveying a painting, art impresario Juliana Force cuts an imposing figure—even when only seen from the back. Her porcelain white skin and flame red hair are offset by a black fur boa and low-cut dark gown in this arresting oil painting by artist Guy Pené du Bois. One of the most important figures of the New York art world in the early 20th century, Force organized influential contemporary American exhibitions at the behest of, and with money provided by, Gertrude Vanderbilt Whitney, and would eventually be named the first director of the Whitney museum.

as Edgar Degas and Claude Monet (Palmer purchased 32 of Monet's paintings alone). In the process, they helped introduce Impressionist art to the United States.

At the center of the Impressionist art world in Paris was another Gilded Age American—painter Mary Cassatt. She had moved to Paris to become a serious artist, and she earned the admiration of her French peers, most of them men. "No woman has the right to draw like that," Degas said grudgingly of her work. In turn, Cassatt was an unabashed advocate of her fellow Impressionists. One Parisian art dealer recalled, "It was with a sort of frenzy that generous Mary Cassatt laboured for the success of her comrades."

Her unflagging enthusiasm inspired collectors like Bertha Palmer and Louisine Havemeyer, Cassatt's old friend from Philadelphia, to purchase the finest contemporary art. Louisine recalled Cassatt's passion: "[She] suddenly looked up from her coffee, and holding the little spoon in her hand, she made a convincing gesture and said emphatically: 'To make a great collection it is necessary to have the modern note in it.'" Cassatt astutely guided Louisine in her purchases, persuading her (even before her marriage to the fabulously wealthy sugar baron, Henry Havemeyer) to buy her first Degas, a pastel, for 500 francs. The two women—with the indulgence of Louisine's husband, Henry, who provided the funds and generally acquiesced to his wife's wishes—amassed one of the greatest art collections of the late 19th century. Louisine referred to Cassatt as the collection's "godmother"—and in truth she was. Cassatt steered her friend not only to the Impressionists, but also to paintings by Goya and El Greco, whose art was almost entirely unknown to Americans at the time. The Metropolitan was the beneficiary of this magnificent collection; after Louisine's death nearly 2,000 works of art went to the museum.

Similarly, Bertha Palmer would eventually bequeath her priceless collection of French Impressionist paintings to the Art Institute of Chicago, enriching that museum immeasurably. The doyenne of Chicago society and a shrewd businesswoman in her own right (after her husband's death she would manage his hotel, the Palmer House, and double her fortune), Bertha's forays into the studios and salons of France always caused a stir, as she was a voracious collector and a tough bargainer.

In 1892 she commissioned Mary Cassatt to paint a 12-by-58-foot mural entitled "Modern Woman"; it would be used in the Woman's Building planned for the upcoming World's Columbian Exposition in Chicago. At first Cassatt was reluctant to take on the project, but she eventually said yes, in part driven by Degas's response to it: "As the bare idea of such a thing put Degas in a rage and he did not spare every criticism he could think of, I got my spirit up and said I would not give up the idea for anything. Now one only has to mention Chicago to set him off." Cassatt's massive painting indeed graced the Woman's Building, and some of Bertha's choicest Impressionist paintings were loaned to the Exposition in Chicago.

At home, Bertha showcased her art in a private gallery she had built in her turreted Chicago mansion. Dubbed Palmer Castle, the granite-and-sandstone pile boasted an 80-foot tower and such an extravagant mélange of styles that it was described as both "sumptuous and abominable." Husband Potter Palmer built the mansion specifically for his wife, in order to set her up properly as queen of Chicago society. He originally intended spending some $90,000 for the house, but as costs began to spin out of control, Palmer finally told his accountant to stop keeping count—he did not want to know the final tally. It came to a hefty million. Bertha certainly lived in regal style, but her Boston counterpart, Isabella Stewart Gardner, was not impressed by the ostentatious display. When shown Bertha's gold table service for 50, Isabella sniffed, "And what do you do when you have a large dinner party?"

Isabella Stewart Gardner, a larger-than-life Gilded Age character, entertained grandly in Boston, where she often flouted Puritan sensibilities—and seemed to take pleasure in doing so. She never contradicted a good story about herself, whether it was true or not. Described as "effervescent, exuberant, reckless, [and] witty," she attended lectures at Harvard as well as prizefights. Once she served tea in a drawing room with an unusual sideshow—posing behind a gauzy curtain was Sandow the Strong Man, variously described as wearing only trunks, or a fig leaf. Strong-willed and unconventional, Isabella gathered artists, musicians, and writers around her whom she encouraged and often supported financially. John Singer Sargent painted her and novelist Henry James heaped praise on her: "I think of you," he wrote, "as a figure on a wondrous cinquecento tapestry—and of myself as one of the small quaint accessory domestic animals, a harmless worm, or the rabbit who is very proud and happy to be in the same general composition with you."

After her husband's death in 1898, Isabella set out to re-create a Venetian-style palace on a tract of reclaimed Boston marshlands. The place took three years to build and she

"No woman has the right to draw like that."

EDGAR DEGAS
ON MARY CASSATT

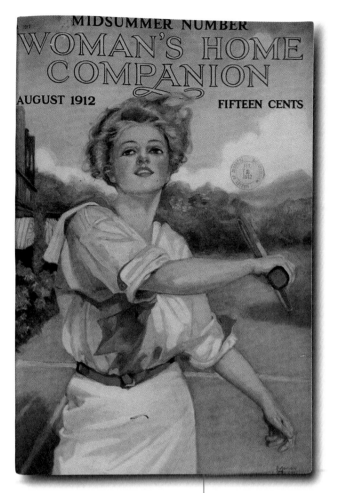

MIDSUMMER NUMBER

WOMAN'S HOME COMPANION

AUGUST 1912   FIFTEEN CENTS

Athletic grace typified the idealized young woman on this 1912 magazine cover, reflecting the new freedom emerging among American women around the turn of the 20th century. The young photographer Alice Austen poked some fun at the image of the "New Woman" by staging a humorous—and brazen—photo of herself and friend (the daughter of an Episcopalian minister) smoking in petticoats and masks.

personally supervised the construction, eating lunch with the workmen. She had signals to summon particular workers—one blast on a cornet indicated a mason, two meant a steamfitter, and so on. On New Year's night in 1903 she unveiled one of the greatest private art collections in the world—2,500 art objects housed in a stunning palace that includes a grand courtyard rising four stories. Isabella lived amidst her treasures until her death in 1924.

While Isabella Stewart Gardner gathered an eclectic mix of art that ranged from Egyptian antiquities to Renaissance tapestries to late 19th-century European paintings, Gertrude Vanderbilt Whitney stunned the art world by championing contemporary American artists. "What do you mean by American art?" a trustee of the Metropolitan Museum of Art asked incredulously in 1909. "Do you mean English or French or what? There is nothing American worth notice." Gertrude thought otherwise. A seminal show featuring "ashcan" artists who portrayed everyday aspects of American life had opened in New York the year before. Gertrude, captivated, had purchased a number of works, an act that the painter John Sloan described as "almost as revolutionary as painting them."

Daughter of Cornelius Vanderbilt II, one of the richest men in the world, and wife of Harry Payne Whitney, fabulously wealthy in his own right, Gertrude lived at the pinnacle of Gilded Age society. Yet she searched for meaning in her life as she moved restlessly between the Whitney mansion on Fifth Avenue, their 600-acre estate on Long Island, their Newport "cottage," and various other properties. Her husband, Harry, a womanizer and heavy drinker, spent much of his time on the polo fields. In a dream that transformed her life, Gertrude saw herself creating the figure of a man. She decided to become a sculptor, and took it up with great energy and success. Her straight-laced mother, Alice, had some qualms. After viewing one of her daughter's male nude sculptures, Alice blurted out, "Do give him a scarf. The fig leaf is so little!"

In 1907 Gertrude took over a former carriage house on a cul-de-sac in Greenwich Village and turned it into her studio; out of these quarters the Whitney Museum of American Art would eventually grow. Drawn into the bohemian world around her, Gertrude began to sponsor shows featuring the work of artists spurned by other mainstream gal-

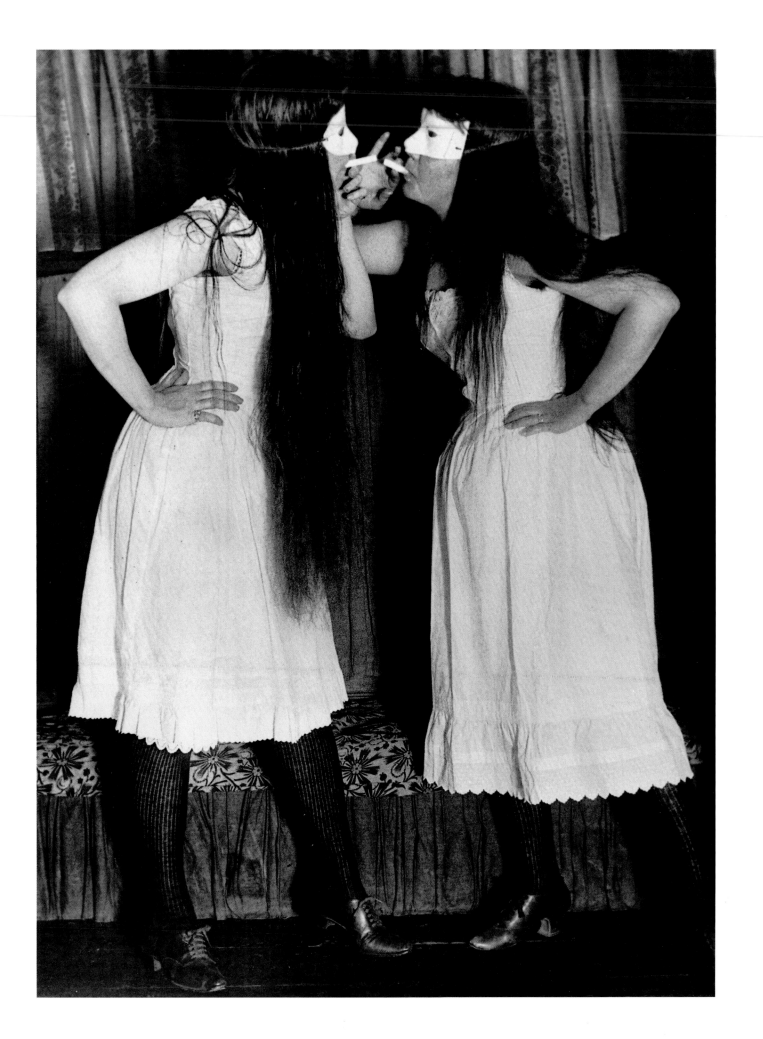

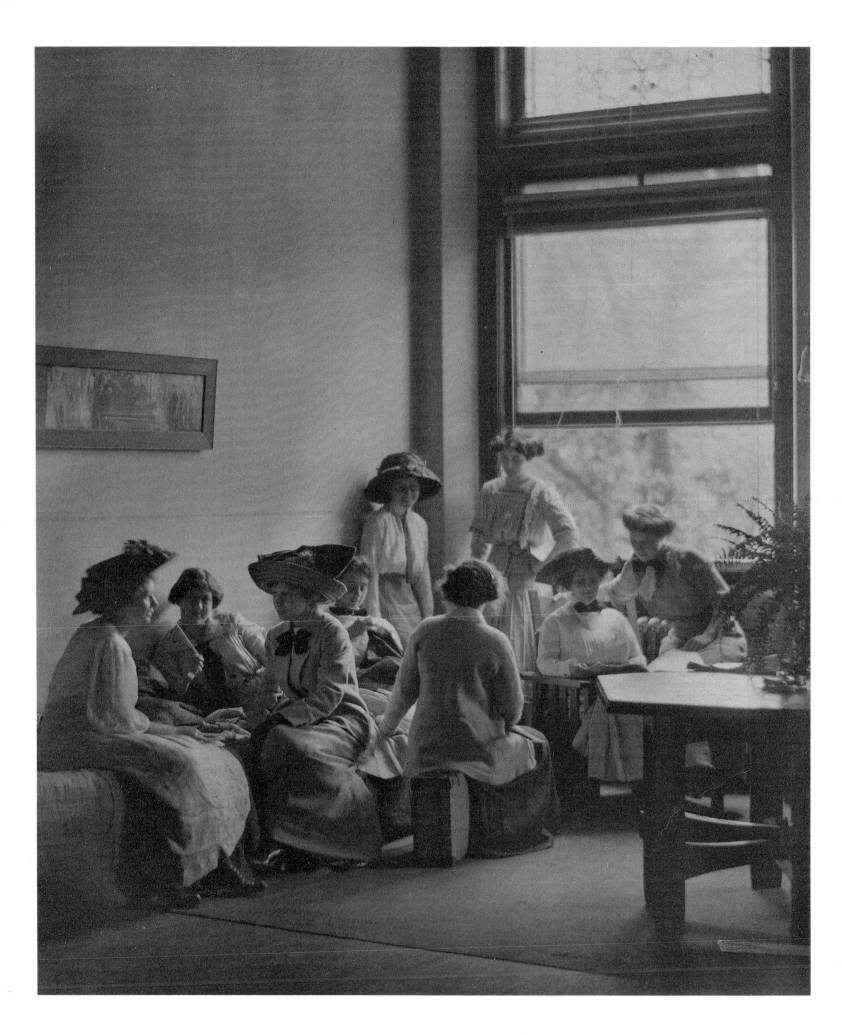

leries. She collaborated with Juliana Force, an energetic force in her own right, who brilliantly organized the shows. Red-haired and theatrical, Force was said to have "a personal magnetism that struck one instantly…like a physical sensation. The social temperature would go up ten degrees when she entered a room."

Gertrude Whitney's collection of American art grew so large that she eventually deputized Force to approach the Metropolitan Museum of Art about giving it to them, along with five million dollars to build a wing for the collection. Force never got around to mentioning the money. The director of the Metropolitan had little use for the paintings: "What will we do with them, my dear lady?" he said dismissively. "We have a cellar of those things already." His rejection led to the creation of the Whitney Museum of American Art—a major addition to the art world—with Juliana Force as the first director.

A free-spirited woman, Gertrude Vanderbilt Whitney defied the rules of Gilded Age society. She was not alone. By the end of the 19th century the "New Woman" began taking shape in America. Idealized in the pages of popular magazines and novels, she had an athletic bearing and exuded a sense of freedom. She longed to live a meaningful life. The energetic and fresh-faced Gibson girl became the American ideal at the turn of the 20th century. She was animated, took to the outdoors—and even enjoyed sports. A creation of the illustrator Charles Dana Gibson, the Gibson girl was supposedly modeled after his wife, the beautiful Irene Langhorne of Virginia.

But the young woman who perhaps best personified the Gibson girl was President Theodore Roosevelt's sassy daughter, Alice. She delighted in creating a stir—she smoked in public, ate asparagus while wearing gloves, and even waved from the inaugural stand, prompting her father to demand her to stop because "this is *my* inauguration!" In the midst of his Presidency, Teddy Roosevelt confessed: "I can do one of two things. I can be President of the United States, or I can control Alice. I cannot possibly do both." The country loved her spirit. A product of the Gilded Age, she lived until 1980 and spent most of the 20th century outraging proper Washington, D.C., society. "If you can't say something good about someone, sit right here by me," she had embroidered on one of her pillows. And in her parting shot, just moments before she died, she stuck her tongue out at a family friend.

Women students socialize at Columbia Teacher's College in New York City in 1912. During the Gilded Age, educational opportunities for middle-class women expanded significantly as state universities in the West and Midwest increasingly opened their doors to female students, and women's colleges in the East offered rigorous academic programs. By 1920 nearly 50 percent of college students were women.

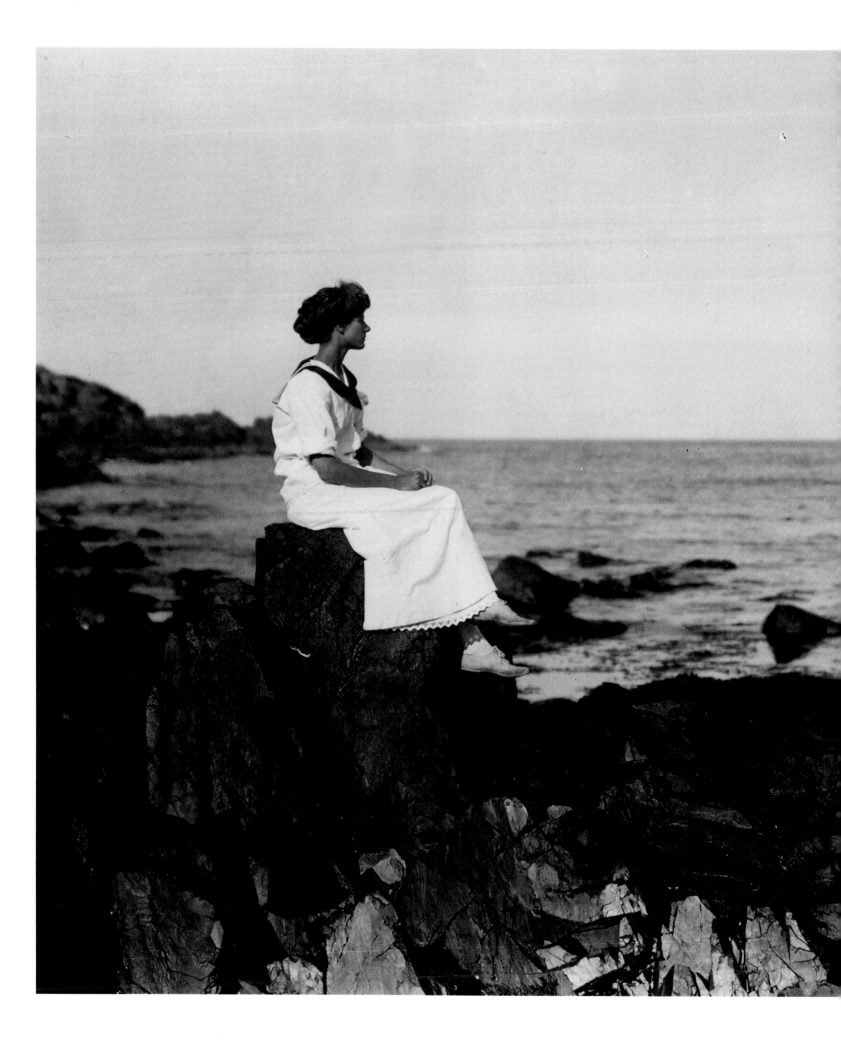

Perched on the Maine coastline, Dorothy Emmons gazes out to sea in an evocative portrait done around 1910 by her mother, professional photographer Chansonetta Stanley Emmons.

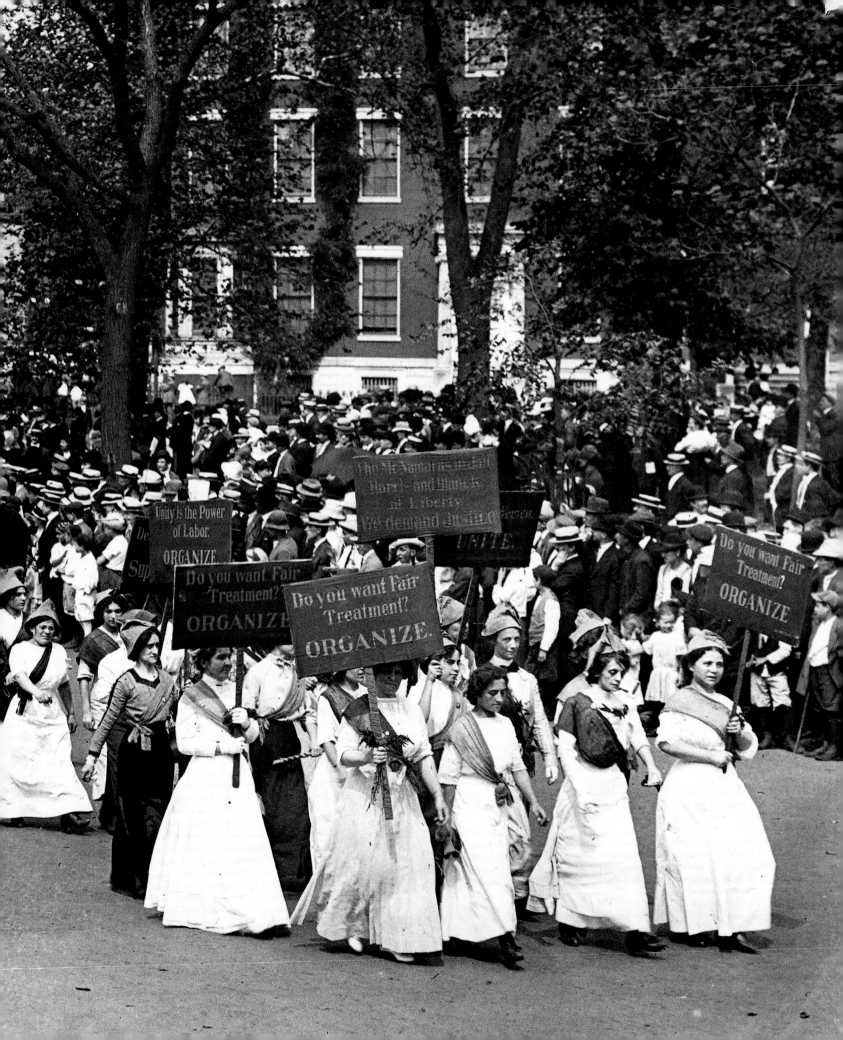

WOMEN ON
THE MARCH

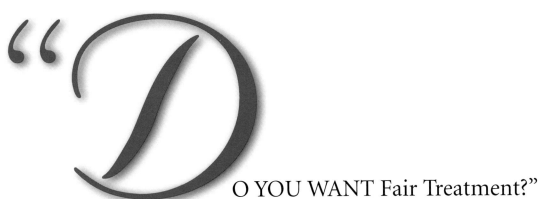"O YOU WANT Fair Treatment?"
the placards at left demanded. If so, the answer was clear:
"ORGANIZE"—and march. And women did so in droves at
the dawn of the 20th century. Immigrant seamstresses joined
with social mavens turned suffragists to fight for the vote
and protest squalid working and living conditions for the
new urban poor. Fifteen thousand women and a smaller
contingent of male supporters marched up New York's Fifth
Avenue in May 1912; the *New York Tribune* called it "the

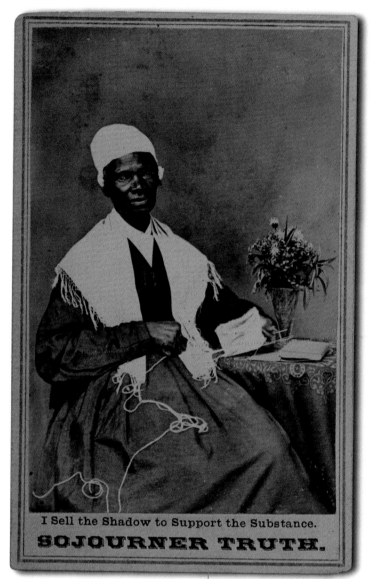

I Sell the Shadow to Support the Substance.

SOJOURNER TRUTH.

greatest demonstration of women in American history."

The march was indeed a spectacular show of solidarity and might, but such political activism was nothing new. For nearly a century women had been in the forefront of the battle for social justice and reform—and in the process they had helped transform America. In the late 1830s Dorothea Dix single-handedly set out to improve inhumane conditions in prisons and insane asylums; her work set in motion state and federal legislative reform.

Women played a key role in the abolitionist movement, and two remarkable women—Sojourner Truth and Harriet Beecher Stowe—helped inject a new element into the debate over slavery: the very humanity of enslaved people. Sojourner Truth, an ex-slave nearly six feet tall with a mesmerizing speaking and singing voice, traveled the country for 30 years denouncing slavery and promoting women's rights and temperance. Her performances—and they were truly that, being a cross between theater and preaching—began with gospel singing. She would then tell stories, holding her audience rapt with her Dutch-inflected voice (one of her owners had been a rich Dutch patroon). Though illiterate, Truth possessed remarkable charisma. Harriet Beecher Stowe said that she had never known anyone with such a powerful personal presence.

Truth's passion could not be denied. Standing before an 1851 gathering she presented herself, in all her flesh and blood reality, and posed a rhetorical question: "And ar'n't I a woman?" The audience was electrified. On another occasion, she was confronted by foes who called her very gender into question; they believed that such an effective abolitionist could not possibly be a woman. She dramatically bared her breast, instantly shaming—and silencing—her critics.

Sojourner Truth became the very embodiment of slavery; she put a human face on that faceless and heartless institution. She herself had suffered from its horrors—born into slavery around 1797 as Isabella, she had been taken from her own family when she was nine years old and sold for $100. History would repeat itself. In 1826, as slavery was coming to an end in New York, her six-year-old son Peter was illegally sold to a family in Alabama, a fate that meant permanent bondage for him. Isabella (as Truth was still called) fought back. She begged the white families involved in the sale to spare her son, but they ignored her pleas. The situation seemed hopeless. As a slave, she lacked both money and legal status; nonetheless, her strong belief in God made her feel "so *tall within...*as if the *power of a nation* was within me!" Remarkably, she succeeded. She went to court, sued for her son's return, and won.

Deeply religious, she underwent a series of conversions. In 1843 she claimed a heavenly spirit told her to set off and tell the truth—thus she changed her name to Sojourner Truth and began her lecture campaign against injustice, supporting herself through the sales of photographs and copies of her ghost written autobiography. During the Civil War she collected food and clothing for black soldiers; in 1864 she met the Great Emancipator himself in the White House. (The meeting had been arranged through Mary Todd Lincoln's African-American seamstress, Elizabeth Keckley.) During her stay in Washington, Truth felt the sting of segregation. After a streetcar conductor tried to physically remove her from a car, she stood her ground and had him arrested for assault and battery. He was dismissed from his post and convicted. "It is hard for the old slaveholding spirit to die," Truth said of the persistent racism, "but die it must."

In the 1850s Truth visited the literary sensation, Harriet Beecher Stowe, to ask for an advertising blurb for her own autobiography. Stowe eventually wrote a full-scale article about the abolitionist preacher which appeared in *Atlantic Monthly* in 1863. Her article turned the mesmerizing orator into a national figure overnight.

Stowe's own rise to fame had been meteoric—and unexpected. The seventh of thirteen children in a household bursting with intellectual fervor and physical activity, Harriet had to work hard to earn her father's attention. (Her mother died when Harriet was five years old.) Her father Lyman, a leading theologian of the day and thunderous orator, bred a family of hard-driving reformers. Harriet's eldest sister Catharine became a well-known educator of young women; her abolitionist brother Henry Ward inspired his congregation at Plymouth Church in Brooklyn to send boxes of rifles, known as "Beecher's Bibles," to antislavery colonists settling Kansas in the 1850s.

Harriet would outshine them all. Upon the publication of *Uncle Tom's Cabin* in 1852

This grandmotherly portrait of Sojourner Truth (opposite) made around 1850 belies the ex-slave's steely resolve and electrifying personal presence. An itinerant evangelist, abolitionist, and crusader for women's rights, she sold these inexpensive mounted photos known as "cartes-de-viste" to finance her work; thus she captioned them, "I sell the Shadow [of my image] to Support the Substance."

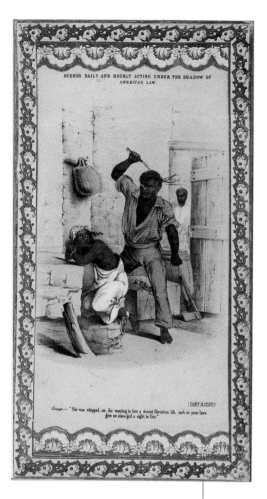

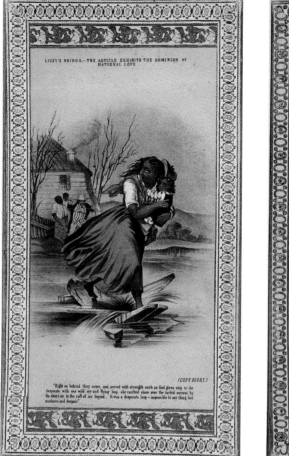

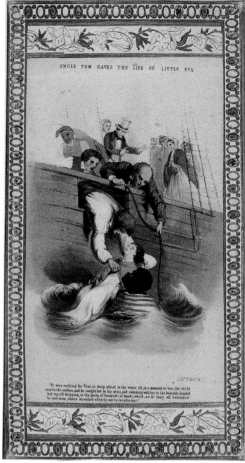

Panels from an accordion-style screen depict dramatic events from Harriet Beecher Stowe's *Uncle Tom's Cabin*. Probably produced in England, this screen was used to decorate the mantel in a Victorian parlor. Stowe's book was such a national and international sensation that it spawned an entire industry of memorabilia.

she achieved a level of celebrity that no American woman had ever experienced. Her previous writings—tracts on temperance and domestic sketches that appeared in *Godey's Lady's Book* for two dollars a page—did not hint at what was in store. Only her husband Calvin took her seriously as a writer. "Get a good stock of health and brush up your mind," he advised. Having yet only written short pieces, Stowe set down to write in the spring of 1851, and promptly produced her masterpiece. It surprised her as much as everyone else. She claimed that it had come to her as a vision; years later she said that "God wrote it." It came indeed from the deepest recesses of her heart, and from a reality that was far from her own life, and yet within sight.

When Harriet was a young woman, her father accepted a post in Cincinnati, Ohio, and moved the family there. Across the Ohio River lay the slave state of Kentucky. In Cincinnati, Harriet opened a Sunday school for African-American children, and in the confines of her own household heard searing stories about life in bondage from her cook, an ex-slave named Eliza Buck. Buck described how she would steal away at night to care for other slaves who had been "lacerated by the whip." She also admitted to Harriet that her children had been fathered by her Kentucky slave master—a shocking revelation for a clergyman's daughter and wife. (Harriet had since married Calvin Stowe, a teacher in

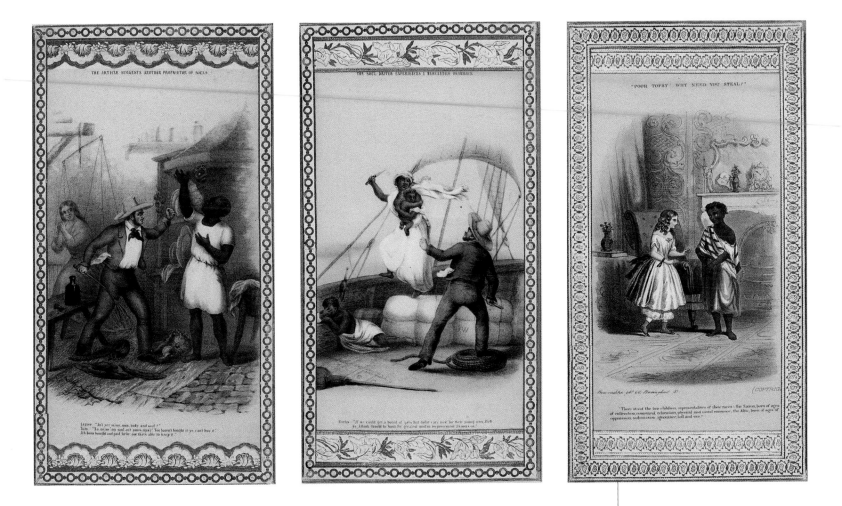

her father's theological seminary.) "You know, Mrs. Stowe," the cook told her employer, "slave women cannot help themselves."

Harriet spent 18 years in Cincinnati absorbing such stories and even witnessing her own scenes of horror—on one occasion she saw an enslaved couple being separated from one another by a slave trader. According to family lore, another incident hit even closer to home. When word reached the Stowe household that a servant working for them was in danger of being seized and forced back into slavery in Kentucky, Harriet's husband and brother Henry armed themselves and whisked away the black woman, delivering her to a stop on the Underground Railroad.

A personal tragedy in Cincinnati broadened Stowe's perspective on human suffering. She stood by helplessly as her sixth child, an 18-month-old boy named Charley, died of cholera. She was overcome with grief, and it became a transforming event in her life and work. "It was at his dying bed, and at his grave," she would later write, "that I learnt what a poor slave mother may feel when her child is torn away from her."

Such a notion—that an enslaved mother would share the same intense feeling for her child as a white mother would—was practically unthinkable at the time. The genius of Stowe's *Uncle Tom's Cabin,* and the reason it struck such a deep chord in the

American psyche, was its emotional and human portrayal of slaves. Despite the stereotypes that she fell into in her characterizations (the heroic, yet servile, Uncle Tom, for instance), Stowe made the reader feel the brutality of slavery and its effect on individuals. Heretofore, the "peculiar institution" (particularly in the North) had been an abstract moral issue argued over in drawing rooms; *Uncle Tom's Cabin* made slavery come alive. The book vividly detailed the profoundly corrupt nature of the system and its cost in human terms.

Initially serialized in an abolitionist paper, *Uncle Tom's Cabin* came out in two volumes in 1852. The publisher had limited expectations: He warned Stowe that the novel was too long and the subject matter too unappealing. Given the option of a 50-50 split of the profits (or losses) or a 10 percent royalty on each book sold, Stowe opted for the safer 10 percent. The book was an overnight sensation. Within a week of publication 10,000 copies had been sold, within a year over 300,000 in the United States alone. Sales abroad were even more astounding. In the course of a year, a million and a half copies were sold in England, where Stowe received no royalties at all because she did not have copyright protection there.

Harriet, her husband, and several other family members sailed for England; the author was hailed as a heroine everywhere she went. An English duchess presented Stowe with a bracelet shaped in the form of slave shackles. One of the links was engraved with the date of the abolition of slavery in the British colonies; another link was left blank, to be filled in with the date marking the end of American slavery. "The memorial you placed on my wrist will ever be dear to me— mournfully dear," Stowe later wrote to her hostess. "I may not live to have engraved there the glorious date of emancipation in America, but my *children will* if I do not."

The southern press rose up to denounce *Uncle Tom's Cabin* and its author. A reviewer for the *Southern Quarterly Review* dismissed the book as "the loathsome rakings of a foul fancy." Southerners seethed, and they made their fury known with death threats. One small package arrived with revolting contents—an ear that had been hacked off the head of a slave.

Stowe stood her ground and answered her critics. She weathered the storm of protest and became a national icon. During the Civil War the tiny author (she was less than five

75 Young Women

From 15 to 35 Years of Age,

WANTED TO WORK IN THE

COTTON MILLS!

IN LOWELL AND CHICOPEE, MASS.

I am authorized by the Agents of said Mills to make the following proposition to persons suitable for their work, viz:—They will be paid $1.00 per week, and board, for the first month. It is presumed they will then be able to go to work at job prices. They will be considered as engaged for one year, cases of sickness excepted. I will pay the expenses of those who have not the means to pay for themselves, and the girls will pay it to the Company by their first labor. All that remain in the employ of the Company eighteen months will have the amount of their expenses to the Mills refunded to them. They will be properly cared for in sickness. It is hoped that none will go except those whose circumstances will admit of their staying at least one year. None but active and healthy girls will be engaged for this work, as it would not be advisable for either the girls or the Company.

I shall be at the Howard Hotel, Burlington, on Monday, July 25th; at Farnham's, St. Albans, Tuesday forenoon, 26th, at Keyes's, Swanton, in the afternoon; at the Massachusetts' House, Rouses Point, on Wednesday, the 27th, to engage girls,—such as would like a place in the Mills would do well to improve the present opportunity, as new hands will not be wanted late in the season. I shall start with my Company, for the Mills, on Friday morning, the 29th inst., from Rouses Point, at 6 o'clock. Such as do not have an opportunity to see me at the above places, can take the cars and go with me the same as though I had engaged them.

I will be responsible for the safety of all baggage that is marked in care of I. M. BOYNTON, and delivered to my charge.

I. M. BOYNTON,

Agent for Procuring Help for the Mills.

A New England textile mill agent advertises for "active and healthy girls" like the ones opposite, who hold the tools of their trade—shuttles for weaving thread on looms. In 1834 Lowell visitor Davy Crockett thought the women looked as if they were "coming from a quilting frolic." It was no frolic; the work was grueling, and conditions and pay worsened over time.

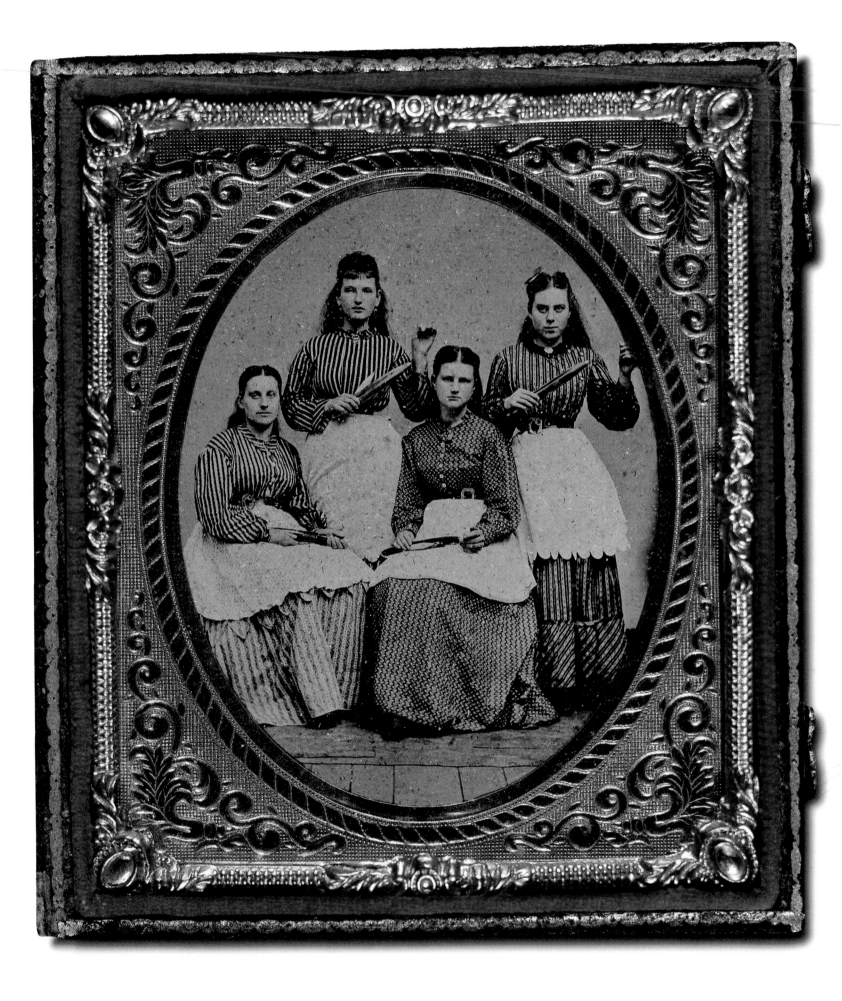

feet tall) met with the lanky Abraham Lincoln in the White House. "So you're the little woman who wrote the book that started this great war!" is how he reputedly greeted her. On the day that the Emancipation Proclamation took effect, Harriet Beecher Stowe was attending a concert in Boston. The momentous event was announced on stage, and someone shouted that the famous author was present. As one, the audience rose and cheered. Harriet Beecher Stowe stood and bowed, accepting their plaudits.

The women who toiled in the early textile mills of New England never achieved the individual fame that Harriet Beecher Stowe did. Yet they created their own quiet revolution—and the beginnings of an effective labor movement in the United States. In 1813 Francis Cabot Lowell, scion of an old-line New England family, decided to copy the new power-loom technology then in use in Britain that enabled both the spinning and weaving of textiles to take place under one roof. He established the first completely power-driven integrated mill in the nation; raw cotton could now be turned into finished cloth in a single location. Lowell's pioneering cotton factory was in Waltham, Massachusetts. It was a huge success, and similar factories began to sprout up on rivers across New England. Lowell and other mill owners brilliantly tapped into a new source of labor—unmarried New England farm girls (who were known as "spinsters" because they would often spin yarn in their own households). Such women could be hired for half or even a third of what it would cost to hire men; for the women it opened a great new window of opportunity. Hitherto, options for them outside the family farm were limited. Teaching (and those jobs were scarce indeed for women), sewing, and working as a servant were alternatives—but the factory paid far better than any of those jobs. The mills offered an escape. "In almost every New England home [was] an unmarried woman, sitting solitary, sometimes welcome, more often unwelcome.... From a condition of almost pauperism, they could earn money and spend it as they pleased," one female veteran of the mills wrote. "For the first time in this country woman's labor had a money value."

In an effort to recruit young women, and to placate parents who worried that their daughters might lose their virtue and even their marriageability, factory owners took on a paternalistic role. They built boardinghouses for workers that were overseen by nononsense matrons. Curfews were strictly enforced, as were rules forbidding smoking and requiring Sunday attendance at church. Mill owners fostered the idea that respectable young women could work in their factories for several years as "an honorable mode of securing a dower"; at that point the "mill girls" would marry and leave the factory, making way for a fresh wave of young workers.

The combination of respectability and income proved irresistible; white New England women flocked to the factory towns. Lowell, Massachusetts, became the nation's first planned—and largest—textile manufacturing center. Located at the confluence of the Concord and Merrimack Rivers, it grew from a tiny hamlet of 200 in 1820 to over 25,000 in 1845. More than 30 separate mills run by different corporations lined Lowell's riverbanks and canals, and the vast majority of the labor force was female.

After a long day's work, many women took advantage of educational opportunities that mill towns provided; in fact, that is what drew some workers in the first place. Mill hand Lucy Larcom recalled that "many of us were resolutely bent upon obtaining a better education." Corporate money in Lowell helped fund both a library and a Lyceum, where workers could take in 25 lectures per season for 50 cents—a bargain, especially considering the roster of speakers, which included the likes of Henry David Thoreau, Ralph Waldo Emerson, Horace Greeley, and John Quincy Adams. Young women banded together into "improvement circles" and took up pen, writing poems, essays, novels, even translations from Latin. Literary magazines sprang up in mill towns, the most famous publication being the *Lowell Offering*. Charles Dickens, chronicler of the miseries of industrialism in Britain, was impressed by the energetic women tending the looms in Lowell and their quest for self-improvement. Visiting the mill town in 1841, the author was amazed to find that one group of women had pooled their resources to buy a piano for their boardinghouse. He left with a stack of issues of the *Lowell Offering*.

But for all the cultural trimmings and prim moral tone, life in Lowell and other mill towns was grim. Work was long, hard, and dangerous—and grew ever more so over the years. A system of bells regulated the grueling daily schedule, from the 4:30 a.m. wake-up call to the end of the work day at 6:30 p.m. (the fall and winter schedule was pushed back half an hour). Work often began and ended in the dark, and mill hands depended on the light shed from oil lamps know as "petticoat lamps" fastened to the looms. They worked six days a week, in rooms with little or no ventilation—some windows were reportedly nailed shut to keep the humidity in and prevent brittle threads from snapping. The air was thick with cotton lint, which clung to the walls, as well as to the hair and lungs of the young women. The noise was earsplitting. One woman wrote that

"So you're the little woman who wrote the book that started this great war!"

ABRAHAM LINCOLN ON MEETING
HARRIET BEECHER STOWE

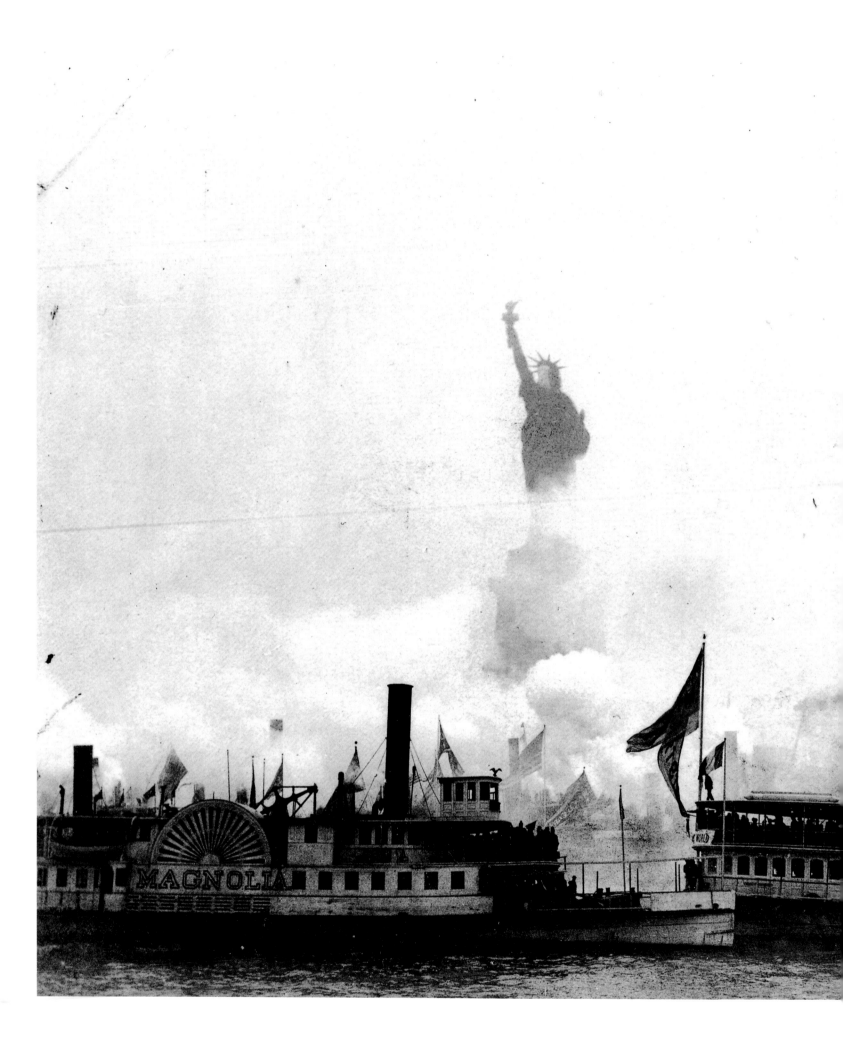

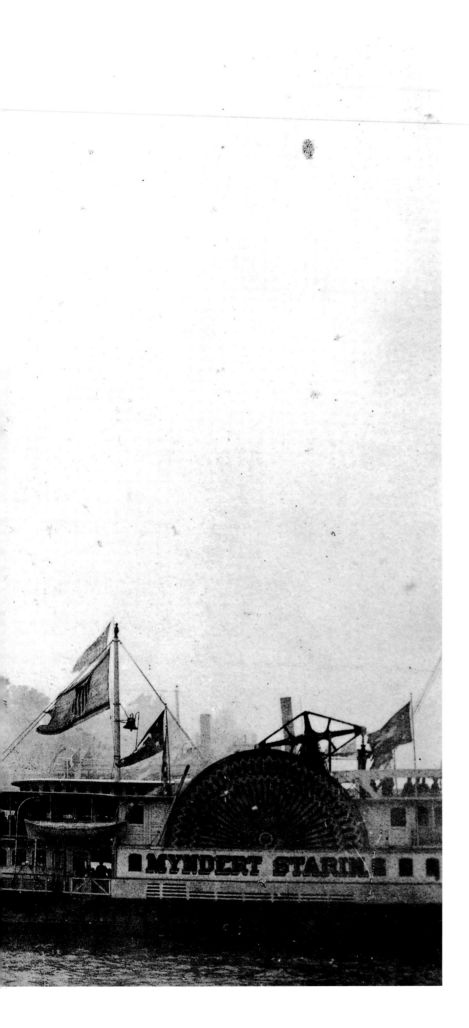

The New Colossus.

Not like the brazen giant of Greek fame,
With conquering limbs astride from land to land;
Here at our sea-washed, sunset-gates shall stand
A mighty woman with a torch, whose flame
Is the imprisoned lightning, and her name
Mother of Exiles. From her beacon-hand
Glows world-wide welcome, her mild eyes
 command
The air-bridged harbor that twin-cities frame.

"Keep, ancient lands, your storied pomp!" cries she
With silent lips. "Give me your tired, your poor,
Your huddled masses yearning to breathe free,
The wretched refuse of your teeming shore,
Send these, the homeless, tempest-tost to me,
I lift my lamp beside the golden door!"

Emma Lazarus.

November 2nd 1883.

Poet Emma Lazarus gave full voice to the promise of America. "Give me your tired, your poor, Your Huddled masses yearning to breathe free," she wrote in a sonnet composed to help raise money for the Statue of Liberty, shown at its 1886 unveiling (left).

223

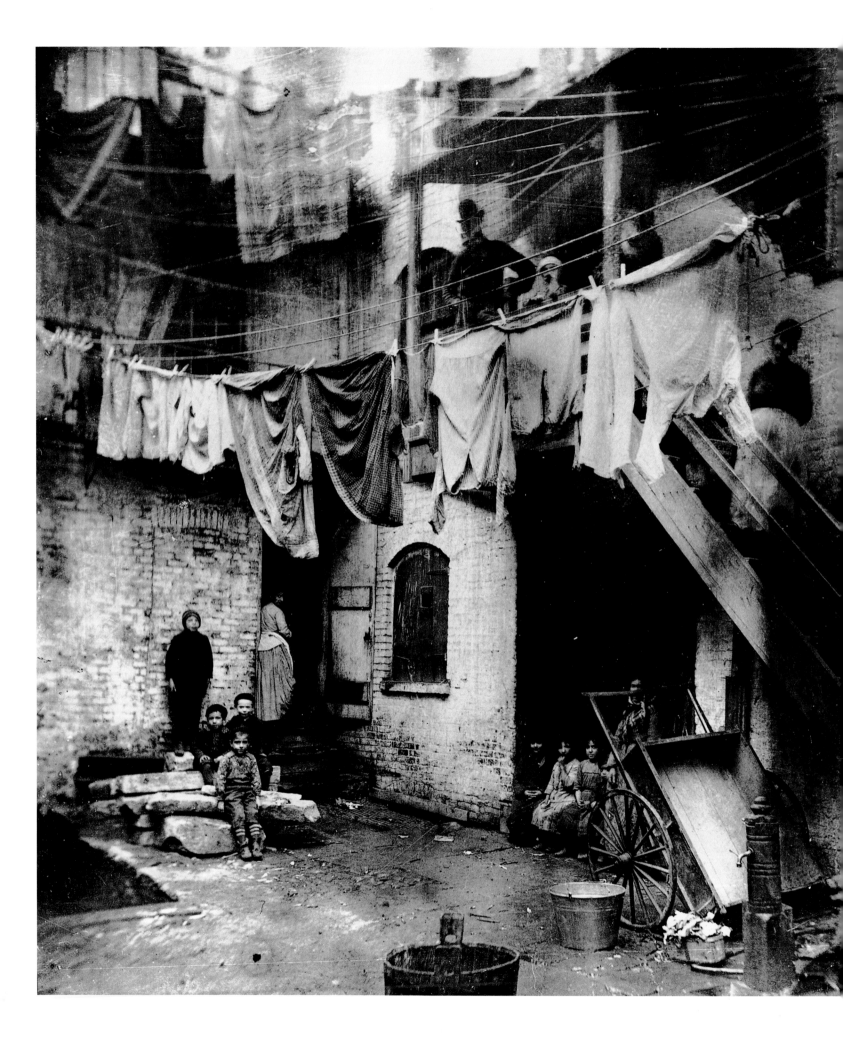

at night she still heard the mill pounding in her head, like the sound of "crickets, frogs, and Jew-harps, all mingled together in a strange discord."

In 1836 one overcrowded weaving room had 55 operators tending 110 looms; they had so little room to maneuver that their hair and clothing frequently got caught in the machinery. Flying shuttles also posed a serious threat to workers—that is, until a woman found a solution. When she was 12 years old, factory worker Margaret Knight of Springfield, Massachusetts, had seen a shuttle fly loose and injure a man; years later she invented an emergency stopping device.

A two-tiered salary system prevailed in the mills. Male workers, generally overseers and mechanics, earned substantially more than women. In addition, men were paid a flat weekly salary. Women's pay was based on piecework; the more they produced, the more they earned. This led to unorthodox and potentially dangerous timesaving techniques. To rethread the shuttle eye quickly, women sucked the thread through with their mouths. A perfect way to spread tuberculosis and other diseases, this method became known as the "kiss of death." Women workers earned between $2.50 and $5.50 per week; management would then deduct $1.25 to cover room and board.

As time went on and textile profits declined, owners stepped up the work pace—and reduced wages at the same time. By the late 1830s, 50 or 60 women might be crowded into one boardinghouse, 10 or 12 to a room, 2 to a bed; at the same time, boarding charges rose. The women "turned out," or went on strike, in 1834 and again in 1836. Over 1,500 workers paraded in the streets in 1836, singing:

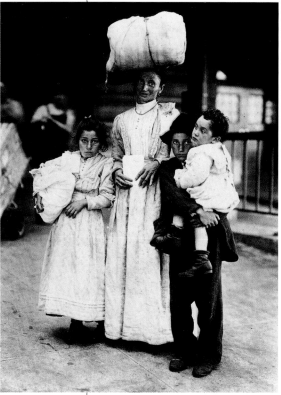

At Ellis Island the faces of an Italian mother and her children register both excitement and fear. Many immigrants ended up in unsanitary and overcrowded slum housing, such as this New York City tenement (opposite) photographed in 1888.

> *Oh! isn't it a pity, such a pretty girl as I—*
> *Should be sent to the factory to pine away and die?*
> *Oh! I cannot be a slave,*
> *I will not be a slave,*
> *For I'm so fond of liberty*
> *That I cannot be a slave.*

Though the strikes themselves were not particularly effective, the women mill workers were newly politicized and bound together by their cause. "As our fathers have resisted unto blood the lordly avarice of the British ministry, so we, their daughters, never will wear the yoke which has been prepared for us," militant factory women declared in 1836. The Factory Girls Association was formed to coordinate the Lowell strike that year, and its membership eventually reached 2,500. Protests continued in the 1840s, and in 1845 mill worker Sarah Bagley organized the Lowell Female Labor Reform Association to demand a ten-hour work day. Bagley gathered over 2,000 signatures on a petition and testified before the Massachusetts Legislature.

Simple farm girls turned mill hands were lifting their voices in mass protests. Management was dumbstruck—and also outraged. In one year alone, a Lowell mill fired 28 women for a variety of reasons, among them "misconduct," "impudence," and "mutiny." These women were willing to break conventional roles in an effort to bring about social change. They acted courageously and placed their own well-being in jeopardy for the greater good. In the process, these pioneering activists helped sow the seeds for labor reform that would come decades late.

Working conditions in the late 19th century continued to deteriorate as factory owners took advantage of a new and plentiful supply of cheap labor. Immigration increased steadily from the 1840s onward; by the turn of the 20th century it had become a tidal wave—from 1880 to 1920 alone, 20 million foreigners would arrive on American soil. Many came expecting instant riches, but the reality was quite different. "I came to America because I heard the streets were paved with gold," was one oft-told Italian tale. "When I got here, I found...they weren't paved at all; I was expected to pave them."

The vast majority of the newcomers were peasants accustomed to rural life; in the United States most of them followed work opportunities and relatives to teeming urban areas. The scale and complexion of the landscape completely overwhelmed the country folk—buildings cheek by jowl for as far as the eye could see, screeching trolleys and overhead railways, an endless sea of faces, and a cacophony of indistinguishable languages. "Going to America then was almost like going to the moon," said one 1906 Russian-Jewish immigrant named Goldie Mabovitch (better known years later as Golda Meir, the formidable Israeli leader). It was said that "the crush and the stench were enough to suffocate one." The new arrivals crowded into narrow tenement buildings overlooking alley-

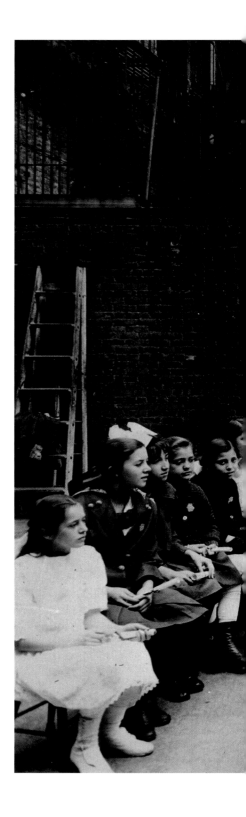

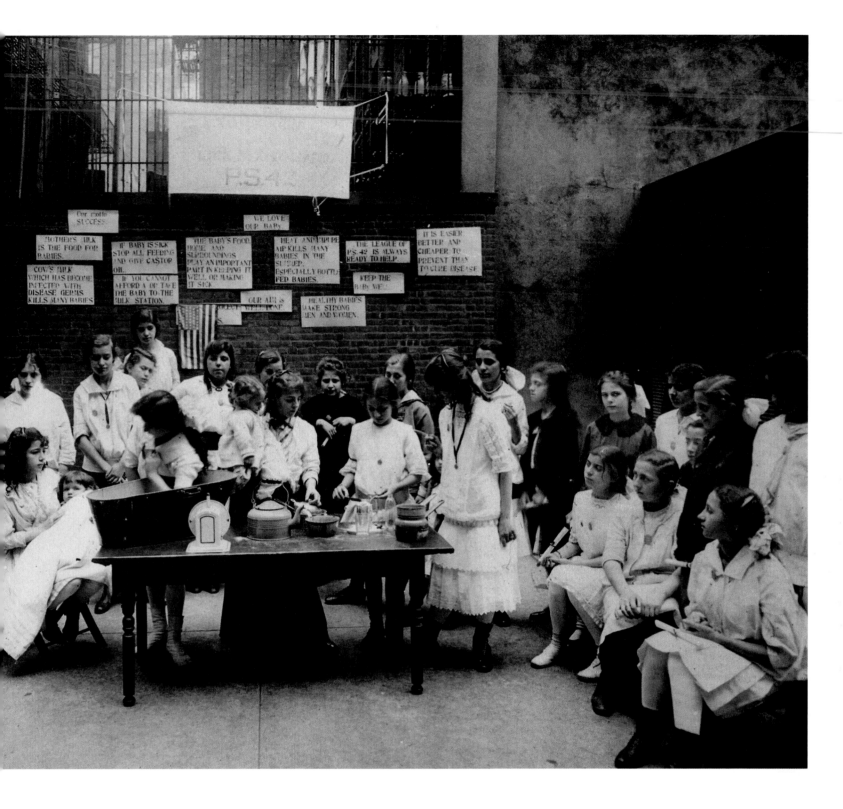

Around the turn of the 20th century, young New York City school girls learn how to care for babies in a public health class sponsored by the Department of Health. One sign on the brick wall behind them reads, "HEAT AND IMPURE AIR KILLS MANY BABIES IN THE SUMMER." Summer heat could turn deadly in poorly ventilated buildings—in 1896 some 420 tenement dwellers died in New York during an eight-day heat wave.

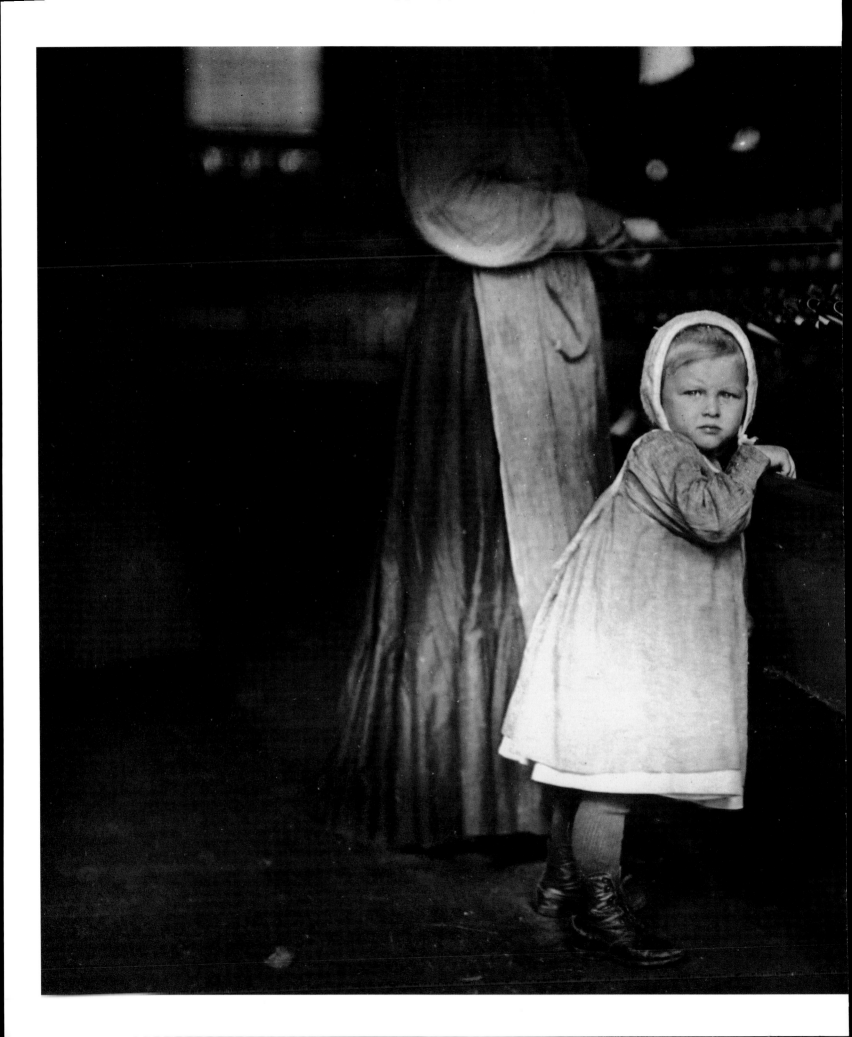

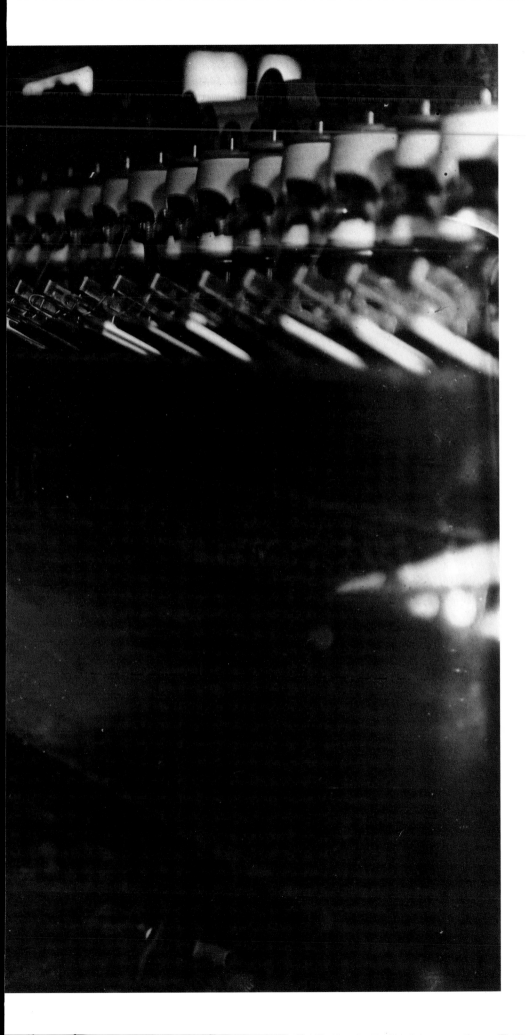

Three-year-old Ivey Mill, daughter of the overseer, spends her day in a North Carolina textile factory in 1908. Children not much older than she would work a 12-hour day in such factories and earn ten cents—the price of a loaf of bread. Girls generally tended the yarn as it spun furiously. "The tangles were always worst when I was tiredest," one child explained while working a night shift. Women helped lead the fight against child labor.

ways or air shafts. Ventilation was poor and daylight scarce—it was "a place so dark it seemed as if there weren't no sky" according to one young resident. Into the 1870s and 1880s indoor plumbing was extremely rare in these poor districts. Entire neighborhoods sometimes had to share one streetside water pump. Out of roughly 4,000 New York City tenements in the 1890s, only 50 had private toilets; even fewer could boast bathtubs. Infectious diseases spread through the slums like "the track of a tornado through a forest," according to an observer. Starvation claimed other lives—especially those of children. In one particularly poor immigrant district in Chicago, three out of every five babies died before reaching their first birthday.

Survival demanded that as many family members as possible earn money—including women and children. Paid by the number of pieces they produced, entire families rolled cigars, made artificial flowers and hat trimmings, and stitched clothing in cramped apartments. By 1900 the thriving garment industry in New York spawned thousands of sweatshops in high-rise factories and tenements, and most of the workers were women. Conditions were appalling. One young woman described her shop in the *New York Evening Journal* of November 28, 1909:

> *Regular work pays about $6 a week and the girls have to be at their machines at 7 o'clock in the morning and they stay at them until 8 o'clock at night, with just one-half hour for lunch....There is just one row of machines that the daylight ever gets to—that is the front row, nearest the window. The girls at all the other rows...work by gaslight, by day as well as by night.... The bosses in the shop are hardly what you would call educated men, and the girls to them are part of the machines they are running. They yell at the girls and "call them down"....The shops are unsanitary— that's the word that is generally used, but there ought to be a worse one.*

Women who toiled in these shops could barely make a living wage. They were subjected to arbitrary fines for laughing, talking, singing, for imperfect stitching, or for inadvertently soiling pieces of fabric with machine oil. Owners charged garment workers for everything they used, including the sewing machines, needles, electricity, thread, and the water they drank.

In the first few decades of the 20th century, women began to gravitate toward labor unions. Leaders such as Rose Schneiderman, who created the first women's local within the United Hat and Cap Makers Union, emerged to fight for basic rights. On one occasion Schneiderman confronted an owner who enjoyed pinching all of the women in his shop. He responded, "Why Miss Schneiderman, these girls are like my children." The woman who had filed the complaint shot back, "We'd rather be orphans."

Management naturally detested even the idea of unions in their shops, and did all they could to discourage membership. In 1909, the Triangle Shirtwaist Company in New York, one of the city's largest producers of women's blouses, fired employees suspected of promoting unionization. Triangle workers walked off the job in protest and were joined by garment workers from another shop. Management stood firm, hiring prostitutes to taunt the strikers and thugs to beat them. A citywide meeting of shirtwaist workers was called in November 1909. Speeches dragged on for several hours, seemingly leading nowhere, until a young woman worker who looked to be in her teens asked for the floor. Clara Lemlich, a protest veteran whose ribs had been broken by police while on a picket line, came to the platform. "I am a working girl, and one of those who are on strike against intolerable conditions," she told the audience. "I am tired of listening to speakers who talk in general terms. What we are here for is to decide whether or not we shall strike. I offer a resolution that a general strike be declared—now!" The crowd roared its approval.

Between 20,000 and 30,000 garment workers—75 percent of them women—joined the strike. "From every waist-making factory in New York and Brooklyn, the girls poured forth," wrote a contemporary. "It was like a mighty army rising in the night, and demanding to be heard." Overnight, union membership exploded. Women took to the picket lines en masse. Police clubbed hundreds of them and dragged them off to jail. The law came down on the side of the owners, one judge lecturing a striker: "You are on strike against God and Nature, whose prime law it is that man shall earn his bread in the sweat of his brow. You are on strike against God." From across the Atlantic, George Bernard Shaw cabled: "Delightful. Medieval America always in intimate personal confidence of the Almighty."

Women from across all social classes were horrified by the harsh treatment accorded the strikers, and impressed by their courage. Mrs. Oliver Hazard Perry Belmont (the former Alva Vanderbilt), grande dame of the Gilded Age, helped secure bond money for the arrested protesters, putting up a mansion as security. Muckraking journalist Ida Tar-

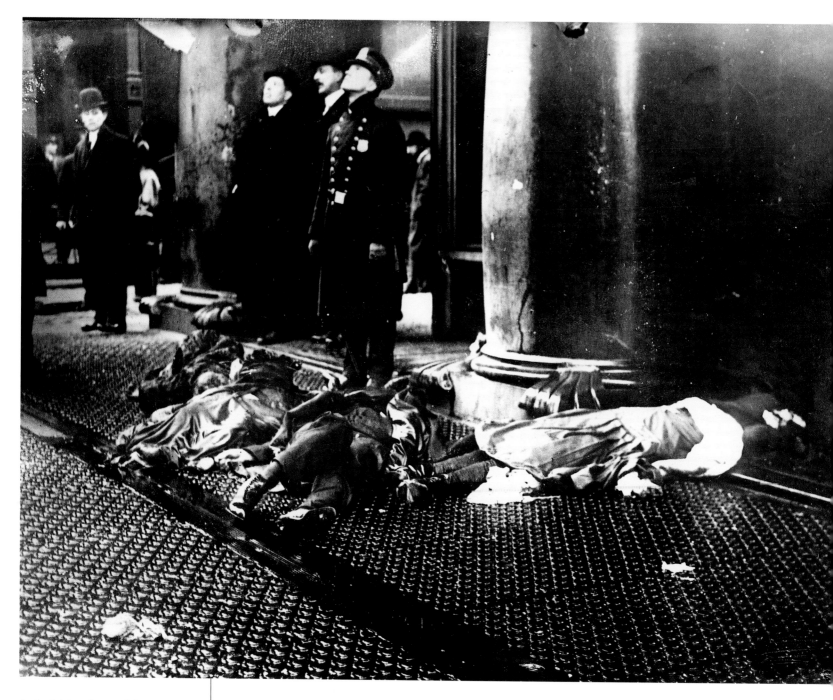

As firefighters (opposite) desperately try to control the Triangle Shirtwaist fire in 1911, young women garment workers, trapped in flames on the top three floors, jump out the windows. Bystanders watch helplessly as over 50 workers leaped to their deaths.

bell vehemently objected how the strikers were being treated.

For 13 cold weeks during the winter of 1909-1910, the shirtwaist makers—primarily young women between the ages of 16 and 25, many of them mothers—held out. During that time an estimated 1,250 babies were born to strikers or strikers' wives. A union official recalled visiting an Italian mother with a newborn and three other hungry children. "It is not only bread we give our children," said the mother. "We live by freedom, and I will fight till I die to give it to my children."

In February 1910 the strike ended. Though a new era had emerged—women were now involved in the labor movement on a massive scale—the strikers had won few concessions. The owners showed their utter disregard for the women workers by doing little to change the intolerable conditions in the factories. That contempt for female lives led to the notorious disaster—really an industrial mass murder—known as the Triangle Shirtwaist fire.

On Saturday, March 25, 1911, barely a year after the great strike, 500 employees at the shirtwaist factory were working overtime to fill back orders. Located on the top three floors of a ten-story loft building just off Washington Square in Manhattan, the factory produced an array of shirtwaists: pleated, ruffled, or fashionably embroidered blouses. The clatter of the machines came to an abrupt end at 4:30 p.m., and the young Jewish and Italian immigrant women began to leave the sewing room. What happened next no one knows for sure. The New York City Fire Chief would later suggest that a cigarette spark had ignited the fire. One man saw the fire in a rag bin; he threw buckets of water onto it "but it was like there was kerosene in the water; it just seemed to spread it." The place was full of flammable material: bins overflowing with rags, baskets piled high with finished waists, floors soaked in machine oil, the air and walls covered with cotton lint. The factory just erupted in flames. The building's hallway hose would not work.

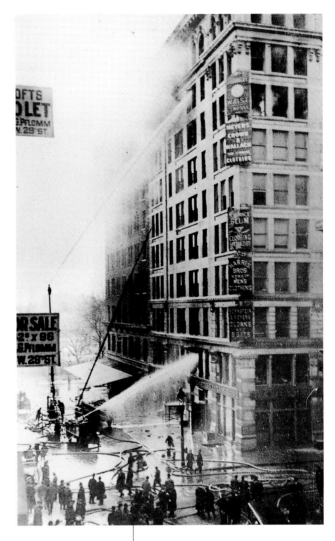

Panic ensued. Fire blocked the freight elevator on the eighth floor. The stairwells on the eighth and ninth floors were locked. Some said it was to prevent workers from pilfering material; others said the locked doors were intended to keep workers at their machines in case of a sudden strike. Whatever the reason, the effect was disastrous. The workers were trapped with flames licking all around them. There was only one fire escape—an 18-inch-wide stairway that led to an interior courtyard that soon filled with smoke and flames. Fewer than 20 made their way to safety on the lone escape ladder.

The fire department arrived three minutes after the alarm, but already it was too late. Before they could even hook up the hoses, a nightmarish scene unfolded. The workers, mostly young women, some still girls, began leaping to their deaths. According to the fire chief, "People were jumping from the windows so fast that before we could turn the water on our line was buried under bodies and we had to lift them off before we could get to work." The ladders were too short to reach the factory floors; the longest one reached only to the sixth floor. The victims kept jumping. Three young girls jumped together, as if there were safety in numbers. A fire captain estimated that each person hit the pavement with the force of 11,000 pounds.

A reporter who happened upon the scene gave a chilling eyewitness account:

I was walking through Washington Square when a puff of smoke issuing from the factory building caught my eye. I reached the building before the alarm was sounded. I saw every feature of the tragedy visible from outside the building. I learned a new sound—a more horrible sound than description can picture. It was the thud of a speeding, living body on a stone sidewalk. Thud—dead, thud—dead, thud—dead, thud—dead. Sixty-two thud—deads. I call them that, because the sound and the thought of death came to me each time, at the same instant. There was plenty of chance to watch them as they came down. The height was eighty feet...

The floods of water from the firemen's hose that ran into the gutter were actually stained red with blood. I looked upon the heap of dead bodies and I remembered these girls were the shirtwaist makers. I remembered their great strike of last year in which these same girls had demanded more sanitary conditions and more safety precautions in the shops. These dead bodies were the answer.

The final toll was staggering: around 150 dead, the vast majority of them women. Mass protests broke out in neighborhoods where the shirtwaist workers had lived.

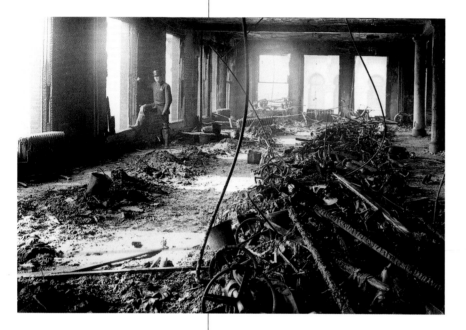

In the wake of the Triangle Shirtwaist fire, the ruins of the factory were overshadowed by the sickening sight (opposite) of the dead women lined up in coffins for identification. Around 150 died in the disastrous fire, most of them young women immigrants. The city buried the unclaimed bodies in seven coffins; an eighth "contained the dismembered fragments picked up...by the police." The tragedy helped spur labor reform.

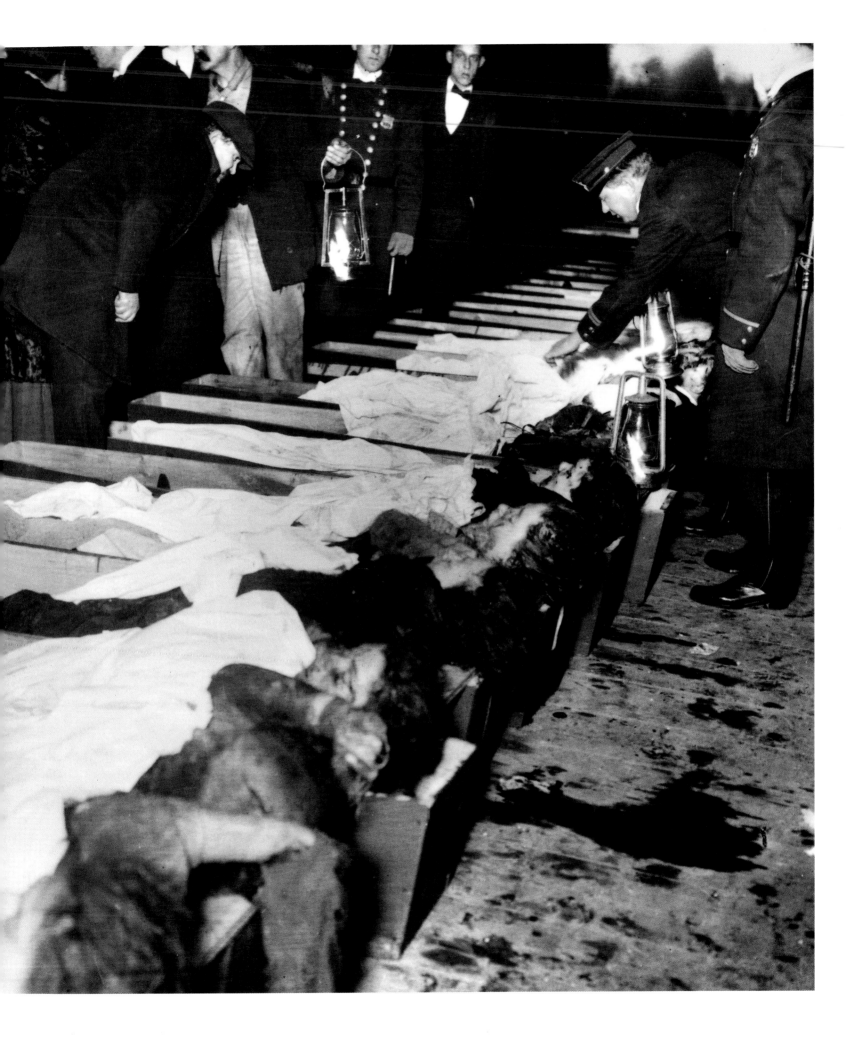

Uptown at the Metropolitan Opera House, philanthropists as well as union members gathered for a memorial service. Labor leader Rose Schneiderman gave an impassioned address. Three days later a heartrending funeral service took place. Eighty thousand workers marched for four hours through the streets of New York in a drenching rain— "the skies wept," in the words of a New York *World* reporter. Over 250,000 silent spectators lined the sidewalks. When the marchers came within sight of the building where the Triangle factory had been, a reporter wrote that "the women gave vent to their sorrow. It was a long-drawn-out, heart-piercing cry, the mingling of thousands of voices, a sort of human thunder in the elemental storm—a cry that was perhaps the most impressive expression of human grief ever heard in this city."

In the wake of the tragedy, the Triangle Shirtwaist employers were charged with manslaughter and acquitted; one partner was fined $20. An outraged journalist reported that they "offered to pay one week's wages to the families of the dead girls—as though it were summer and they are giving them a vacation!" Three days after the fire, the company advertised in trade papers that they had reopened for business in a new location. When city officials quickly inspected the place, they discovered that the manufacturing firm had not learned its lesson: Two rows of sewing machines blocked the exit to the only fire escape.

The public outcry over the fire helped transform labor conditions throughout the country. The New York State Legislature appointed a Factory Investigating Commission that gathered testimony about workplace conditions; out of it came a new Industrial Code safeguarding workers. This code in turn became a model for other states.

Women's voices were raised throughout the country demanding reform of all kinds in the early decades of the 20th century. Ida Tarbell personally took on John D. Rockefeller's ruthless monopoly of the oil business in a remarkable series of articles that appeared in *McClure's* Magazine. Mother Jones, the Irish-born rabble-rouser who fought for 50 years for the rights of workers, organized the wives of striking miners to attack scabs with household weapons—brooms, mops, and dishpans. Enraged by what she encountered during a Pennsylvania textile strike in 1903—of the 75,000 workers, 10,000 were children, many not over the age of 10, many of whom were maimed and stoop shouldered—she decided to take action. A master of the flamboyant gesture—and of publicity—Mother Jones led a group of these children east with the intention of bringing them to Theodore Roosevelt's home in Oyster Bay, Long Island. "I thought that President Roosevelt might see these mill children and compare them with his own little ones who were spending the summer on the seashore." Roosevelt refused to greet the ragtag army of children, but the publicity helped push through child labor laws.

With the American entry into World War I in April 1917, women proved their patriotism—and their mettle. Thousands rushed to Europe to nurse the wounded, fry doughnuts for the troops, drive ambulances, and operate switchboards. On the homefront, women flocked to the factory work once the province of men only: They undertook jobs manufacturing explosives and steel; they worked in smelting plants and oil refineries. They became elevator operators, streetcar conductors, and postal workers. They made bandages, organized food drives, and sold Liberty Bonds. Women did all that and more for the war effort, yet they still did not have the vote.

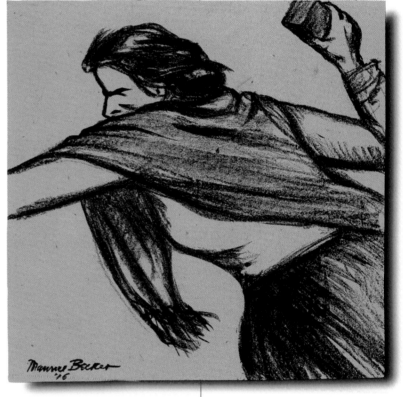

For some 70 years, suffragists had been fighting for the vote—with little success except in the western states. The movement had begun quietly; in fact, a key moment in its birth had been a teatime gathering of four women, including Lucretia Mott and the redoubtable Elizabeth Cady Stanton, who took the occasion to pour out "the torrent of my long-accumulating discontent, with such vehemence and indignation that I stirred myself as well as the rest of the party to do and dare anything." They decided then and there to hold a "public meeting for protest and discussion," and posted a single advertisement in the *Seneca County Courier* announcing a two-day long "convention to discuss the conditions and rights of Woman." It was to be held in a chapel in Seneca Falls, in rural upstate New York. On July 19, 1848, the appointed opening day, Stanton arrived only to find that the door was locked and that the key, as well as the minister (who had perhaps changed his mind about such a suspicious event), were nowhere to be found. Undeterred, those already assembled

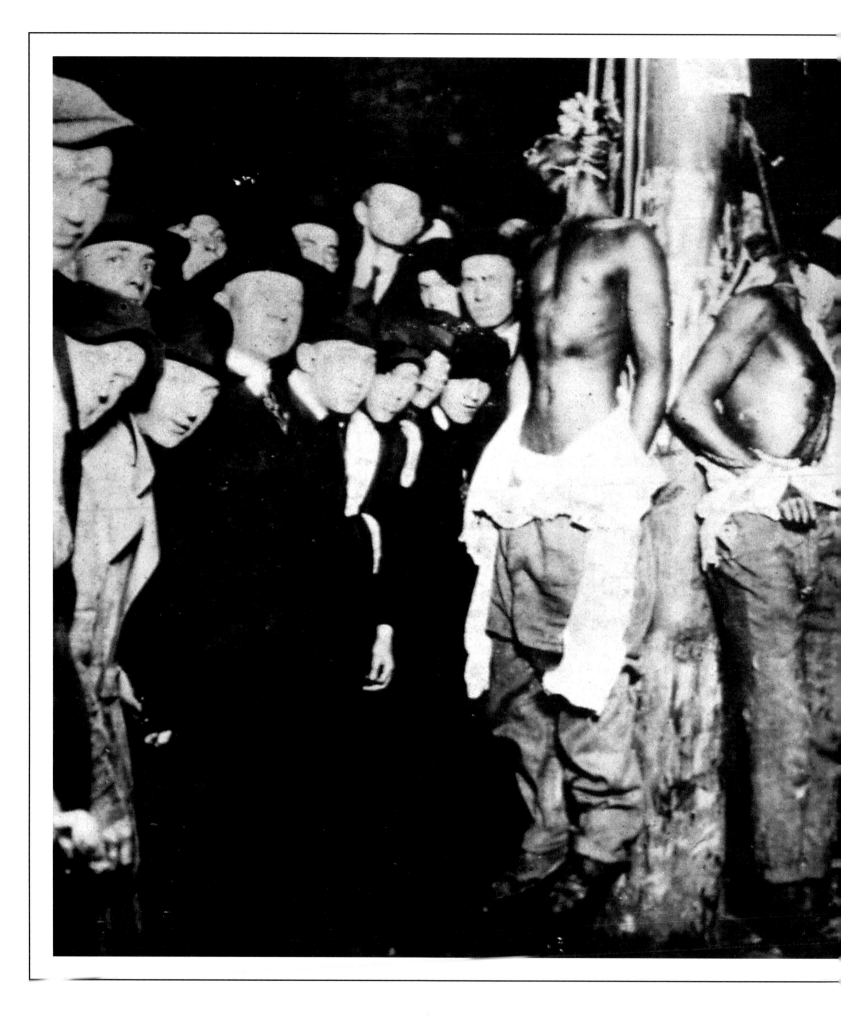

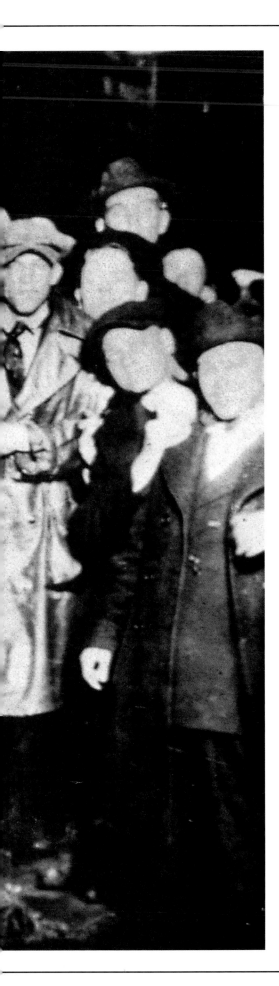

CRUSADING AGAINST TERROR

"I felt if I could take one lyncher with me, this would even up the score a little bit."

IDA WELLS-BARNETT

On a Sunday afternoon in Georgia, 1899, over 2,000 white men, women, and children gathered to witness the lynching of African-American Sam Hose, accused of murdering his boss and raping the white man's wife. No jury had convicted Hose, but the crowd's blood-lust was fierce: they stripped him, chained him to a tree, and cut off his fingers, ears, and genitals. Then they burned him alive and took souvenirs: bits of heart, liver, and bone.

One woman fought back. Ida Wells-Barnett organized an investigation of the charges. In the end, the white man's wife admitted that Hose had killed her husband in self-defense; she had not been touched. Sickening scenes like the one at left took place across the country in the late 19th and early 20th century. Waging a campaign against lynching, Wells-Barnett penned impassioned editorials for her newspaper in Memphis; a white mob destroyed the printing presses and set the building on fire. Ida's life was threatened. Undeterred, she packed a pistol and went to small southern towns to investigate lynchings, publishing a detailed account in 1895. Her crusade led to an international outcry against lynching, and helped lay the groundwork for the Civil Rights movement of the 1960s. ■

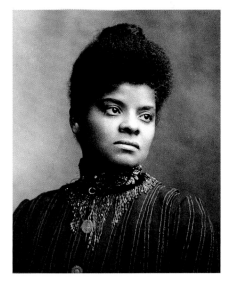

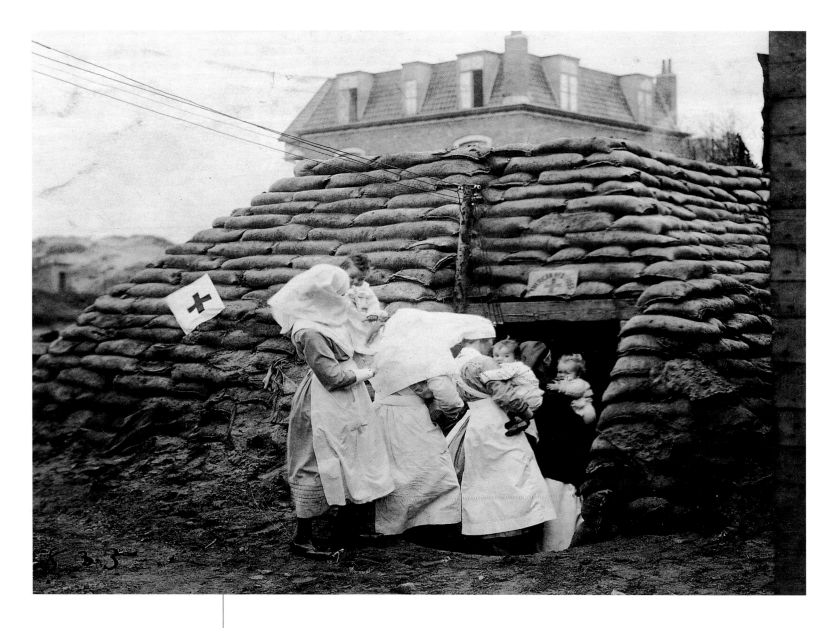

boosted Stanton's nephew through a window to unlock the door.

By the second day, over 300 men and women filled the chapel, including the abolitionist ex-slave, Frederick Douglass. Also present was Charlotte Woodward, a 19-year-old farm girl who dreamed of becoming a typesetter—a profession deemed unsuitable for a woman at that time. She and a half dozen friends had come by wagon and they listened intently to the speeches. Elizabeth Cady Stanton presented the "Declaration of Sentiments," a document based on the Declaration of Independence, which set forth a specific political agenda: Women should have the same rights as men to own property, to testify in a courtroom and bring lawsuits, and to have access to educational and professional opportunities. The crowd enthusiastically accepted all of those points; another one, however, was greeted with skepticism. The resolution calling for women to have the right to vote was passed—but by only a small margin. At the end of the convention 68 women and 32 men signed the declaration; among the signatories was Charlotte Woodward—the only woman among all those present at the convention who would live long enough to vote in a presidential election. That would not come until 1920.

Committed women of all colors and social classes struggled for generations to win the fight. Most of the early leaders were veterans of the abolitionist movement—including Sojourner Truth, Lucretia Mott, Lucy Stone, and the Grimké sisters, who were members of a prominent slaveholding family in Charleston. "I ask no favors for my sex," Sarah Grimké wrote eloquently in 1838. "All I ask of our brethren is that they will take their feet from off our necks and permit us to stand upright on the ground which God has deigned us to occupy." For her part, Lucy Stone took more direct action: She returned her 1858 tax bill, unpaid, to the local tax collector noting, "Women suffer taxation, and yet have no representation, which is not only unjust to one-half of the adult population, but is contrary to our theory of government." Unmoved, the tax collector auctioned off some of her possessions—including her daughter's cradle—to cover the bill.

A similar battle was fought in Glastonbury, Connecticut, in the 1870s—but this one was waged over the fate of seven Alderney cows. Julia and Abby Smith, elderly unmarried sisters, ran a farm and held strong political views. In November 1873, a tax collector appeared at their door to inform the sisters that the value of their property had risen, and so had their taxes. Oddly enough, property belonging to two local widows had also been reassessed at a higher level, while not a single male taxpayer had his land reappraised. The Smiths were outraged and took on the town fathers. It was not the amount of money involved, but the principle; "It increased our tax but little," Abby later wrote, "but what is unjust in least is unjust in much."

Seventy-seven-year-old Abby gave an impassioned address at a town meeting. It was met with complete silence; the meeting resumed as if she had never spoken. Julia and Abby made up their minds: They would pay no more taxes until they had some say in the town's finances. When the tax collector came back to their house, the sisters ignored his bill for $101.39 saying, "It really does not belong to us to assist in any way, having no voice in the matter." Instead of money he took seven of their cows and marched them off to auction. The sisters outbid all other rivals to buy back four of their seven cows. The story caught on nationally, and overnight the seven cows became symbols of resistance. Money and letters of support poured in from across the country. Lucy Stone came

Fleeing a German bombardment, Red Cross nurses hurriedly carry orphans into a sandbagged bunker in Belgium during World War I. Many American women rushed to join the Red Cross and other relief organizations during the war. When trainloads of Belgian orphans arrived dazed and filthy in Paris in 1915, the expatriate American writer Edith Wharton took charge of them, arranging for their care and a schoolhouse. Wharton was deeply enmeshed in the war effort—heading rescue committees, raising funds for refugees, and making a number of tours of the front. "The sadness of all things is beyond words," she wrote to a friend, "and hard work is the only escape from it."

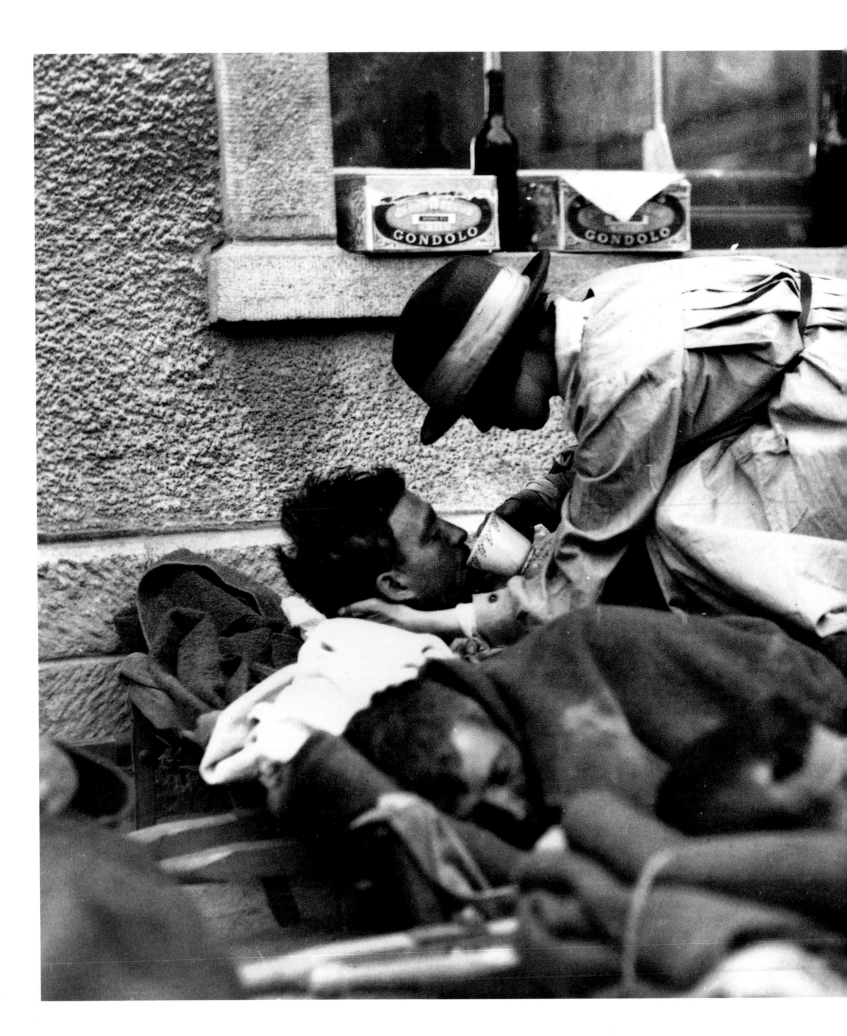

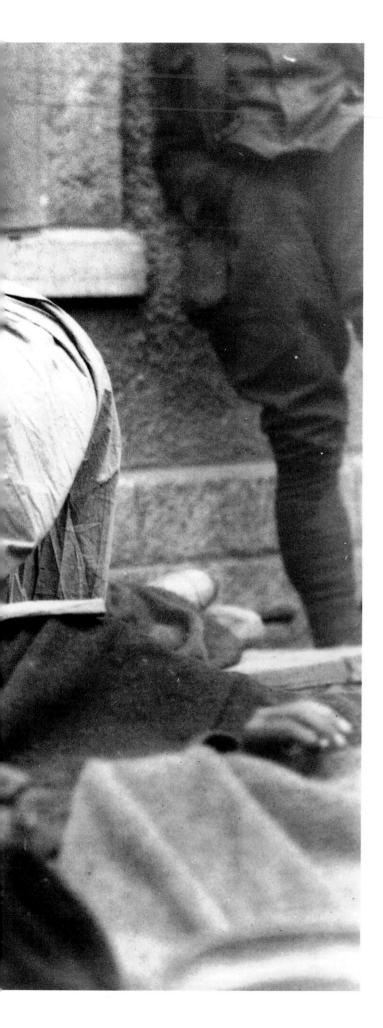

In a poignant scene, an American Red Cross worker gives water to a badly wounded British soldier on a railroad platform at Montmirail, France, in May 1918. Another American woman, a poet, even ventured to battlefield wastelands to read verse to shell-shocked troops. When memory failed her while she was reciting the famous poem "Trees," a young sergeant chimed in: It was the author of the poem, Joyce Kilmer. A month later he was killed in battle.

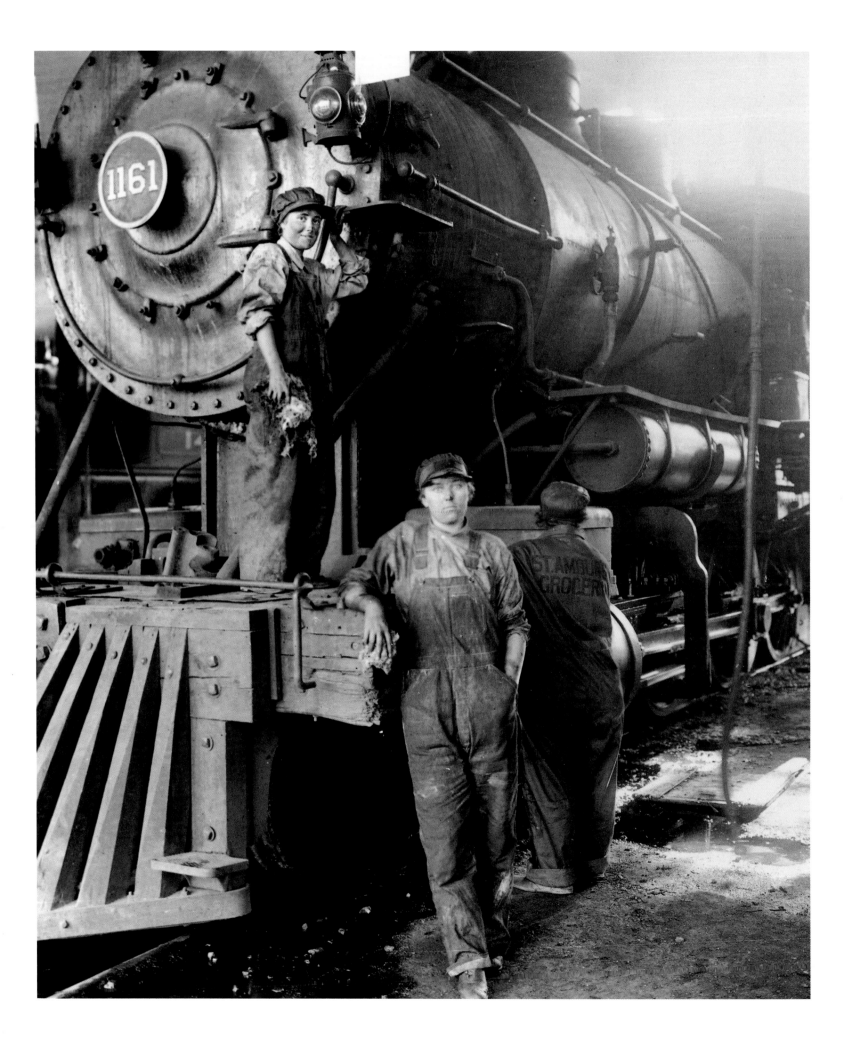

to visit and likened the Smiths' homestead to Bunker Hill. Abby, for her part, discovered that public speaking suited her; at a woman suffrage convention in Worcester she declared that the town officials "can't shut us up as they did our cows."

The tax collector, not to be outdone, announced the sale of 15 acres of their pastureland; at the last moment he changed the location where the auction was to take place. The sisters arrived too late; a greedy neighbor had just purchased their land for $78.35 (though its market value was nearly $2,000). Abby and Julia brought suit, and the appeals dragged on for several years. The skirmishing continued. In 1876 their cows were paraded two more times to auction. For every punch, the sisters counterpunched. By the end of 1876, the final court verdict came down in favor of the feisty sisters: Their property would not be touched. Victorious, the two sisters became sought-after speakers at suffrage events, and even went to Washington to appear at a Senate hearing and to see the President. (They decided to go without a suitcase. They wore all of their clothes at once, just changing the top layer depending on the occasion.)

In an effort to win the vote, women throughout the nation committed acts of civil disobedience, including the act of voting itself. Suffragist Susan B. Anthony cast her vote in Rochester, New York, in an 1872 national election. Her act created headlines; it also brought her an indictment. Tried in a federal court for voting while "being then and there a person of the female sex," Susan B. Anthony lost the case and was fined $100. She never paid it. Eight years later Elizabeth Cady Stanton went to the polls in New Jersey; She was rebuffed, but later wrote to her son, "We had great fun frightening and muddling these old Dutch inspectors. The whole town is agape with my act."

As the 20th century moved into its second decade, suffragists grew increasingly impatient with the indifference of national political leaders. When asked about his stance on woman suffrage, newly elected President Woodrow Wilson claimed that the issue had not come to his attention. That was hardly the case. On the eve of his inauguration in 1913, Wilson had arrived in Washington, D.C., anticipating a huge crowd of well-wishers. No one was there. When he inquired where the crowds were, he was told that they were all on Pennsylvania Avenue watching the woman suffrage march. The peaceful march turned into a near riot. Five thousand women had to fight through jeering mobs of men, abetted by the police who joined the crowd in hurling insults. Calvary troops had to be summoned from nearby Fort Myer to restore order. The march

Grease-stained and eager to do their part in the war effort, women (opposite) take over maintenance duties on the Great Northern Railway in Great Falls, Montana, around 1918. With a shortage of male workers, women filled the gap—working in railroad yards, munitions plants, steel mills, and other hitherto all-male preserves. Following pages: Handsome posters produced during World War I urged women to raise and can food in order to "Sow the seeds of Victory!" And artist Paul Honoré created a stirring tribute to "The Spirit of Women-Power" in the homefront battle to win the war.

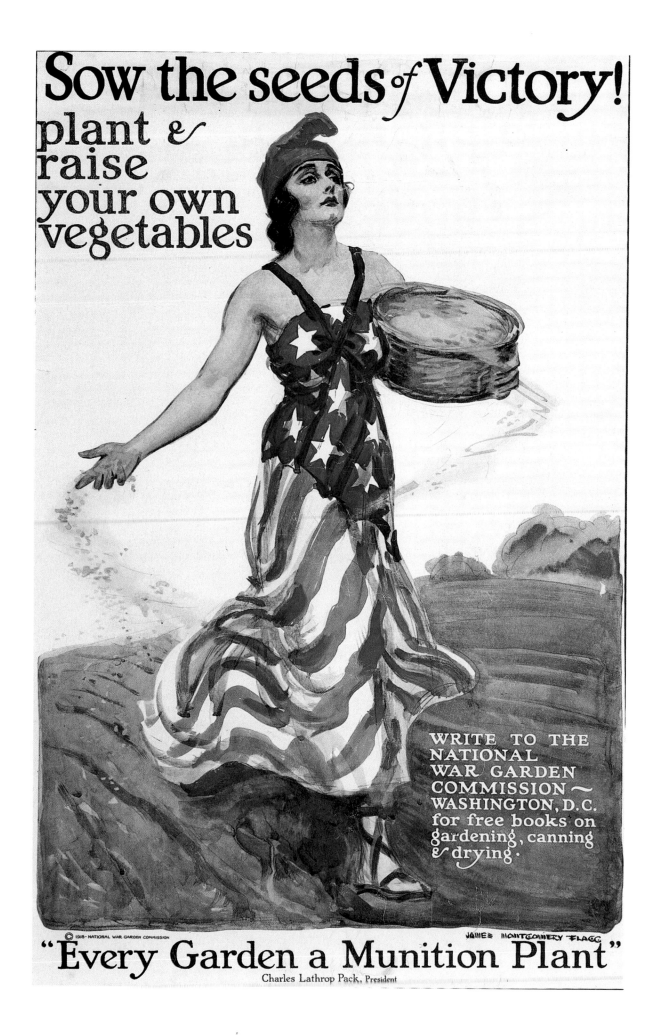

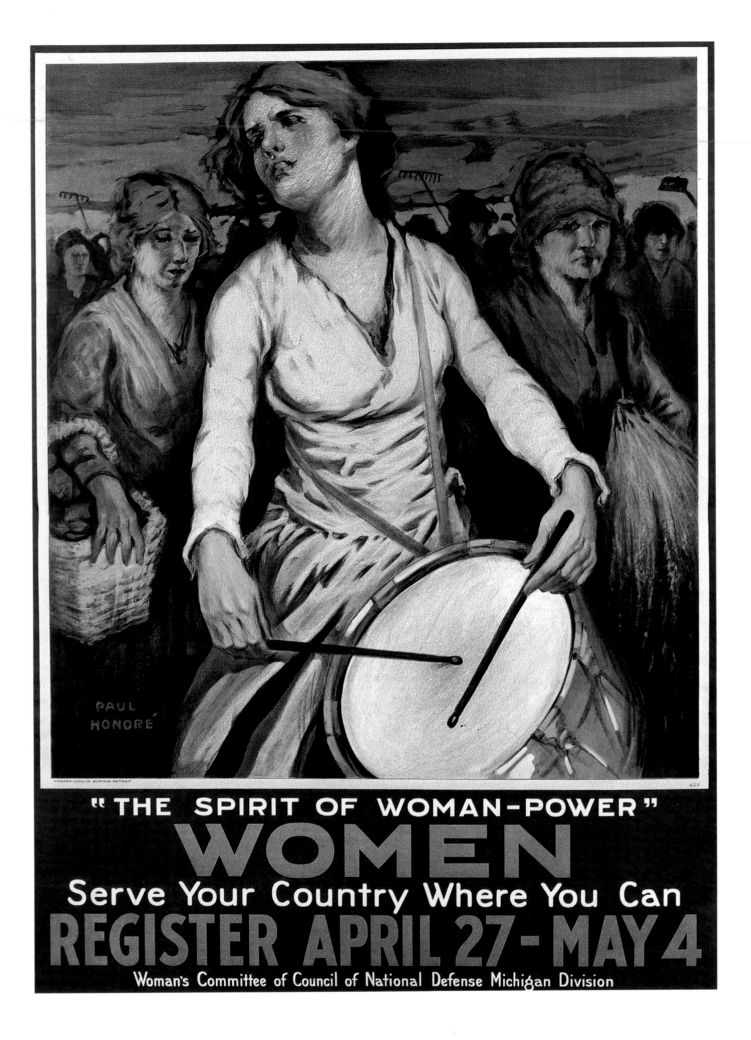

had been organized by Alice Paul, a Quaker who had studied militant feminist tactics in England. When America entered World War I, Paul, head of the National Woman's Party, urged suffragists to keep up the homefront fight for the vote. In 1917 silent pickets holding banners stood motionless outside the gates of the White House. The women came day after day, rain or shine, holding signs with messages such as "Mr. President, What Will You Do For Woman Suffrage" and "How Long Must Women Wait for Liberty?" President Wilson could no longer plead ignorance.

The protesting women were abused by male hecklers; their signs were torn from their hands. The men had resorted to violence, but it was the women who were arrested. They were sent to a notorious workhouse in Virginia where the conditions were abominable. When the women prisoners, including Alice Paul, went on a hunger strike, authorities inserted tubes through their nostrils and force-fed them. The brutality backfired: It turned the prisoners into martyrs and helped the women's cause. Alice Paul's will was so strong that prison officials believed she was insane. A doctor reported: "This is a spirit like Joan of Arc, and it is useless to try to change it. She will die, but she will never give up."

Women could be held back no longer. Even President Wilson admitted as much. In January 1918, the day before the proposed constitutional amendment granting suffrage to women was to be voted on in the House of Representatives, Wilson advised fellow Democrats that backing the amendment would be "an act of right and justice to the women of the country and of the world."

The tally was going to be close. Four congressmen were ill or injured; nonetheless they came to cast their votes (one actually arrived on a stretcher). Representative Hicks of New York left his wife on her deathbed—at her urging, as she was an ardent suffragist—to come to Washington for the final vote. He returned home for her funeral. His courage—and his wife's—had been crucial; the amendment passed the House of Representatives without a vote to spare. It would take over a year before the Senate approved the measure, and another year before a sufficient number of states ratified the amendment. With victory finally secured, women proudly went to the polls on November 2, 1920, and for the first time cast their votes in a presidential election. It was said that in New York "every woman not suffering from Spanish influenza voted." It was a glorious triumph for American women.

Just months before women finally secured the right to vote, the federated Women's Clubs of Massachusetts presented a statue to the commonwealth. It was a memorial to Anne Hutchinson, the great religious dissident of the 1600s. The timing was perfect: As women were poised to partake fully in the electoral process for the first time in the country's history, the nation could look back upon the arc of history and pay tribute to one of its earliest heroines. Certainly the painful trials that Anne Hutchinson endured helped shape the very nature of our government and its clear separation of church and state. A woman of deep religious beliefs and principles, she risked—and lost—everything to follow her conscience.

Yet Hutchinson's life and legacy still created such ripples in Massachusetts that the legislature hemmed and hawed over the statue—it took the lawmakers three years before they decided to accept the gift. It was never formally dedicated. Even after 300 years, Hutchinson still rankled the authorities in Massachusetts. When pressed on the issue by a reporter, one 1920s legislator mentioned that she was deemed too "aggressive." In other words, she did not "know her place." Fortunately for our country, she and many other courageous women failed to accept their place—they followed their hearts and their deep-seated beliefs rather than the dictates of social convention.

Clearly, women had a profound impact on the nation before they ever walked into a voting booth. Fettered by restrictions of all kinds, women cleverly circumvented them—or simply ignored them. Their ingenuity and persistence were awe-inspiring. Women helped form the conscience of the New World, as well as its backbone. They worked side by side with men to create America's wealth and fabled institutions. With imagination, vigor, and joy, they helped fashion a society, create a world of art and beauty, and refine a political and economic system. For 300 years women helped shape and define what it is to be American. All this without even having the vote. The possibilities, it turned out, were limitless.

In an unusual advertising gambit, suffragists take their message to the skies. As the grassroots campaign spread, women of all social classes banded together and made their opinions known. Secretaries and housewives proudly wore yellow corsages of buttercups or jonquils—yellow being the traditional color of the cause. For her part, society doyenne Alva Belmont custom-ordered from England a tea service emblazoned with the slogan "Votes for Women."

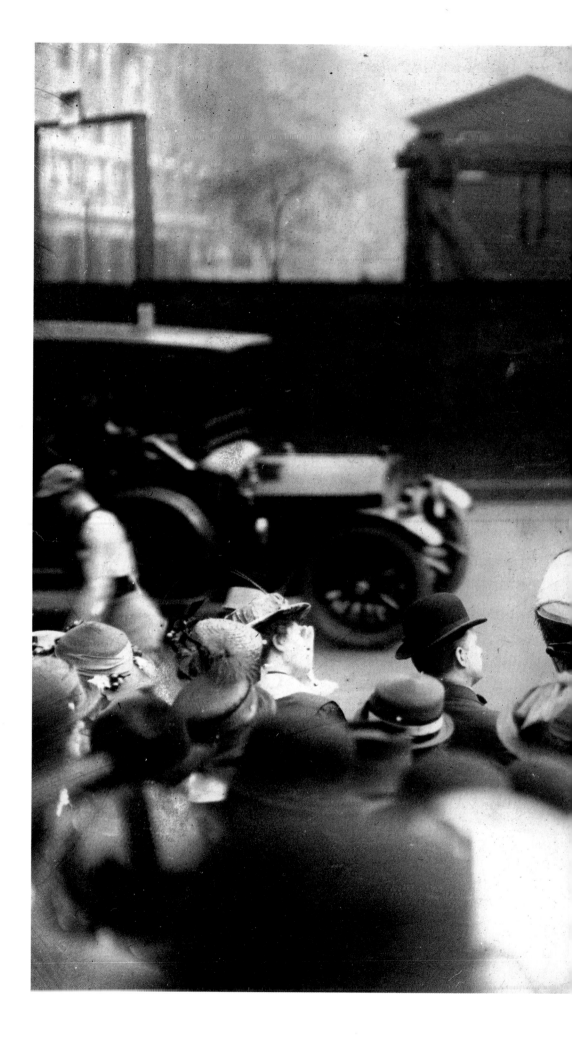

An impassioned suffragist harangues a crowd from the back of an open automobile. Women marched, held rallies, and lobbied Congress to remind the nation that "by keeping women out of politics, the soul of our country is diminished by one-half." On June 4, 1919, women finally won the right to vote.

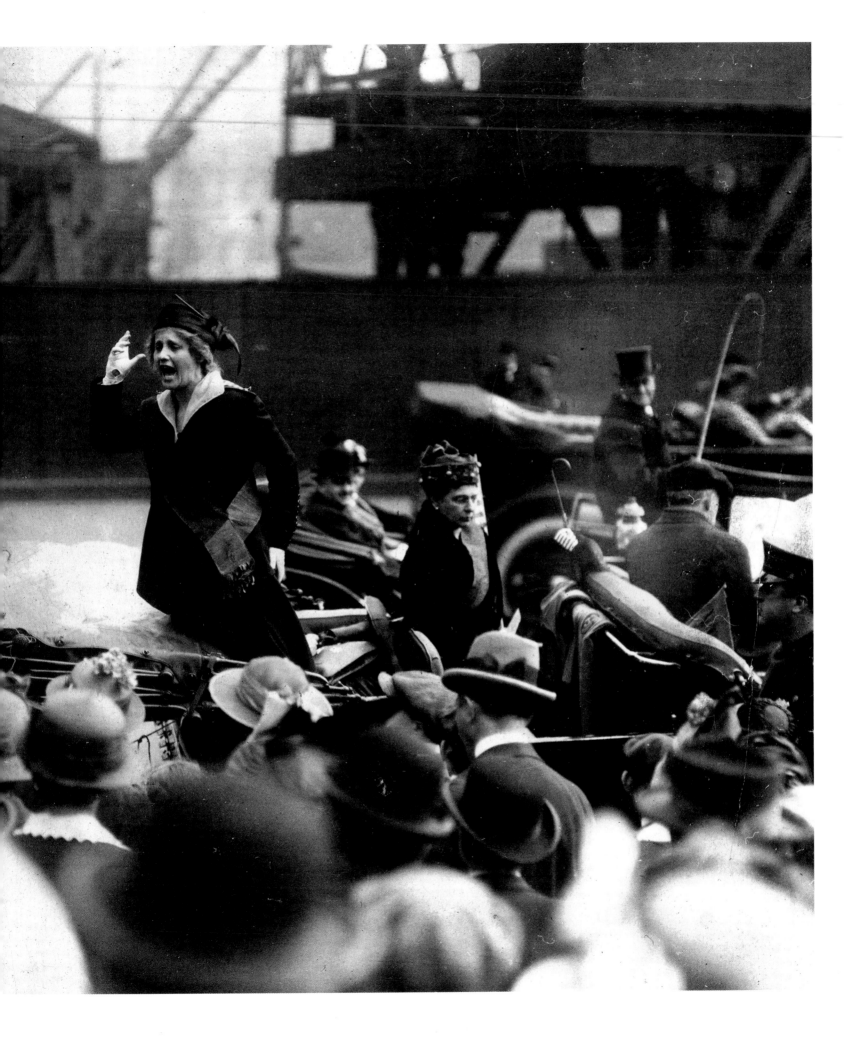

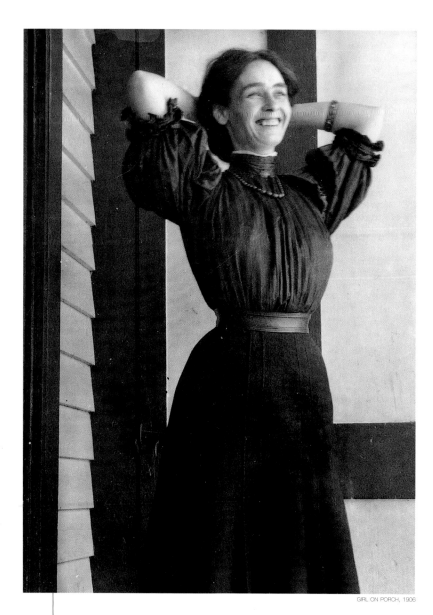

GIRL ON PORCH, 1906

INDEX

NOTE: **Boldface** indicates illustrations.

ILLUSTRATIONS CREDITS

I DWELL IN POSSIBILITY

By Donna M. Lucey

Published by the National Geographic Society

John M. Fahey, Jr. *President and Chief Executive Officer*
Gilbert M. Grosvenor *Chairman of the Board*
Nina D. Hoffman *Executive Vice President*

Prepared by the Book Division
Kevin Mulroy *Vice President and Editor-in-Chief*
Charles Kogod *Illustrations Director*
Barbara A. Payne *Editorial Director*
Marianne R. Koszorus *Design Director*

Staff for this Book
Barbara Brownell *Project Editor*
Marianne R. Koszorus *Art Director*
Donna M. Lucey *Illustrations Editor*
Rebecca Beall Barns *Editor and Researcher*
Roxie France-Nuriddin *Researcher*
R. Gary Colbert *Production Director*
Lewis R. Bassford *Production Project Manager*
Melissa Farris *Design Assistant*
Sharon Kocsis Berry *Illustrations Assistant*
Melissa Hunsiker *Assistant Editor*
Connie D. Binder *Indexer*

Manufacturing and Quality Management
George V. White *Director*
Clifton M. Brown *Manager*
Phillip L. Schlosser *Financial Analyst*

The world's largest nonprofit scientific and educational organization, the National Geographic Society was founded in 1888 "for the increase and diffusion of geographic knowledge." Since then it has supported scientific exploration and spread information to its more than eight million members worldwide.

The National Geographic Society educates and inspires millions every day through magazines, books, television programs, videos, maps and atlases, research grants, the National Geographic Bee, teacher workshops, and innovative classroom materials.

The Society is supported through membership dues, charitable gifts, and income from the sale of its educational products. Members receive NATIONAL GEOGRAPHIC magazine—the Society's official journal—discounts on Society products, and other benefits.

For more information about the National Geographic Society, its educational programs, publications, or ways to support its work, please call 1-800-NGS-LINE (647-5463), or write to the following address:

NATIONAL GEOGRAPHIC SOCIETY
1145 17th Street N.W.
Washington, D.C. 20036-4688 U.S.A.

Visit the Society's Web site at
www.nationalgeographic.com

Printed in the U.S.A.

AUTHOR DONNA LUCEY is a writer and illustrations editor who wrote the award-winning 1990 book *Photographing Montana 1894-1928: The Life and Work of Evelyn Cameron,* which was reissued in 2001. She co-authored the *National Geographic Guide to America's Great Houses* and has contributed to books produced for Time-Life, Reader's Digest, and Rolling Stone Press, and to magazines such as *People, Money, American Heritage,* and *GEO.* She lives in Charlottesville, Virginia, with her husband, Henry, and her son, Henry.

ADDITIONAL READING: Berkin, Carol, *First Generations: Women in Colonial America;* Cable, Mary, *Top Drawer: American High Society from the Gilded Age to the Roaring Twenties;* Clinton, Catherine, *Tara Revisited: Women, War, & the Plantation Legend;* Demos, John, *The Unredeemed Captive: A Family Story from Early America;* De Pauw, Linda Grant, *Founding Mothers: Women of America in the Revolutionary Era;* Faust, Drew Gilpin, *Mothers of Invention: Women of the Slaveholding South in the American Civil War;* Foner, Philip S., editor, *The Factory Girls;* Hedrick, Joan D., *Harriet Beecher Stowe: A Life;* Hill, Tom and Richard W. Hill Sr., editors, *Creation's Journey: Native American Identity and Belief;* Lewis, R.W.B. *Edith Wharton: A Biography;* Lucey, Donna M., *Photographing Montana 1894-1928: The Life and Work of Evelyn Cameron;* Painter, Nell Irvin, *Sojourner Truth;* Schlissel, Lillian, *Women's Diaries of the Westward Journey;* Sterling, Dorothy, editor, *We Are Your Sisters: Black Women in the Nineteenth Century;* Wiencek, Henry, *The Hairstons: An American Family in Black and White;* Withey, Lynne, *Dearest Friend: A Life of Abigail Adams;* Tomkins, Calvin, *Merchants and Masterpieces: The Story of the Metropolitan Museum of Art.*

ACKNOWLEDGMENTS: This book owes a great debt to the scholars currently doing groundbreaking work on various aspects of women's history, including Theda Perdue, Laurel Thatcher Ulrich, Betty Ring, Mary Beth Norton, Linda Kerber, Linda Grant DePauw, Drew Gilpin Faust, Gladys-Marie Fry, Carol Berkin, Elizabeth Fox-Genovese, Sandra Myers, Glenda Riley, Lillian Schlissel, Christine Stansell, Nell Irvin Painter, Kathryn Kish Sklar, and especially Catherine Clinton, who served so ably as consultant on the project. I am extremely grateful to the curators and librarians at museums, archives, and libraries across the country who helped lead me to both visual and literary treasures in their collections. Special thanks to Tony Guzzi at The Hermitage in Tennessee; photography collector, Mr. James Allen; Andrea Mons from the U.S. General Services Administration; Reginald Washington from the National Archives; collector Michael Bliss of Fort Collins, Colorado; John E. Carter of the Nebraska State Historical Society; and Professor Stephen Railton of the University of Virginia. Nancy Malan of the National Archives served as both expert guide to the massive collections at the Archives as well as genial hostess. Jane Colihan provided much needed moral support as well as critical help. Rebecca Barns worked tirelessly on the manuscript to whip it into shape. My thanks to Roxie France-Nuriddin who worked on the illustrations. Among the staff members at National Geographic I must make special mention of Sharon Berry, Melissa Hunsiker, Dale-Marie Herring, Gary Colbert, Lewis Bassford, and Chris Brown, as well as the designer Marianne Koszorus. Barbara Brownell was the guiding light from start to finish. Finally, all my love and thanks to my two Henrys.

Library of Congress Cataloging-in-Publication Data
Lucey, Donna M.,1951-
    I dwell in possibility : women build a nation, 1600-1920 / Donna M. Lucey
      p. cm.
    Includes bibliographical references and index.
    ISBN 0-7922-6360-X
      1. Women–United States–History. 2. Women–United States–History–Pictorial works. I. Title.

HQ1410.L83 2001
305.4'0973–dc21

                             2001032682